The Complete Cat Book

RICHARD H. GEBHARDT

WHSMITH
EXCLUSIVE
· BOOKS ·

This edition is produced exclusively for W.H. Smith Ltd.
ISBN 1-873901-00-3

This book was created and produced by
Mirabel Books Limited, P.O. Box 1214, London SW6 7ES

Special Photography by Bill Buckner

Editor: Phil Maggitti

Editorial Assistants: David Shumaker and Patricia Ford

Design by Chris McLeod and Peter Simmonett

Separation by Oceanic Graphic Printing, Inc.

Printed and bound in Hong Kong by C & C Offset Printing

NOTE:
The Author wishes to thank the Governing Council of the Cat Fancy for agreeing to allow an abbreviated version of the Official Standard of Points to be published in the English version of this book.

Acknowledgements

As I wrote this book, there was never a doubt in my mind about the person to whom it should be dedicated: my lifelong partner, collaborator, and friend John Bannon, whose loyalty and love of animals made possible my achievements. John, who shared my heartaches and highlights, has given me a sense of pride few people experience.

I was fortunate to have been surrounded with persons of great talent and achievement during my years in the cat fancy, and I should like to acknowledge my mentors in the Cat Fanciers' Association: Elsie Hydon, Rita Swenson, Jean Rose, Lillias Bloem, Louise Sample, Matil Rotter, and Robert Winn.

In addition, I have enjoyed lasting friendships with some of England's legendary cat fanciers: Kathleen Yorke, Joan Thompson, Grace Pond, and Brian Sterling-Webb.

I must also mention my wonderful family, who endured all my ambitions with their love and support—and last but not least, the beloved four-legged members of my household. Each and every one has been a special part of my life.

Finally, I would like to acknowledge the help I received from the following individuals who supplied information or assistance in the preparation of this book: Carolann Bannon, Bud and Betty Cowles, Tom Dent and Allene Sergei of the Cat Fanciers' Association, Marna and Joe Fogarty, the Garden Cat Club, the Garden State Cat Club, Phil and Mary Ann Maggitti, Vicky and Peter Markstein, Douglas Myers, Daphne Negus, John and Gina Philpot, Lesley Pring and Eric Wickham-Ruffle of the Governing Council of the Cat Fancy, Janice Reichle, Allen Scruggs, Barbara St. Georges, Eric and Helena Thom, Betty White-Ludden, and Herb Zwecker.

Contents

Preface

Cats are becoming increasingly popular as pets and it is essential that prospective cat owners are fully aware of the responsibility inherent in bringing home a new kitten. Mr Richard Gebhardt's book gives excellent advice on all aspects of ownership and care of cats; in the ideal world, anyone who is considering buying a cat would read and appreciate the very practical advice he is offering.

A large section of the book deals in great detail with Pedigree cats and as Honorary Secretary of the Governing Council of the Cat Fancy I am of course principally interested in this section. In particular, there are major differences in the Long Haired Persian cats, the Burmese, Abyssinian and the Havana, as seen in the United States and this country.

In the early eighties in Britain, judges, and veterinary surgeons began to notice that some pedigree breeding was having an adverse effect on the health of cats. Problems with the cats' mouths, uneven jaws and teeth, and flattened noses were all results of this breeding. This situation persuaded the Governing Council to take a long hard look at all cat breeding. Their work resulted in the introduction of a Standard List for Faults of all breeds which explains all the defects thought to put cats at risk. This List of Faults is reproduced on page 217. Since its introduction, and despite the worries of many breeders, who felt it was impossible to produce the desired type in their cats without producing these defects, the worst problems are already beginning to disappear.

Notwithstanding my comments about these problems' the vast majority of cats are healthy, lovable animals which are a delight to welcome into your home. Their requirements are relatively simple: they need good food, a warm dry place indoors to sleep, human company and a caring owner who will know when they are feeling a little under the weather and need veterinary attention. In return for these simple requirements they will give hours of companionship to people of all ages. It does not matter whether the cat you own is a rescued cat, pedigree cat or one from the farm just up the road; all these animals will provide equal pleasure in return for a little care and consideration. It is important when you are buying a cat to consider which variety will be the best for you. If you decide on a pedigree, I suggest that you try to attend a cat show before you look for a kitten, then you can see if the cat in real life does, in fact, resemble the one you fell in love with in a book. This will also give you the opportunity to talk to other owners and to find out their views about differences in temperament of the various breeds.

I hope that on your first visit to a breeder you will find litters of healthy fit kittens and will only be faced with the problem of which one to choose. My advice is, you choose the one that chooses you. Kittens seem to have a great ability to recognise an affinity with a person on first sight, unlike their human counterparts who frequently realise that first impressions of fellow humans are not always so reliable.

Mr Eric Wickham-Ruffle kindly agreed to work on the Long Hair section of the breeds and also the section on judging. Eric is a Long Hair judge of many years experience. I am grateful to him for agreeing to undertake these specialist sections with which he was far better qualified to deal. I would also like to thank my various friends in the Fancy who have supplied me with information when it fell outside my own experience.

Cat lovers in the United Kingdom are indeed fortunate that this book has been produced in this country. They will be able to enjoy the excellent advice given by Richard Gebhardt and benefit from his very long experience of breeding and judging cats.

Lesley Pring
Honorary Secretary, The Governing Council
of the Cat Fancy

Before You Buy Your Cat

HOW TO LOCATE BREEDERS

People seeking a pedigreed kitten can find the names of breeders from Club Kitten registers whose phone numbers are available from GCCF Office, or the breeders' ads in *Cats* or *Cat World* magazines, and the classified section of the newspaper. Yearbooks, which contain the most pictures of different breeds, can be ordered from *Cats Magazine* and *Cat World*; these are also available at newsstands or at cat shows. Newspapers are available everywhere but such advertisements should be considered carefully. Prospective buyers can meet breeders in person by visiting cat shows, which are advertized in newspapers and cat magazines.

HOW MUCH IS THAT KITTEN IN ...?

The price of a pet kitten is a function of breed, geography, supply, demand, and occasionally—the number of surplus kittens a breeder has to feed. Between £90 and £200 is a reasonable range for most breeds in most parts of the country, though longhairs tend to be priced at the higher end of the range. Prices in the Southeast are sometimes higher, and breeders with new or exotic breeds often equate novelty with increased value, but there is little reason to pay more than £250 for a companion cat that is not going to be used for breeding.

Show kittens are another matter. Price will vary with breed, demand, and potential, but prices will start high and finish higher. Persian kittens are usually the most expensive. It is difficult to find one that will be competitive for less than £200. Of course, the more competitive a kitten is likely to be, the more a breeder is likely to ask for it. Many breeders offer insurance cover for the kitten for the first few weeks in its new home.

The purchase price should include vaccination against feline enteritis and cat 'flu. Buyers are also advised to have kittens tested for Feline Leukaemia Virus prior to purchase – an extra fee may be charged for this.

BASIC CONCERNS

Contrary to their reputation for being aloof, cats are charming and devoted companions who provide us with affection and amuse us with their antics. What's more, they are meticulously clean and supremely self-sufficient—perfectly content to spend the day at home when we are away at work and delighted to see us when we return. Just as their ancestors have adapted to meet the earth's changing conditions over the last three million years, modern-day cats adapt well to the restrictions of urban living and the busy schedules of two-career families or single-parent homes.

Like people, kittens come in a variety of personalities, from shy to scintillating, and people who go to look at a kitten should observe carefully. Watch as a kitten plays with litter mates. If a kitten is right in the middle of the rolling and tumbling that kittens love, chances are he's in good health and developing normally. A wallflower that sits quietly while the others play might not be feeling well or might be the kind of kitten that requires a little more patience and attention than the average.

Two simple personality tests involve wiggling a few fingers along the floor about six inches in front of a kitten, or dangling a small toy back and forth. Does the kitten scamper over to investigate, or back away as though feeling threatened? A well-adjusted kitten will be curious to find out what this human is about. A nervous or a timid kitten will be more cautious. A poorly adjusted or immature kitten will disappear under the nearest chair.

For persons who have other pets or children at home, the curious, pleased-to-meet-you kitten is the best choice. This is the type more apt to adjust quickly and to get along with other family members. The timid kitten will probably make a fine companion, too, but may need more time to adjust, and might prefer more quiet surroundings. As for the little one under the sofa, perhaps the perfect owner will come along one day, but chances are he doesn't think it's today.

No matter what personality suits a new owner best, a kitten is not suitable at all if it isn't healthy. While making a kitten's acquaintance, a person should be making observations about the animal's health and general condition. Did the kitten follow alertly the toy that was waved about nearby? Are his eyes bright, shiny, and clear? Is his nose cool and slightly damp? Are his gums free of inflammation? Is the area around his tail clean?

Kittens love to climb and play in containers of all sorts

Kittens enjoy supervised outdoor play

Beware the kitten with a dry, warm-feeling nose or teary eyes. These are frequently signs of poor health. Inflamed gums are often an indication of gingivitis. Dirt or wetness in the area around a kitten's tail may signal diarrhoea or urine scalding, which may in turn be signs of ill health.

A kitten's ears should be clean and free of wax or dirt. The body should be soft and smooth, a little lean, perhaps, but not skinny. The coat should be free of bald patches or flea dirt; skin should be free of scabs or scratches. Bald patches or scabs could mean ringworm. Flea dirt always means fleas.

Even if the prospective new member of the family appears healthy, a kitten should come with a money-back guarantee, and the new owner should agree a short period in which to take a kitten to a veterinary surgeon for an examination. The vet will check the kitten's temperature, listen to the kitten's heart and lungs, weigh the kitten, and test him for leukaemia and other contagious diseases if this has not been done prior to purchase. If the vet discovers any serious, pre-existing conditions such as leukaemia or cat 'flu, the buyer should have the right to return the kitten and to have the purchase price refunded.

Though most cat breeders are reputable, kitten buyers should allow for the possibility that the person they're dealing with is not. If a breeder asks for a deposit on a kitten, the buyer should write 'deposit for such-and-such kitten' on the cheque. Buyers should also ask for a receipt for that deposit and should find out in advance—preferably in writing—if the deposit is refundable should they decide not to take the kitten. The same cautions apply when a person sends the cheque for the balance of the purchase price.

Many breeders will send the buyer a sales contract

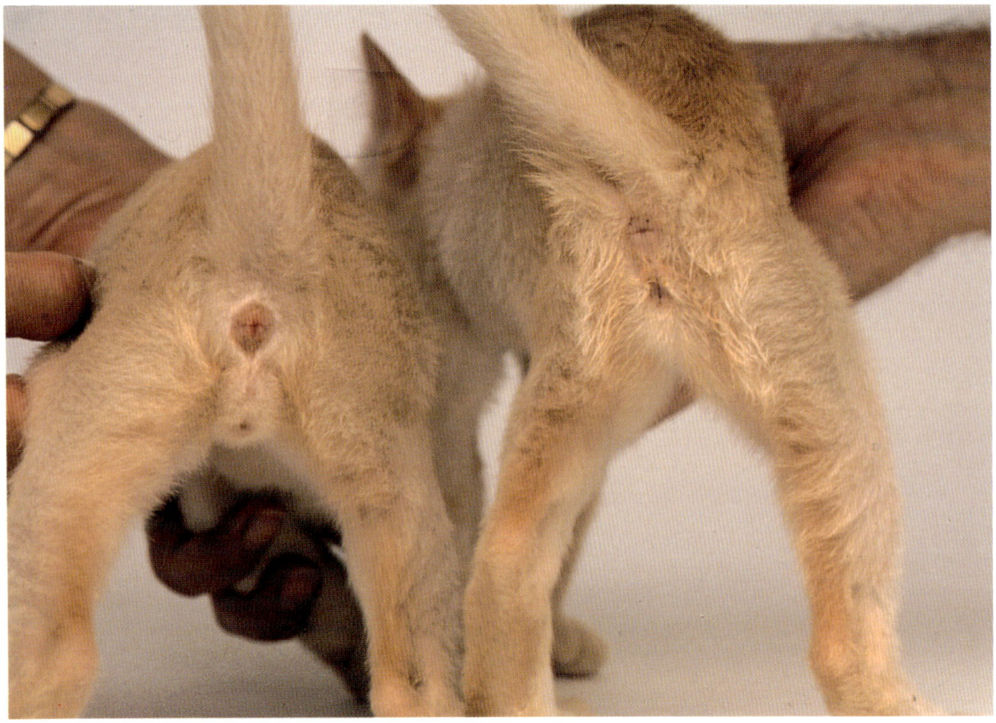

At roughly eight to ten weeks, the young male's accoutrements (left) are quite visible; but even at birth the difference between the sexes is apparent. The male genital area resembles a colon (:), and the female's looks like an inverted exclamation mark (¡)

before they sell a kitten. Buyers should read the contract carefully and question any stipulations they do not understand or would not feel comfortable meeting.

Occasionally breeders who sell a kitten will say they haven't registered the kitten yet, but when they do, they'll send along its 'pink slip'—the application for transfer of ownership. If buyers accept a kitten under this condition, they should ask the breeder to send them a note to the effect that 'papers will follow within thirty to sixty days' after the breeder has sold the kitten.

No matter how eager a person is to buy a kitten, a responsible breeder never lets a kitten go before it is twelve weeks of age. A kitten approaching twelve weeks has been properly weaned and has been eating solid food for some time. It is nursing infrequently, if at all, and has begun to make the transition from being a dependent to an independent creature. And by that time it has had all its vaccinations.

Kittens that are six to ten weeks old are still babies. If they're taken away from their mothers, the stress of going to a new home may cause them to become sick, to forget their litter training, or to chew on blankets or sofa cushions as a substitute for nursing—a habit they often keep the rest of their lives. So no matter how cute or tempting an eight-week-old might be, the kitten will adjust better—and so will the owner—if the transition to a new home is made when the kitten is at least three weeks older. Barring misfortune, the average cat will live ten to fourteen years, so the serious owner ought to be able to be patient for twenty-one extra days.

ABOUT BREEDS AND PERSONALITIES

There are so many breeds to choose from, that a prospective owner should be able to find a kitten that suits any aesthetic taste, purse, or living arrangement. As one might expect—and contrary to what one frequently hears—every breed does not have a unique personality distinct from every other breed's. There aren't that many distinct personalities among people, and there are far more breeds of people than there are of cats.

In truth, feline personality is more related to body type than it is to breed. For example, the slim, elegant Siamese is the most active, vocal, curious—and some would say the most intelligent—cat. Siamese share these traits to varying degrees with other svelte, tubular breeds like the Oriental Shorthair, Balinese, Abyssinian, and Cornish Rex. At the other end of the personality spectrum, the Persian is the most easygoing cat. It holds this trait in common with other foursquare, stocky breeds like the Sacred Cat of Burma, the Exotic Shorthair and the British Shorthair which resembles its 'moggie' relative about as much as steak tartare resembles mince.

In the middle of the spectrum for body type and personality is the Abyssinian or Russian Blue. On a personality scale of one to ten, these breeds are a perfect, middle-of-the-road five.

No matter what the breed, the process of domestication retards the development of certain adult behaviours. Domesticated animals never, in short, quite grow up. We don't want them to. A lingering immaturity is part of their appeal. The self-sufficient, aggressive, urine-marking animal which is the adult of any feline species is not something we want running about in our homes.

The tendency of domesticated cats to be forever young is amplified by their socialization. In studies involving domestic cats conducted at Temple University in Philadelphia in the early 1980s, Eileen Karsh, Ph.D., found that kittens which were handled for as little as five minutes a day from the time they were three weeks old until they were fourteen weeks old became more attached to people than kittens which were handled daily from seven to fourteen weeks of age or kittens which were not handled at all. Early handled kittens were more likely to tolerate being held ventral side up, and they approached humans almost four times as quickly as late or nonhandled kittens. These and other user-friendly characteristics are the traits one hopes to find in kittens that are advertised as having been 'raised underfoot with a lot of TLC (tender loving care).' The proof of the advertisement, however, is always in the handling.

TIPS ON SELECTING A SHOW CAT

Though some people prefer male or female cats as pets, either sex, if given love and attention and a place on the bed at night, will make a wonderful companion.

This British Shorthair is sturdy and correct

An American Shorthair in a classic tabby pattern

Anyone planning to breed cats, however, should buy the best female he or she can find. This task is more complex, time consuming, and costly than locating a pet kitten. Some novices mistakenly believe that because a kitten can be registered it can automatically be shown. That's true, as far as it goes, but there's a difference between buying a cat that can be shown and buying a show cat. In fact, just because a kitten is said to be show quality and is sold at a show-quality price do not always guarantee that it is good enough to be shown.

One way to find out how well a kitten is likely to do at a show—and to save oneself disappointment—is to buy a young adult or an older kitten that has been shown a few times. Some breeders like to show their kittens but do not have room to keep them all. Thus, a new owner might find a cat that's less than a year old and has a few wins to its credit. If a person is willing to forgo the pleasure of watching a kitten grow up—and is willing to pay a little more for a proven winner—the older kitten or young adult might be a better choice than the untried adolescent.

In every case, it is better to wait until a show-quality kitten is older than twelve weeks before buying it. Kittens can change overnight, and it's difficult to predict how a kitten is going to develop when it is only twelve weeks old—no matter what glowing predictions a breeder might make. A five- or six-month-old kitten is less subject to change without notice.

No matter how old the show cat a person buys—or whether the cat is longhaired or short, male or female, adult or kitten—that person should do some homework before writing the cheque: visit shows, talk to breeders who are working with a particular breed, watch the cats in that breed being judged, and walk round several show halls to see what the winning representatives of a breed look like. The prospective buyer should also consult the breed Standard (See Breeds Section), and take a copy of that Standard along when looking at kittens. The buyer should ask the kitten's breeder to show where a kitten meets the Standard and where it doesn't. If possible, the buyer should also take an experienced breeder along when looking at a prospective show kitten.

Anyone interested in buying a kitten from a breeder who lives too far away to visit, should ask to see pictures of the kitten. If the pictures are not clear, ask to see more. Ask the breeder to say, preferably in writing, where a kitten meets the Standard and where it falls short, and try and get an informed independent opinion if possible.

Persons buying kittens should remember that they're buying the genetic influence of several generations. Buyers should look at a kitten's pedigree to see what titles its family members have won, especially those in the first two generations, for the parents and grandparents wield the greatest influence on a kitten's potential. If neither the parents nor the grandparents are grand champions, they either were not shown or they were not good enough to do well when shown. If they were not shown, ask why. If several of them were shown but did not achieve 'grand,' status think at least twice about buying the kitten. And ask the breeder how many grand champions the sire and dam of the kitten have produced. Just as thoroughbred breeders put great stock in equine families, so, too, should the prospective cat breeder or exhibitor.

Although pedigree documents are written in English of a sort, they are manuscripts in a foreign tongue to newcomers. Yet the breeder who does not learn the language might just as well be pondering graffiti on a dark wall under a bad light if he or she hopes to use pedigrees as an aid to acquiring or producing a good cat.

Part of the knack of learning to understand pedigrees involves the ability to read between the lines, that is to say, have a look at as many of the cats and their backgrounds as possible in the first three generations of a pedigree, even if the examination is only a pictorial one. The astute buyer also tries to examine the littermates of the cats and their backgrounds which are on a pedigree document. This is particularly important if one is considering buying a cat that is inbred. While that cat may not have an extra ear, one should not consider buying it if one of its littermates did.

Nearly three hundred years ago William Penn remarked that 'men are generally more careful of the breed of their [animals] than of their children.' Penn's observation is, perhaps, too cynical to apply to modern day cat breeders, but the touchstone of good breeding has remained the same since Penn's day: to buy a kitten with a pedigree that is stronger than either of its parents' pedigrees taken alone, one that will advance a breeder toward his or her goals.

Pedigree of one of Britain's Grand Champion Chinchillas

LYNCHARD CHINCHILLAS
LYNDA TAYLOR B.SC.
COLESGROVE FARM
GOFFS LANE
CHESHUNT
HERTS EN7 5EN

Lynchard Chinchillas

Owner LYNDA TAYLOR
Address COLESGROVE FARM
GOFFS LANE
CHESHUNT, HERTS EN7 5EN
Tel. No. 0992 22705

Pedigree of: GRAND CHAMPION LYNCHARD SILVER SURPRISE — G.C.C.F.) NS Regd. No.) 301501 — Breed No. 10 — Colour. USUAL — Sex. FEMALE — Date of Birth. 24.7.85

Parents	Grand-Parents	Great Grand-Parents	Great Great Grand-Parents
SIRE Reg. No. NS 224121 — GRAND CHAMPION LYNCHARD SILVER BARNUM — Breed No. 10 Colour. USUAL	Sire Reg. No. NS 107970 — GRAND CHAMPION ADELISIA ROMULUS — Breed No. 10 Colour. USUAL	Sire CHAMPION TUIDENE KYNAN (N.Z IMPORT) Reg. No. NS 15261 Breed No. 10	Sire CHAMPION TUIDENE ROYAL SHAH Br. No. 10
			Dam TUIDENE MEGAN Br. No. 10
		Dam CHAMPION EXCELSIOR CHE SARA Reg. No. NS 54599 Breed No. 10	Sire CHAMPION SNOWBLOOM PHILE'MON Br. No. 10
			Dam EXCELSIOR PRINCESS UTOPIA Br. No. 10
	Dam Reg. No. NS 178042 — NONOARTICA — Breed No. 10 Colour. USUAL	Sire GRAND CHAMPION ADELISIA ROMULUS Reg. No. NS 107970 Breed No. 10	Sire CHAMPION TUIDENE KYNAN Br. No. 10
			Dam CHAMPION EXCELSIOR CHE SARA Br. No. 10
		Dam MORROWMERE MELODY Reg. No. NS 118473 Breed No. 10	Sire GRAND CHAMPION CLICQUOT ROMULUS Br. No. 10
			Dam DEDANNAN WILD SILK Br. No. 10
DAM Reg. No. NS 271042 — LYNCHARD SILVER DEONIE — Breed No. 10 Colour. USUAL	Sire Reg. No. NS 107970 — GRAND CHAMPION ADELISIA ROMULUS — Breed No. 10 Colour. USUAL	Sire CHAMPION TUIDENE KYNAN (N.Z IMPORT) Reg. No. NS 15261 Breed No. 10	Sire CHAMPION TUIDENE ROYAL SHAH Br. No. 10
			Dam TUIDENE MEGAN Br. No. 10
		Dam CHAMPION EXCELSIOR CHE SARA Reg. No. NS 54599 Breed No. 10	Sire CHAMPION SNOWBLOOM PHILE'MON Br. No. 10
			Dam EXCELSIOR PRINCESS UTOPIA Br. No. 10
	Dam Reg. No. NS 230001 — MORROWMERE LEONIE — Breed No. 10 Colour. USUAL	Sire CHAMPION SONATA SILVER KING Reg. No. NS 192312 Breed No. 10	Sire SONATA OCTAYE Br. No. 10
			Dam SONATA COPPELIA Br. No. 10
		Dam CHAMPION MORROWMERE RENARTA Reg. No. NS 118474 Breed No. 10	Sire GRAND CHAMPION CLICQUOT ROMULUS Br. No. 10
			Dam DEDANNAN WILD SILK Br. No. 10

AWARDS:

I certify that this Pedigree is correct to the best of my knowledge.

Signed. Lynda J.R. Taylor Date.

Choosing a cat or a kitten is like falling in love: the heart has the upper hand. The divorce rate being what it is, however, people should learn everything they can about their intended breeds before promising to love, honour, and support a cat in the manner to which it would like to become accustomed. Someone looking for a four-legged companion who requires little more than the occasional scratch behind the ears, for example, will not be satisfied with an in-your-face breed. Nor will the individual who craves constant fawning discover eternal wedded bliss with a prim, reserved cat who dresses for dinner.

The following chart contains evaluations of the activity level and grooming needs—high, medium, or low—of every recognized breed. These are important considerations to anyone buying a pedigreed cat. The chart also contains information of interest to anyone thinking about breeding cats: are all the kittens in a breed showable? Are there genetic considerations that make one breed more challenging than others? These questions are answered Yes or No. Not all American Wirehair kittens, to mention one example, are showable. Some are born with straight coats. And Manx present a challenge to breeders because of the spinal problems and weak hindquarters that plague this breed.

	Activity Level	Grooming Needs	All Kittens Showable?	Genetic Concerns
Abyssinian	H	L	Y	Y[1]
American Curl	M	M	N[2]	N
American Shorthair	M	L	Y	N
American Wirehair	M	L	N[3]	Y[4]
Balinese	H	L	Y	N
Bengal	M	L	N[5]	N
Birman	L	M	Y	N
Bombay	H	L	N[6]	Y[7]
British Shorthair	L	L	Y	N
Burmese	H	L	Y	Y[8]
Burmilla	M	L	Y[9]	N
Chartreux	M	L	Y	N
Colourpoint Shorthair	H	L	Y	N
Cornish Rex	H	L	Y	N
Cymric	M	M	N[10]	Y[11]
Devon Rex	H	L	N[12]	Y[13]
Egyptian Mau	H	L	Y	N
Exotic Shorthair	M	M	N[14]	N
Foreign Burmese	H	L	Y	N
Havana Brown	M	L	Y	N
Himalayan	L	H	Y	N
Japanese Bobtail	M	L	Y	N
Javanese	H	L	Y	N
Kashmir	L	H	Y	N
Korat	M	L	Y	N
Maine Coon	M	H	Y	N
Manx	M	L	N[15]	Y[16]
Norwegian Forest Cat	M	M	Y	N
Ocicat	M	L	N[17]	N
Oriental Longhair	H	L	N[18]	N
Oriental Shorthair	H	L	N[19]	N
Persian	L	H	Y	N
Peke-faced Persian	L	H	Y	N
Ragdoll	L	H	Y	N
Russian Blue	H	L	Y	N
Scottish Fold	M	L	N[20]	Y[21]
Scottish Fold Longhair	M	M	N[22]	Y[23]
Siamese	H	L	Y	N
Singapura	M	L	N[24]	N
Somali	M	M	N[25]	N
Sphynx	M	L	Y	Y[26]
Tonkinese	H	L	N[27]	N
Turkish Angora	M	L	Y	N
Turkish Van	M	M	Y	N

1 Susceptibility to kidney problems is embedded in many lines.
2 Produces some straight-eared kittens.
3 Produces some straight-coated kittens.
4 This breed is slow to develop an immune-system response, leaving cats prone to sneezing and other upper-respiratory symptoms.
5 Produces some nonspotted kittens.
6 Produces some brown kittens that cannot be shown in most associations.
7 Cranial deformities occur frequently in many lines.
8 Cranial deformities occur frequently in many lines.
9 Has achieved provisional status only thus far.
10 Produces some tailed and partially tailed kittens.
11 Lethal gene prevents development of one fourth of all kittens in the womb. Spinal problems and weak hindquarters are also frequent in this breed.
12 Produces straight-coated kittens when outcrossed to American or British shorthairs.
13 Spasticity occurs in some lines.
14 Produces some longhaired kittens that cannot be shown in most associations.
15 Produces some tailed and partially tailed kittens.
16 Lethal gene prevents development of one fourth of all kittens in the womb. Spinal problems and weak hindquarters are also frequent in this breed.
17 Produces some nonspotted kittens.
18 Can produce pointed kittens when outcrossed to Balinese.
19 Can produce Siamese-coloured kittens that cannot be shown in all associations.
20 Produces some straight-eared kittens.
21 Fold-to-Fold breedings produce a percentage of kittens with short, inflexible tails and hindquarter crippling.
22 Produces some straight-eared kittens.
23 Fold-to-Fold breedings produce a percentage of kittens with short, inflexible tails and hindquarter crippling.
24 Produces nonticked kittens occasionally.
25 Produces shorthaired kittens when crossed to an Abyssinian. These cannot be shown in most associations.
26 Has had a tendency in the past to ineffective immune system development.
27 Produces some colours and patterns which cannot be shown in most associations.

Origins and Domestication of the Cat

THE WORLD'S FIRST CATS

All cats belong to the mammalian, carnivorous family known as *Felidae* or felids. About fifty-four million years ago felids began to evolve from miacids—small, tree-climbing creatures that resembled today's marten.

Fossil remains suggest, however, that felids exhibiting close similarities to twentieth-century domestic cats did not appear until roughly twelve million years ago.

Felids can be classified most simply into three genera: *Panthera,* which includes cats that can roar—the lion, tiger, leopard, snow leopard, clouded leopard, and jaguar; *Felis,* which includes all non roaring cats but the cheetah; *Acinonyx,* a Genus awarded to

The Domestic Cat's Pedigree

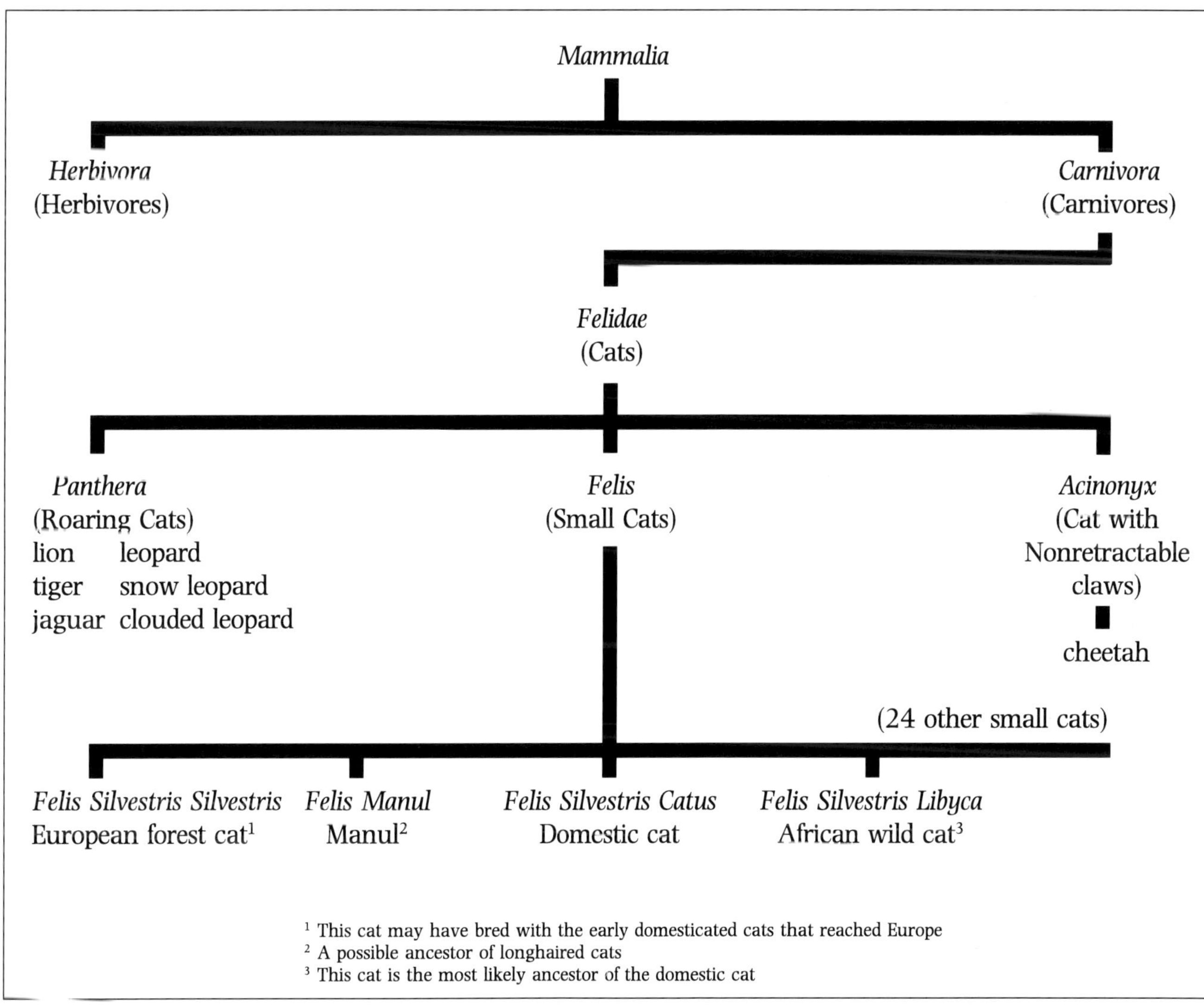

the cheetah because its claws aren't fully retractable. The genus *Felis*, to which domestic cats belong, was well established when *Homo sapiens* appeared thirty thousand to thirty-five thousand years ago. In many places cats were contemporaries of prehistoric people, but were not domesticated by them. Our ancestors had domesticated at least a dozen animals—beginning with dogs, reindeer, goats, and sheep during the preagricultural phase more than ten thousand years ago—before coming to terms with the cat.

ANCESTORS OF THE DOMESTIC CAT

Most researchers believe that the African wild cat (*Felis silvestris libyca*)—a yellow, faintly striped animal somewhat larger than present-day felines, that is found primarily in deserts throughout Africa, Syria, Arabia, and parts of India—is the probable ancestor of the domestic cat. Chief among the reasons for this conclusion are correlations between human and feline habitats during the period when domestication is most likely to have occurred; morphological and behavioural adaptations in the domestic cat—including a hearing apparatus suited to open spaces like the desert; behavioural evidence—the African wild cat is docile and is still easily tamed today; and etymological evidence—the English word *cat*, the French *chat*, the German *Katze*, the Spanish *gato*, the fourth-century Latin *cattus*, and the modern Arabic *quttah*, appear to be derived from the Nubian word *kadiz*, meaning a cat.

Two other varieties may have contributed also to the cat's development: Pallas's cat (*Felis manul*), a long-coated resident of the steppes in Northern and Central Asia, is believed by some to be the longhaired cat's

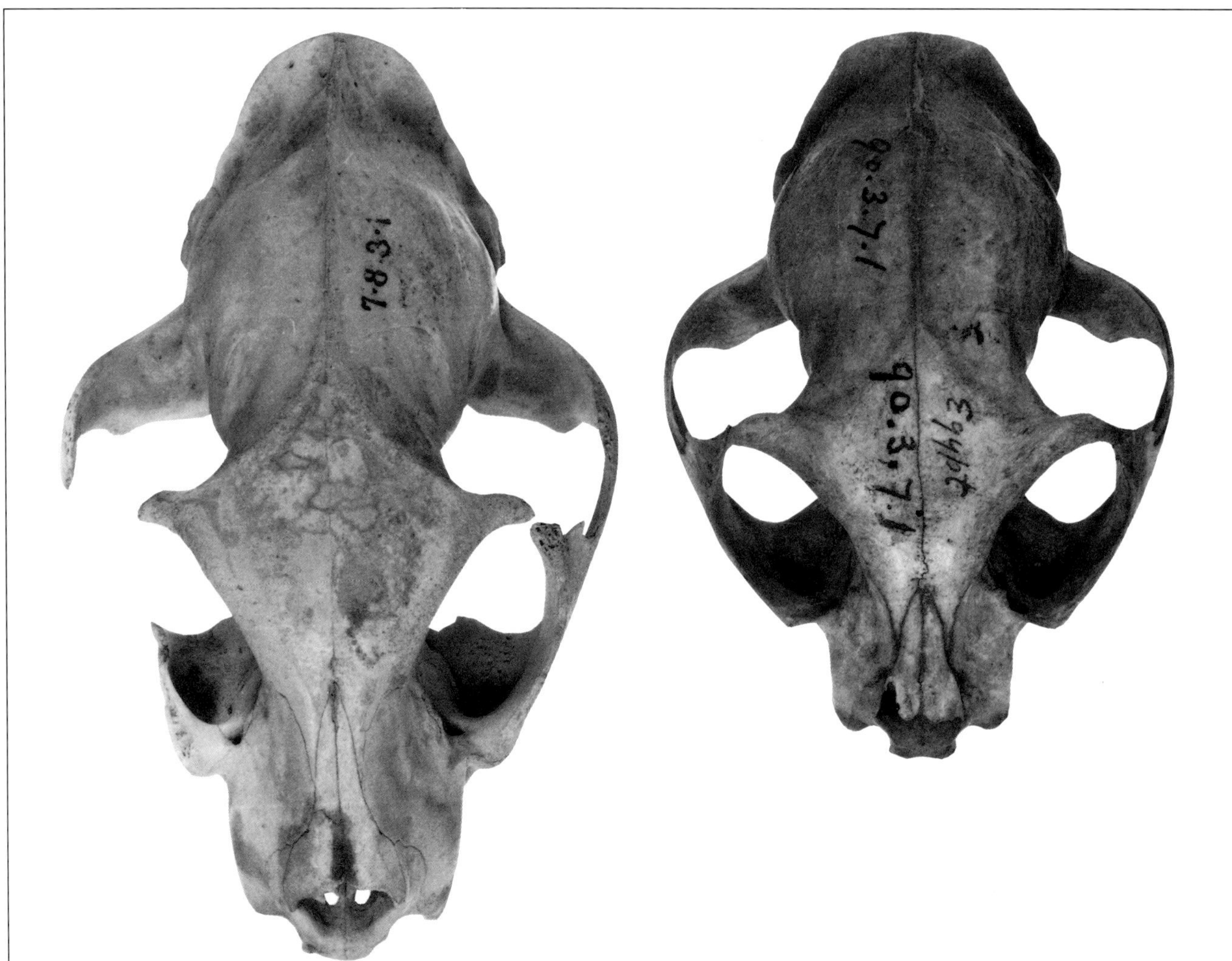

Skulls from mummified Egyptian cats

distant ancestor; and the never-domesticated European wild cat *(Felis silvestris silvestris)* may have interbred with domesticated cats once they had spread throughout Europe beginning in the fourth century, thereby contributing genes for darker tabby markings to the more lightly marked descendants of the African wild cat. The ancestors of the modern-day cat were either ticked, mackerel, or spotted tabbies. The classic (or blotched) tabby pattern seen in the show ring does not occur in any other member of the cat family except *Felis catus,* the domestic cat, in whom it appeared as an ordinary gene mutation.

Egyptian cats in bronze (left) and earthenware

Dessins sans paroles des chats by Theophile Steinlen (1859-1923), a French lithographer

WHEN THE CAT WAS DOMESTICATED

'It is likely,' says one animal behaviourist, 'that the cat was first domesticated in Egypt, but the probable date of this event is, at best, an approximation. The earliest pictorial representations of cats from Egypt date from the third millennium B.C., but it is often difficult to ascertain whether these animals were wild or domestic. From about 1600 B.C. onwards [however] paintings and effigies of cats become increasingly abundant in Egypt, and it [seems] that these animals were fully domesticated.'

HOW THE CAT WAS DOMESTICATED

Nearly all zoologists agree with their colleague Paul Leyhausen, who wrote: 'There is no evidence that at any time during its history the cat's way of life and its reception into human homesteads were purposely planned and directed by humans, as was the case with all other domestic animals at least from a very early stage of their association. In every sense the cat domesticated himself—if with some unimagined assistance from man.'

Cats were domesticated—whether by themselves or by humans—to hunt vermin and, to a lesser extent, for companionship. As agrarian societies developed, wild cats moved closer to towns and villages, attracted by food refuse and the large populations of rats and mice that thrived in granaries. When cats proved their skill at protecting grain, farmers began feeding them, hoping they would stay on the job.

IS THE CAT TRULY DOMESTICATED?

Although its ancestors formed an alliance with humans more than 3,500 years ago, the cat remains, according to one zoologist, 'an instructive example of a species which is only in the first stage of domestication ... perfectly capable of still becoming feral, and comparatively little altered' by its association with humankind. Indeed, cats are the most wild among the tame animals and the most tame among the wild. Two circumstances unique to the cat have accounted for this development.

Except for the lion and the cheetah, all cats, unlike other domesticated animals, are solitary creatures. Their survival does not depend on membership in a well-structured group. Cats follow their own counsel. Horses, by comparison, follow the lead of the dominant member of the herd, usually the alpha mare. This ancient instinct allows humans to become the dominant animals in the horse's life once domestication occurs. The cat does not transfer its allegiance so easily.

Centuries of complete reproductive freedom have also influenced the cat's personality. Until the late nineteenth century humans exerted almost no control over the cat's choice of mates. Other domesticated animals had been subject to arranged marriages for thousands of years by then, and only the most docile animals were considered fit subjects.

One can argue, therefore, that the cat has been domesticated, if at all, for little more than a hundred years, that its domestication did not commence until people began to exert systematic control over its breeding activities, and that pedigreed cats—especially those of the longest standing—are the first truly domesticated felines. The more extensive the pedigree, the greater the evolution in that animal whose ancestors it records.

Though no one has formally studied differences in temperament between pedigreed and nonpedigreed cats, breeders who have both kinds make some interesting observations. An American Shorthair breeder once took a barn cat into her house and bred it to one of her pedigreed males. When that female had kittens, she would not use the litter pan in the same room where she was raising them. She preferred to eliminate away from the nest, like an animal in the wild. Nor was she comfortable about letting her owner handle her kittens, as females who have descended from generations of indoor cats normally are.

Compared to the tenure of the dog, the interval since the cat was first domesticated has been brief. We can only guess at the personalities of those earliest cats who accepted food from humans, then agreed to accept their companionship as well. In addition, we can only guess at how the cat's personality will be affected by continued selective breeding. One thing, however, is certain: those making the selections ought to base their choices at least as much on temperament as they do on type.

A cat receiving a deputation of mice, by Wenceslaus Hollar (1607-77).
From an 18th-century edition of Aesop's Fables

A Brief History of the Cat Fancy

THE BIRTH OF THE CAT FANCY IN ENGLAND

In 1598, the year that Shakespeare published *Much Ado About Nothing,* a cat show was held at the St. Giles Fair in England. Much apparently did not come of this event, for 273 years passed before the English cat fancy was born. The affair that inspired this birth was a cat show at London's Crystal Palace in 1871. This gathering was organized by Harrison Weir, an Englishman of various talents, who also wrote the Standards by which the entries were appraised, and served as one of the show's three judges.

The breeds exhibited at nineteenth-century British cat shows were the Abyssinian; Manx; Royal Cat of Siam, which included both pointed and solid-chocolate cats; shorthairs, which were no doubt the descendants of cats brought to England by the Romans nine centuries before; and longhairs, which were judged by one Standard and which included Persians, Angoras, and a few cats from Russia. There were also classes for hybrids between wild and domestic cats, the heaviest cats, gelded cats, and 'Cats Belonging to Working Men.' The entrance fee in the latter was one third the fee in other classes, and the prize money offered to the first three finishers in the class was similarly reduced.

Harrison Weir with a prize-winning Persian cat

The popularity of cat shows in England led to the formation of the National Cat Club in 1887, with Harrison Weir as president. The NCC, whose motto was 'Beauty Lives by Kindness,' was both club and governing body. It established a national stud book and register to record the lineage of pedigreed cats.

The Cat Club, a rival to the NCC, was founded in 1898 by Lady Marcus Beresford and 'some of the most important people in the land,' according to one writer. Since TCC maintained its own stud book and register, persons who entered their cats in its shows had to enrol them in that association, too. After five years of stormy coexistence with the NCC, The Cat Club disbanded. Finally, in March 1910, the various clubs in England agreed to amalgamate. They formed the Governing Council of the Cat Fancy, which remains the oldest and the largest cat association in Great Britain today.

THE BIRTH OF THE CAT FANCY IN THE UNITED STATES

The cat fancy in the United States was officially born on May 8, 1895, when an Englishman named James T Hyde organized a cat show in Madison Square Garden in New York. One hundred and twenty-five exhibitors—and 176 cats—endured temperatures as high as ninety six degrees inside the Garden that day. This show—where the best cat was a brown tabby Maine Coon male—was the first to attract significant attention, but there had been other cat shows in the United States. For many years Maine Coon fanciers had promoted exhibitions of their cats in New England; and a handful of shows for all breeds of cats—frequently included as adjuncts to pigeon or poultry shows—had been held in Boston, Philadelphia, and Newburgh, New York.

In 1896 the Madison Square Garden show attracted

Catalogues from cat shows in England

only 130 entries. Nevertheless, at the close of the show a group of cat fanciers created the American Cat Club, the first registry in the United States. Its functions included verifying pedigrees, maintaining a stud book, sponsoring shows, and promoting the welfare of cats. The club was disbanded a year later, and for several years there were no shows at Madison Square Garden.

Cat fanciers in Chicago organized two clubs in 1899. The first was the Chicago Cat Club. It was followed and eventually eclipsed by the Beresford club. Then, as now, no crown can be counted secure in the cat world.

THE CAT FANCY IN TWENTIETH CENTURY BRITAIN

During this period cat breeding was becoming increasingly popular and in 1911 a large show was organized at the Crystal Palace at which 747 cats were entered and there were eight judges including the well known cat artist Louis Wain. The show lasted for two days and the best in show was a white longhair named White Satin and the reserve was a brown tabby called Brayfort Vector. Pictures of these events show the ladies in their imposing Edwardian hats, long skirts and high necked blouses, wearing large white kitchen aprons whilst stewarding. The gentlemen chose large striped butchers' aprons and cloth caps as their uniform.

World War I greatly reduced the activities but after the war things appeared to improve again and by 1939 there were seventeen affiliated cat clubs, seven more than in 1910. The Fancy had a great difficulty in surviving World War II and by the end there were very few pedigree cats left but by the early fifties there were twenty two clubs and over 2,100 prefixes listed in the stud book. Cat Shows were normally run by cat clubs but in October 1953 the GCCF ran the Coronation Cat Show at the Royal Horticultural Hall in London, the show manager was Mr A Towe, whose widow Mrs

E Towe is one of the GCCF Vice-Presidents. Mr Towe also ran the Golden Jubilee Show in 1960 and this was the second GCCF show.

The first Supreme Show was held at Stafford in December 1986. So began a new era for the Fancy. Dr WA Groom, founder of the Supreme, had been talking about a 'Crufts for the Cat Fancy' for years. His vision was of a spectacular event full of interest and colour. In order to achieve this he introduced ring judging so allowing exhibitors to decorate their cats' pens with great ingenuity. Cats have to qualify to enter the Supreme and in the early days the number of entries was quite low but in recent years entries have risen to about 1,400 cats, pedigree and non pedigree in competition and cats on exhibition most of whom appear in beautifully decorated pens.

During World War II the registration of cats had fallen from 1,000 a year up to 1939 to only 400 in 1940, but by the early 1950s registrations were increasing steadily again and in the early 1980s numbers had risen to 25,000 per year. Until this time all the registration work was done by a dedicated band of Registrars working in their own homes, but it became obvious that this would no longer be possible if numbers continued to rise and so it was decided to computerize the register and move into a permanent office. This change started when the Bridgewater office was opened in August 1983 and completed in December 1988 when the last register—the Siamese was moved. In 1990 the number of cats registered rose to over 36,000 and the advantages of the computer had been fully realized.

The number of varieties of cats registered had remained relatively static until the late 1960s when the new colours and patterns of Siamese were accepted. By the early 1970s the Colourpoint cats had received Championship status. This was the first addition to the Persian Longhair list since World War II. In the British Shorthair section, the British Smoke had been recognized

From the 1911 edition of the English magazine Fur and Feather

FUR AND FEATHER. March 17, 1911.

MRS. SLINGSBY'S CH. ROSETTE OF THORPE.
Winner of many championships, including 1st and championship Crystal Palace, 1910, and 1st and championship, and 2nd best Long-haired female, Glasgow, 1911.

THE WELL-KNOWN SILVER TABBY, CH. DON PEDRO OF THORPE.
Winner of 27 1sts and many championships; several times best in show. The property of Mrs. Slingsby.

Photo by] [Russell & Sons, London.
THE CHAMPION RED TABBY FEMALE, AQUILA OF THORPE.

MRS. SLINGSBY'S WELL-KNOWN CH. RED EAGLE OF THORPE.

MRS. SLINGSBY'S SUCCESSFUL CREAM MALE, CH. WILFUL OF THORPE.

These Siamese were among the first ten of their breed to arrive in England. Mrs Parker Brough's Tiam O'Shian IV (left) was imported from Bangkok in 1886 by Mrs Vivian. Below: Mrs Robinson's Champion Wankee, the first Siamese champion in England, was imported from Hong Kong. He earned his title in 1898 at the age of three.

and new colours of Abyssinians were beginning to appear on the show bench. Later in the decade the Persian section increased again with the addition of the Chocolate and Lilac Longhair and the Cameo series of cats, including the Pewter. In the British section the British Tipped, the shorthair equivalent of the Chinchilla, first appeared and this breed has become increasingly popular over the years. The Oriental section also began to grow with recognition of the Foreign Black and the Foreign Blue and the Oriental Spotted Tabby. The Balinese had also been recognized in the Siamese section. As the 1980s wore on, the Exotic Shorthair, the Golden Persian and the Shaded Silver were granted recognition and the Colourpointed British Shorthair appeared on the show bench. The Foreign section was beginning to expand dramatically with the recognition of the Somali, followed by Maine Coon, Norwegian Forest Cat, Ragdoll, the Asian group and finally Tonkinese in early 1991. The Oriental section was also growing with the introduction of the new non-self patterns: Smoke, Shaded, Tipped and Classic, Mackerel and Ticked Tabbies.

During the late 1960s much discussion had taken place about the methods of the appointment of judges and in the early 1970s Joint Advisory Committees were set up to bring together the breed clubs into groups to appoint judges jointly. The first such committee was set up by the Siamese clubs and the early meetings proved to be somewhat stormy as some of the clubs had been founded as break-away clubs originally and were not accustomed to sitting round a table with The Siamese Cat Club, which was the original club for the breed. However, with increasing goodwill and the keen help of the younger, specialist Siamese clubs a system was finally developed which enabled judges to be selected after nomination by the breed clubs and consideration by a panel of judges. Similar systems were followed by the Longhair clubs and later by groups of other breed clubs, including the Burmese and Abyssinian clubs. These schemes ran fairly smoothly until the middle 1980s when considerable dissatisfaction began to arise, particularly

Catalogues from American shows

C.F.A. **FLAGSTONE** A.C.A.

Creams Silvers Blue-eyed Whites

DBL. CH. LAS MONTANAS WALKIE TALKIE

All Southern Chinchilla Male, Best Novice, Angel City, Cal. 1951-C.F.A.; Best Novice, New Orleans All-Breed 1953-A.C.A.; Best Novice, New Orleans, Longhair 1953-A.C.A.; Best Cat and Best Champion, New Orleans All-Breed 1953 - C.F.A.; Best Cat Opp., Best Champion and Second Best Cat, Magic Valley All-Breed 1953-C.F.A.; Second Best Cat, New Orleans All-Breed 1953-A.C.A.

Flagstone's Wins this Year:

All American's	(2)	Best Champion	(3 times)
All Southern	(4)	Best Champion Opp.	(4 times)
Best Cat	(3 times)	Best Novice	(3 times)
Best Cat Opp.	(5 times)	Best Kitten	(4 times)
Second Best Cat	(3 times)	Second Best Kitten	(3 times)

All breeding stock Champions and or Double Champions

MRS. HOWELL J. MUELLER

200 Torcido Drive, San Antonio, Texas, U.S.A.

62

Shorthairs. I asked her what she considered the best cat she ever owned and the answer floored me. I thought it would be Grand Champion Lavender Liberty or Grand Champion Lavender Beau. But no, she said her best cat ever was Champion Lavender Chu-Chu.

When I questioned her regarding show managers and what she considered a requisite she replied: "One with an even disposition who abides by the Association rules. She must try to make the show the sport it should be, win or lose."

is an asset. She avers that she has seen many novices who were genuine and others who had no patience to continue in striving to better their breed.

Breeding show dogs is another phase of Miss Hydon's busy life. She has six different breeds of dogs and one or more champions in every breed.

Some of the Persians that she remembers best are Hiawatha of Hounslow, Lavender Secony Lad, Lavender Regside Gem, Thalia of Culloden, Laughton's Lapine, Lavender Chu-Chu, Garth of Allington, Greyeldo of Allington (all

Champion LAVENDER CHU-CHU, the Blue Longhair rated by Miss Hydon as her "best cat ever."

One of the most outstanding things Judge Hydon has worked for in the Cat Fanciers' Association is trying to keep the breeds pure in blood lines. She feels that the novice is "getting a break" from C.F.A. and that the novice

Blues), and Eastbury Trigo, a Red Tabby. Three of her Blacks became Champions, many others in Creams and Blue-Creams.

Once you have met Miss Hydon and talked with her you will not forget her.

63

Cat association yearbooks are an important historical record of the comings and goings and goings on in the cat fancy

in the Longhair section of the Fancy. This resulted in the decision to set up a new scheme for the appointment of judges; this work was pioneered by the GCCF Chairman of the time, Mrs Kay Burgess and was finally introduced in October 1988. Mrs Burgess guided the scheme through its early teething troubles until her untimely death in December 1989. Many good things resulted from the new scheme including the consolidation of the judging lists, so enabling judges to consider a wide range of colours within their breed instead of being restricted to only one colour. Unfortunately, the scheme has not progressed as had been hoped, probably due to the considerable requirement for both manpower and finance and it is currently being reviewed by the Council.

The growth of cat clubs and cat shows has been keeping pace with the increase in cat breeding and there are now 108 affiliated clubs about half of which are area clubs and half breed clubs. The clubs send delegates to the Council which meets at least three times a year, clubs with 200 members or more send two delegates, smaller clubs send one and the National Cat Club is allowed four delegates in recognition of the powers it relinquished in 1910. The Electoral meeting is held in June each year when the Officers and Committee Members are chosen for the ensuing year. The administration of the Fancy is the responsibility of the Executive Committee and the Finance Committee advises on money matters. The disciplinary powers are the responsibility of three committees; the Investigation, Disciplinary and Appeals Committees. The welfare work of the Fancy is coordinated by the Cat Welfare Liaison Group which works with the affiliated clubs to provide help nationwide.

There has been little change in the functions of the Council during the eighty years of its life and these are to:

Provide for the registration of cats and production of certified pedigrees.

Classify cat breeds and issue Standards of Points for judging cats.

License cat shows and appoint judges.

Prepare, publish, rules to control these functions.

Protect the welfare of and improve breeding of cats.

Protect the interest of cat owners.

Exercise disciplinary powers.

During the 1990's the Cat Fancy in Great Britain will find it necessary to deal with many existing problems. The number of cat shows has proliferated. Until the 1960's the majority of Championship shows were held during the period August to April. Only a few non-Championship shows were held during the early summer months, and breeders had time to relax and concentrate on the breeding and development of good sound stock. New cat clubs then sprang up all over the country, and in many cases specialist breed clubs split for a variety of reasons. Breakaway rival clubs were formed and soon claimed their right to affiliation with the GCCF. In the course of time many of these newly formed clubs became ambitious and decided to apply for permission to hold shows of their own. Very few Saturdays are now left in the year without at least one cat show. On some Saturdays two or three shows are held in different parts of the country. This has inevitably led to an acute shortage of qualified judges.

The author amidst several generations of superb cats, among them three black Persians—1959 Cat of the Year Grand Champion Vel-Vene Voo Doo of Silva-Wyte, 1967 Cat of the Year Grand Champion Silva-Wyte Trafari of JB, and Grand Champion Silva-Wyte Elmer Fudd. Also represented are Grand Champion Silva-Wyte Pola, a white Manx. This portrait [24" x 36"] by Time *magazine cover artist, Roy Andersen, was presented to the author by the Cat Fanciers' Association in commemoration of thirty years of service.*

Grand Champion Silva-Wyte Trafari of JB

From time to time the GCCF has looked at the problem, but no satisfactory solution has yet been found. The most obvious course of action would be to instigate a massive judge training programme. However, there is an obvious problem at once apparent. A cat show is a beauty contest. While many people have the ability to learn and memorise the technical details, not everybody has the inborn ability to assess the aesthetic quality of the entire cat. At any one time, there will always be a limited number of people in the Cat Fancy who possess this artistic perception to a high degree.

The new judge appointment system adopted in 1988 will need radical review. It was then felt more democratic that judge appointment bodies should have broad representation on them from all parts of the Fancy, and no longer consist only of experienced senior judges. The result of this has been that many members of the present Breed Advisory Committees who recommend their approved candidates to Council for appointment as judges, consist of members with only very limited experience. Some have never bred cats.

In 1992 Great Britain will become fully integrated into the European Economic Community. Many experienced cat breeders in England feel that the links with the Continent must become much closer and stronger. Because of the very strict Rabies regulations, which make it compulsory for every imported cat to spend six months in a quarantine cattery, there have been few close links between British cat breeders and their European counterparts. Perhaps the opening of the Channel Tunnel will make easy access to Europe a practical possibility for large numbers of cat breeders. At present it is not possible for them to take their cats to European shows, but it is fairly certain that large numbers will take this first opportunity to drive to Continental shows as visitors.

Although the Rabies restrictions will remain in force, there is the slight possibility that the British Government might review the situation. Race horses are allowed to cross the channel to compete in horse-races under strictly controlled conditions. Perhaps it may become possible to obtain 48 hour passes for cats to be exhibited in Europe. They would be taken in carrying baskets, under careful supervision, and not allowed to roam freely.

Visitors to the exhibitions will find a fascinating contrast between shows held in the United Kingdom and Europe. In Britain no conversation or remarks are allowed between judge and exhibitor until all the judges' classes have been dealt with. In Europe the cats are brought from their pens to the judging area. In all FIFe shows the judge is required to do 'open judging'. After handling and assessing the cat, and writing up a report sheet on each exhibit, the judge will display the cat and give a running commentary. He or she will explain the reasoning behind the order of placing. If a Certificate has been withheld the judge will explain the reason. Faults or defects are discussed, and the exhibitor has every opportunity to ask questions. In this way the judging becomes an educative process.

Out in the Hall the pens are often highly decorated, making a splendid splash of colour. The exhibitors frequently bring portable chairs, food and wine, and have small parties while the judging is going on elsewhere throughout the two days of the show.

It seems probable that within the next decade the GCCF will need to review the current breed numbering system. The one in use has grown piecemeal over a lengthy period and has now become something of a muddle. FIFe have already tackled the problem and produced a new and logical system which appears to be working well.

Design and Function of the Cat

ALL SYSTEMS GO

The cat is a remarkable collection of systems: nervous, endocrine, respiratory, lymphatic, digestive, reproductive, urinary, circulatory, and musculoskeletal.

The nervous system comprises the cerebrum, cerebellum, midbrain, spinal cord, twelve pairs of cranial nerves, and paired sets of peripheral nerves that extend from the spinal cord to all parts of the body. Some functions governed by the agents of the nervous system are learning, reasoning, memory, judgment, and involuntary action—which are controlled by the cerebrum. Blood pressure, respiratory and heart rates are monitored by the midbrain.

The endocrine system comprises the glands that secrete hormones into the bloodstream. The master gland is the pituitary, at the base of the brain. Like a batch file in a computer, the pituitary gland controls the activities of other glands—including the thyroid and adrenal glands, the testicles and ovaries—which in turn control activities of the body. The pituitary gland also produces growth-stimulating hormone.

The respiratory system includes the nose, throat, larynx (voice box), trachea (windpipe), bronchial tubes, and lungs. A cat at rest completes twenty-five to thirty breaths a minute, about twice as many as a human does. In the cat, inhaling, the initial phase of respiration, takes about half as long as exhaling.

The lymphatic system, one of the main defensive systems of the cat's body, is a network of vessels that transport lymph—which is made up of excess tissue fluids, proteins, and other substances. This system functions without benefit of a pump, and carries out its mission through the venous side of the circulatory system. Lymph nodes, another component of the lymphatic system, filter out foreign particles found skulking throughout the body. Lymph nodes contain lymphocytes, a type of white blood cell, which produce antibodies that neutralize bacterial poisons.

The digestive system includes the mouth, teeth, oesophagus, stomach, small and large intestines, liver, pancreas, and rectum. Of all carnivores, cats have the fewest teeth, thirty. Since these were not made for chewing, cats tear their food into small bite pieces, then swallow them whole.

The kidneys, ureters, bladder, and urethra make up the urinary or excretory system in both sexes. In close partnership is the reproductive system. The testicles and sperm ducts comprise the male reproductive system, while the female's ductwork includes fallopian tubes, uterus, womb, and vagina.

The remaining systems of the cat—circulatory and musculoskeletal—warrant some elaboration; the musculoskeletal system because it is the bedrock of conformation, body type at its most elementary, and the circulatory system because it is the medium through which many of the body's other systems function.

THE MUSCULOSKELETAL SYSTEM

THE MUSCLES

From the first time a kitten paddles toward its mother, it is seeking to command the voluntary muscles. These will soon enable the kitten to scuffle with its littermates for a place in the food line, knead contentedly against its mother's belly, crawl, wobble, stand, totter, fall, right itself, look about uncertainly, and then walk.

Voluntary muscles are sometimes called striped or striated muscles because they exhibit longitudinal stripes. They are also called skeletal muscles because their chief function is moving the cat's skeleton from place to place. Secured by tendons to bones, skeletal muscles are always arranged in pairs—antagonists and protagonists that work in cooperative opposition.

When a cat jumps, for example, it crouches on its heels by contracting two muscles: the hamstring, a flexor muscle located behind the thigh bone; and the tibialis, a flexor muscle in front of the tibia and fibula bones. At that point the corresponding extensor

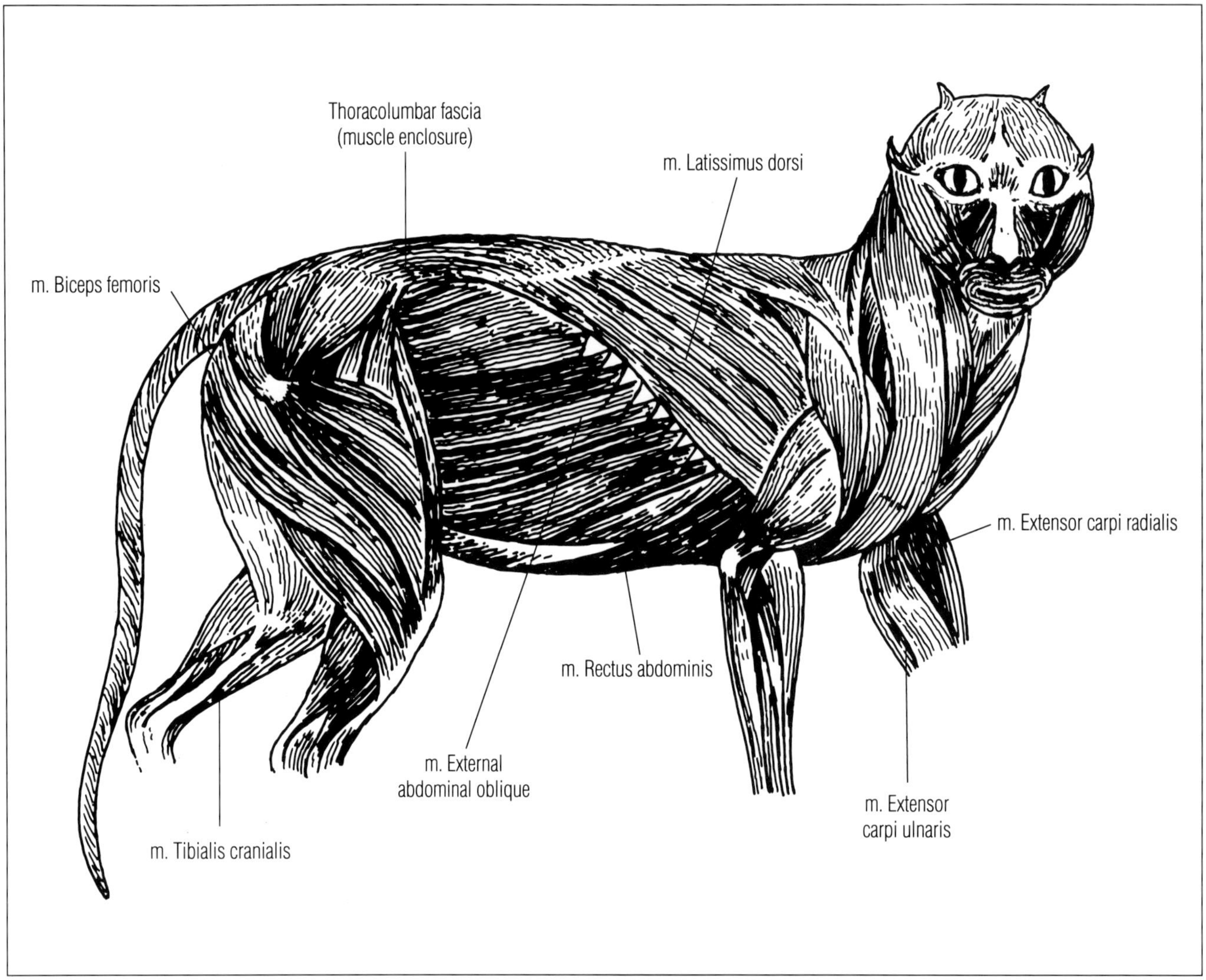

The muscles of the cat

muscles that were stretched while the hamstring and tibialis were contracting, contract powerfully themselves, hurling the cat temporarily beyond gravity's bounds.

Involuntary muscles, which are not consciously controlled by a cat, are already functioning when a kitten begins to crawl. Also known as smooth muscles, the involuntary muscles are found in the alimentary canal, the urinary tract, and the respiratory system.

THE SKELETON

There are 244 bones in the feline skeleton. Together with cartilage they comprise the skeletal system of the cat, and are officially classified as connective tissues that bear weight.

Bone can be catalogued into three classes according to shape: long, flat, and irregular. The radius and ulna in the front legs, as well as the tibia and fibula in the hind legs, are long bones. The scapula or shoulder blade is a flat bone. So are the bones of the skull and face. The metatarsals and metacarpals in the feet are irregular bones.

In addition to occurring in three shapes, bone is formed in three varieties of ossification: intramembranous, endochondral, and heterotopic. The latter, which occurs after birth and under pathologic (disease) conditions, is the formation of bone where bone isn't normally formed. Heterotopic ossification can result in harmless pieces of bone in scars or wounds, or it can result in harmful pieces of bone appearing in vital organs.

Endochondral ossification is the formation of new

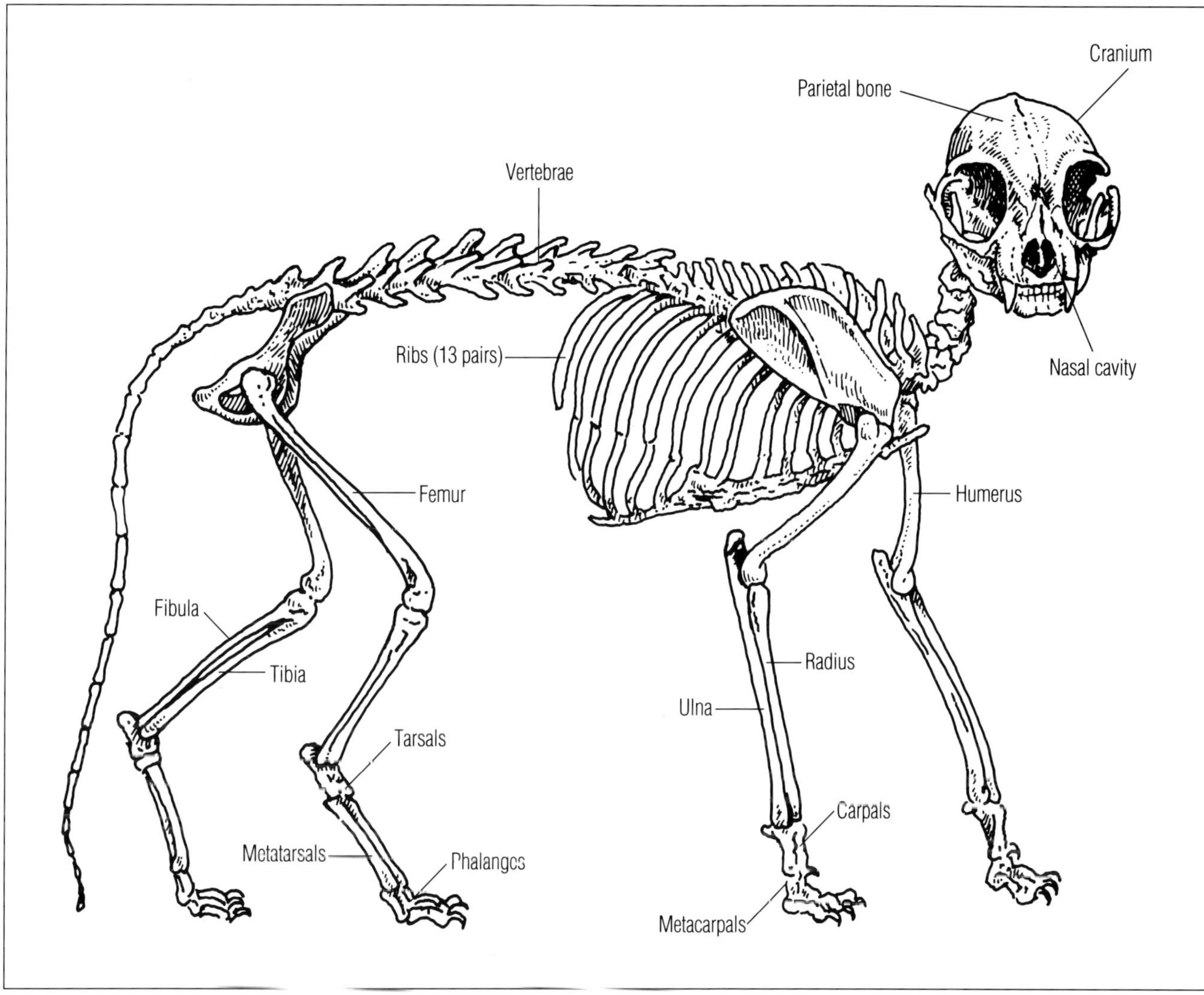

The cat skeleton

bone in an area of existing bone occupied by cartilage. In endochondral ossification, cartilage is removed and replaced by bone. The third type of bone formation, intramembranous ossification, is the development of bone under or within a connective-tissue membrane.

The flat bones in the skull are formed through intramembranous ossification. The bones at the base of the skull and in the face and trunk are formed through a combination of intramembranous and endochondral processes. Bone mass—that is, the compact bone of the shafts of the long and flat bones—is formed intramembranously, while bones grow in length endochondrally.

This means that body conformation in the cat is determined by the relative prominence of each type of bone growth. Some breeds, in which endochondral ossification is paramount, are long, lithe, and fine boned. Other breeds in which intramembranous ossification is prominent are more stocky and substantial.

THE CIRCULATORY SYSTEM

The circulatory system comprises the heart, a network of arteries and veins, and a blood reservoir, the spleen. The cat's heart beats 110 to 140 times a minute, as much as twice the human heart rate. The circulatory system contains half a pint of blood that passes around the body once every eleven seconds. The blood loops first from the heart to the lungs, changing colour from leaden blue to dazzling crimson. The iron atoms in

The cat's narrow chest and well developed hindquarters confer agility and power

haemoglobin molecules of the red blood cells discharge carbon dioxide and latch on to oxygen molecules, freshly inhaled, like riders hooking the rings on a carousel.

That pulmonary circuit completed, blood gathers itself for its journey around the body. The pulsing of the heart sends blood into the aorta and from there into smaller arteries that subdivide in the body's nooks and fissures. The pace diminishes as blood enters smaller passages—called arterioles—that regulate its flow to the body's tissues.

Metarterioles are the conduits between arterioles and capillaries. By the time blood travels through metarterioles and into capillaries, whose walls are but one cell thick, it has been slowed from a torrent to a trickle. Changing courses and complexion in midstream, the blood is now purplish red after exchanging oxygen for carbon dioxide with cells adjacent to the capillary bed. The blood exits the capillaries through venules (tiny veins), which go to veins leading back to the heart, where the eleven-second journey commences again.

There are many workers in the cat's bloodstream: carrying out the oxygen-carbon dioxide exchange and shuttling back and forth between the brain and various tissues and organs. Elements in the bloodstream create the clots that patch up tears, control osmotic pressure and adjust the cat's thermostat toward cool when he is overheated, toward warm when he is in danger of freezing. Blood also defends the cat against invasion by disease, rushes to the stomach after meals, to the lungs during exertion, and (in humans at least) to the face in times of embarrassment.

The bloodstream is also the chief agent of thermoregulation in the body. Heat generated by bodily functions is unloaded into the blood, which conveys part of that heat to other body sites for redistribution and sends the rest on its way to the outside world. Blood's ability to speed to the surface of the skin in large volumes and at a high rate enables it to transport large quantities of heat outward. Conversely, when a cat is cold, it can create muscular heat by shivering; and that heat is carried by the blood to internal organs that cannot produce their own heat.

RED BLOOD CELLS

Red blood cells are the most numerous cells in the body. They exist in the cat in numbers that defy the mind to attach meaning to zeros. The production of red blood cells—which have a life-span of two to six weeks—begins when tissue, anticipating a shortage of oxygen, dispatches a hormone called erythropoietin, via the bloodstream, to the bone marrow located in red blood cell construction sites. This hormone signals a number of primitive cells, so named because they have yet to develop fully, to begin growth.

These dormant cells quickly evolve into rubriblasts, the first recognizable harbingers of mature red blood cells. Each rubriblast divides into two. Three divisions later, the original pair of rubriblasts has turned into sixteen red blood cells (RBCs), composed mainly of water and haemoglobin. There are 270 million haemoglobin molecules in every red blood cell. Each haemoglobin molecule contains four atoms of iron. Therefore each molecule of haemoglobin can transport over 1 billion molecules of oxygen. When haemoglobin accounts for 95 percent of the dry weight of a red blood cell—about day three of the six-day RBC production process—the cell ejects its nucleus. This act of self-sterilization frees the cell from all distractions, leaving only the need to work, which the cell does until it works itself to death. The unperforated-doughnut shape of the mature red blood cell allows the cell to squeeze through the tiniest capillaries to deliver oxygen and haul away carbon dioxide.

GIVING CATS A HEAD START

When assessing a cat, most judges examine the head first, before moving on to look at body, legs, tail and coat. The head type is one of the most distinctive features of a breed and there is no denying that the head sets the standard for the body in a physical sense.

The star pupil in the cat's head is the brain, the valedictorian of the central nervous system. Located in the cranial cavity, the brain is an enlarged, highly modified continuation of the spinal cord. It is divided into two egg-shaped hemispheres whose surfaces are marked by numerous, thick folds. These cerebral hemispheres make up the greater part of the fully developed brain, which is held by the snug-fitting cranial cavity. The posterior wall of this protective compartment (and a portion of its base as well) is formed by the occipital bone, whose lower section is perforated centrally by an almost circular opening. At this point the spinal chord blossoms.

Like wires running to the dashboard of a car, twelve pairs of cranial nerves keep the brain informed of developments affecting the sensory and motor systems. Three of these twelve pairs of nerves—the optic, olfactory, and auditory—serve as couriers of the special senses: sight, sound, and smell. Five pairs of cranial nerves—the oculomotor, abducens, hypoglossal, trochlear, and spinal accessory—serve the motor functions; and the remaining four pairs—the trigeminal, facial, glosso-pharyngeal, and vagus—serve both sensory and motor functions.

Gradually, the one-celled organisms that were the earliest forms of life banded together to form colonies. As cell colonies evolved into sponges, tubeworms, crustaceans, molluscs, fishes, and mammals, the head of each organism—besides playing host to the brain—began to partake in more of the body's functions. Thus, air intake, food intake, and excretory capabilities can all be found in the cat's head, which acts, in a sense, as the body in miniature. The head, for example, produces some digestive enzymes in the salivary glands, located on either side of the face and the adjacent parts of the neck. The largest of these glands is the parotid, named for its proximity to the ear.

Among the substances absorbed in the head are essential oils, which contribute much to the flavour of life. You can feel an example of this absorption when you suck on a cough drop and the tingling in your face tells you that your mucosal membrane is taking up the camphor in the drop. In similar manner, metallic salts and other relatively uncomplicated materials, including the rabies virus, are shed in saliva.

Besides directing sensory-motor activities and participating in vital functions of the body, the head, through the pituitary gland—the principal control gland of the body—influences the endocrine system, too. Nearly a dozen functions in the body are controlled by hormones manufactured, released, or stored by the pituitary gland at the base of the brain. These include everything from growth to the onset of oestrus to the amount of urine secreted by the kidneys.

The head is the dominant part of the cat: because of its evolutionary history, its custody of the brain, its stewardship of the pituitary gland, and its access to feedback from all precincts of the body via the nervous and circulatory systems.

Indeed, the cat's body can be thought of as a member of the servant class, dedicated to the needs of its headstrong master. The muscles of the legs and back, to cite an example, exist to transport the head so that it can obtain food and participate in the other functions essential to life.

The head also claims absolute priority to the body's oxygen and nutrient supplies and to its circulatory capacity. The circulatory system has nervous control mechanisms that deprive the guts, the legs, and the feet of blood to make sure that the cat's head gets an adequate supply. What's more, the brain lives on a diet of simple chemicals. Other cells throughout the body have to work harder for their nutrients—and they have the capacity to do so—but the brain lives well on simple fare.

CONFORMATION

Muscle and bone are the architects of conformation. The 244 bones in the feline skeleton lend support and substance to a cat's body while protecting its internal organs. In some breeds bone is sturdy as an oak; in others it is delicate as scrimshaw. In every breed bone is decorated in wreaths of muscle. By conducting an electrical impulse, and then—through a series of chemical transformations—converting that impulse into contractions, muscle produces movement and, ultimately, the gracefulness that characterizes the cat.

Japanese Bobtail

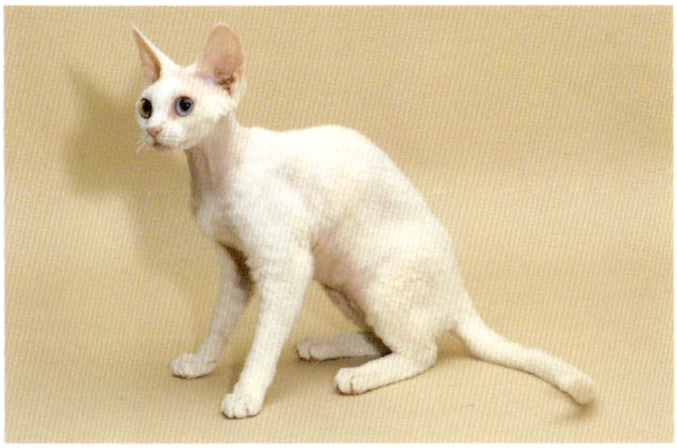

Devon Rex

Burmese

EARS

A cat's ears are decorative as well as functional. They make statements in addition to receiving them. There's no mistaking the message intended by a cat when its ears are pinned back. The upper limit of a cat's hearing is higher than a dog's and almost two octaves higher than ours. From a distance of three feet, cats can discriminate between sources of sound that are as little as three inches apart. They are also able to ignore the sound of their owners' voices from virtually any distance.

Colourpoint Shorthair

British Shorthair

Cornish Rex

EYES

Round, almond shaped, or in between, the cat's eye is a gem that reflects a mysterious lustre. Cats are the most efficient gleaners of light. Their pupils can dilate to a soulful, half-inch width or narrow to the most inscrutable slit. Cats cannot see in absolute darkness, nor are they absolutely colour blind, though they can see red only in the emotional sense. They are, in addition, somewhat farsighted. Their depth of field is in sharpest focus between seven and twenty feet.

Turkish Angora

Maine Coon Cat

Siamese

SIZE

Unlike dog breeders, who are able to work with a variety of sizes, cat fanciers are limited in design. The difference between the largest breed of cat, the Ragdoll, and the smallest, the Singapura, is little more than a dozen pounds and less than one square foot at the extreme; while the difference between the longest and the shortest facial profiles is about two inches. Most other breeds fall into the one-size-fits-all category. Yet within these frugal limits, more than forty breeds have been defined.

Exotic Shorthair

Ragdoll

Singapura

COAT LENGTH

There are thirteen shorthaired and ten longhaired breed types, many of which are further subdivided by colour into separate breeds. Five pairs of breed types are separated by the gene for coat length: Exotic Shorthair/Persian, Abyssinian/Somali, Asian/Tiffanie, Oriental Shorthair/Angora, Siamese/Balinese. Coat length is also one of the factors, together with facial type, body conformation and coat pattern, which divides breeds into their separate sections at GCCF shows.

American Shorthair

Persian

Bombay (an Asian breed)

COAT TYPE

Hair grows from tiny pits in the skin called follicles. Primary or guard hairs, the longest ones in a cat's coat, grow from individual follicles. Secondary hairs—usually classified as awn hairs (bristly tipped and medium in length) or down hairs (fine, crinkled, and short in length)—grow in groups from single openings. Grooming needs are determined not so much by coat length as by coat type. Breeds with thick undercoats (awn and down hairs) are more likely to mat—and hence require more attention—than breeds with less profuse undercoats.

Abyssinian

Birman

Cornish Rex

TAIL

Cats' tails range from long, thin, and whiplike to short, thick, and plumelike. The Siamese' tail ends somewhere over the rainbow; the Manx' tail stops before it begins. The Japanese Bobtail's tail is curled, corkscrewed, pom-pommed, and shaving brushed. It should not, however, be manipulated by a judge. Otherwise, judges check tails for kinks, proper length, and flexibility. They also check to see if a tail is swishing to and fro, which is not a sign of friendly barometric pressure. Cats don't see what all the fuss is about. They use their tails as balancing poles and to keep their noses warm when they sleep.

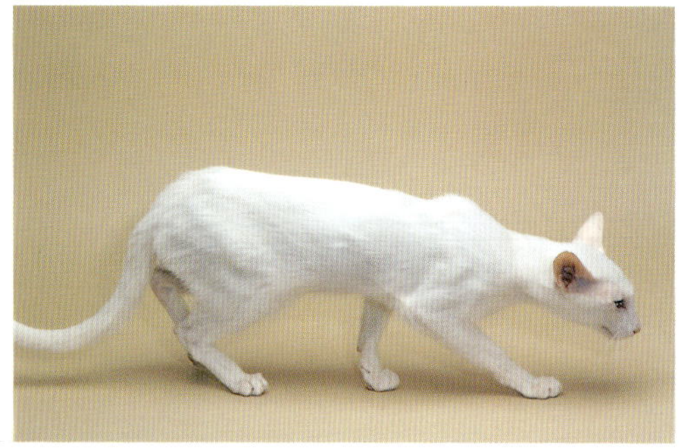

Oriental Shorthair

Scottish Fold

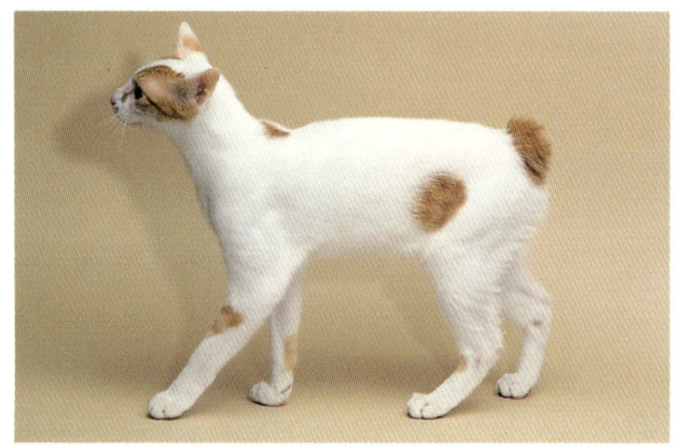

Japanese Bobtail

Introduction to the Breeds

The GCCF is the major registering body in the United Kingdom. They recognise twenty two main breeds of cat for Championship competition.

These include: Abyssinian; Angora; the Asian Group, which are cats of Burmese type and include the Bombay, Tiffany and Burmilla; Balinese; Birman; British Shorthair; Burmese; Cornish and Devon Rex; Exotics; Foreign; Havana; Korat; Longhairs (including Cameos, Chinchillas, Shaded Silvers, Colourpoints, Pewters and Golden Persians) Maine Coon; Manx; Norwegian Forest; Oriental; Ragdoll; Russian Blue; Siamese; Somali and Turkish Van. Peke faced Persians which are popular in the United States are not accepted in the United Kingdom.

The largest registering body in Europe is FIFe (Feline International Federation of Europe) with twenty six countries world wide forming its membership. A number of large Independent Groups in Europe also keep cat pedigree registers and control cat shows. In the United States the Cat Fanciers' Association is the largest registry. Most people register their cats with CFA, even if they also choose to register and exhibit their cats elsewhere.

The CFA Standards of breeds not recognised in the United Kingdom are presented in every case where CFA recognises a breed. In other cases we have attempted to present the Standard of the Association in the United States that recognised a breed first.

In all cases where the standards of other registries differ from the one being used to describe a breed, those differences are discussed in footnotes at the end of the standard. Descriptions of colours found in these breeds which occur in a handful of colours only are provided with the breed standards. Several breeds occur in a multitude of the colours however. The colours for these breeds are listed, but not described, at the end of each breed standard. A discussion of the colours for these breeds begins on page 170. Those breeds in which eye colour must conform to coat colour are identified, and the correspondences between eye colour and coat colour in those breeds are identified on page 173.

In the captions of the Breeds section, different colour descriptions of the same breed sometimes occur. In these cases, the British description appears first, followed by the American in brackets.

Abyssinian

ORIGIN

The legends surrounding the Abyssinian's history are as varied as its splendid coat pattern. One band of believers claims that Abys descended from cats worshipped by the Egyptians more than four thousand years ago. Another group declares that Abys originated in the jungles of North Africa, from which they were brought to England by soldiers returning from the Abyssinian War during the late 1860s. Others argue that the Abys' ancestors were nothing more exotic than ticked tabbies roaming the fields and lanes of Great Britain. But whatever its country of origin, one thing about the Abyssinian is certain: it is obviously a definite and recognizable breed type.

As far as we can determine from available records,

Usual (Ruddy) Abyssinian

the first Abyssinian to reach England was a cat named Zula, who was imported by Mrs. Barrett-Lennard in 1868. According to one writer, Zula 'and possibly other imports were bred with similarly marked cats of partly unknown origin,' and thus the Abyssinian breed was born. By 1882 the Abyssinian was listed as a separate breed in England, and silver Abys, which were also known as chinchillas, were among the early Abyssinian colours. By 1900, however, many authorities declared that the Abyssinian was merely

A Usual (Ruddy) Abyssinian, from England, shorter in the head, body, and legs than the American version.

the result of chance matings among ordinary tabbies, and the name Abyssinian was replaced for a time by 'Ticks' or 'British Ticks' or 'Bunny Cats.' This revisionist opinion was supported by the fact that each of the twelve Abyssinians registered in the Stud Book of the National Cat Club in England for 1900 –1905 was descended from at least one parent of unknown origin.

DEVELOPMENT

The Abyssinian Breed in Britain remained relatively small in numbers prior to the Second World War and during the war the breed came close to dying out. In the GCCF stud book covering the war years, there are only four Abyssinian females and six Abyssinian males listed with the Brunswycke prefix of Mrs Anderson and the Crowham prefix of Major Woodiwiss being the most prominent.

After the war the breed began to increase in numbers very slowly and by the mid fifties the breed was beginning to stabilize. During this time on rare occasions Blue Abyssinian kittens appeared in litters. However, these were not recognized and were normally sold as pets and only the Usual and later the Sorrel Abyssinians were recognized.

During the early sixties a move was made to breed Blue Abyssinians and also to reintroduce the Silver Abyssinians that had not been seen since the turn of the century. This was attempted by outcrossing to silver cats of other breeds. Slowly the range of colours has been increased to include Chocolate and Lilac Abyssinians.

Considerable research has been done into the origins of the blue Abyssinian by George Kennedy in New Zealand. His pedigree research has shown that this colour was found in the early 1950's, if not before. In 1952 two kittens were born in Scotland, Albyn Jason and Ch Albyn Jara and Jason carried the blue colour abroad through his progeny Ch Selborne Catalpa in New Zealand and Ch Abu of Knott Hall of Blue Grass in the United States. His litter sister Jara went to England and her grandson Nigella Kym sired blue kittens in the late fifties.

Towards the end of the 1970s many Abyssinian cats were affected by the Feline Leukemia Virus and the breed numbers were reduced dramatically to such a degree that it was feared that the breed might die out completely.

However, once the mechanism of the virus was understood it enabled breeders to test the stock and only breed from virus free cats. Numbers have slowly increased and by 1990 as many as 750 Abyssinians were being registered by the GCCF each year. The cats have a distinctive temperament and they make excellent pets but are sometimes a little nervous of sudden loud noises.

ABYSSINIAN

General Type Standard

TYPE: Foreign type of medium build, firm, lithe and muscular, never large or coarse. The head to be broad and tapering to a firm wedge set on an elegant neck. The body to be of medium length with fairly long tapering tail. A 'cobby' cat is not permissible.

HEAD AND EARS: Head is a moderate wedge of medium proportions, the brow, cheeks and profile lines showing a gentle contour and the muzzle not sharply pointed. A shallow indentation forming the muzzle is desirable but a pinch is a fault. Ears set wide apart and pricked, broad at base, comparatively large, well cupped and preferably tufted. In profile the head shows a gentle rounding to the brow with a slight nose break leading to a very firm chin.

EYES: Well apart, large, bright and expressive in an oriental setting. A squint is a fault. Colour, amber, hazel and green. A light colour is desirable.

TAIL: Broad at base, fairly long and tapering. Neither a whip nor a kink is permissible.

FEET: Small and oval.

COAT: Short, fine and close lying with double, or preferably treble ticking, i.e. two or three bands of colour on each hair.

MARKINGS: It is required that the appropriate darker hair colour extends well up the back of the hind legs; also showing as a solid tip at the extreme end of the tail, and the absence of either is a fault. A line of dark pigmentation is required round the eyes and the absence of this is also a fault. Undesirable markings are bars on the legs, chest and tail. An unbroken necklet is not permissible. The Abyssinian cat has a tendency to white in the immediate area of the lips and lower jaw and it is a fault if this white area extends on to the neck. A locket and other white markings are not permissible.

ABYSSINIAN COLOURS

USUAL (23): Body colour to be rich golden brown, ticked with black and the base hair ruddy orange or rich apricot. A pale or cold overall colour is a fault and so are black or grey base hairs. The belly and inside of legs to be a ruddy orange or rich apricot to harmonize with the base hair on the rest of the body. Any spinal shading to be of deeper colour. The tip of the tail and the solid colour on the hind legs to be black. Nose leather to be brick red and pads to be black.

SORREL (23a): Body colour to be a lustrous copper, ticked with chocolate and the base hair deep apricot. A pale or sandy colour is a fault. The belly and inside of legs to be a deep apricot to harmonize with the base hair on the rest of the body. Any spinal shading to be a deeper colour. The tip of the tail and the solid colour on the hind legs to be chocolate. Nose leather and pads to be pink.

BLUE (23c): Body colour to be blue-grey with a soft warm effect, ticked with deeper steel blue and the base hair oatmeal. The belly and inside of legs to be oatmeal to harmonize with the base hair on the rest of the body. Any spinal shading to be of deeper colour. The tip of the tail and the solid colour on the hind legs to be steel blue. Nose leather to be dark pink and pads to be mauvish-blue.

NOTE: Any cat displaying a FEATURE which is NOT PERMISSIBLE (i.e. cobby type; whip tail; kink in tail; unbroken necklet; locket; other white markings) shall not be awarded a First Prize, nor a Challenge Certificate nor a Premier Certificate.

Any cat displaying a FAULT may be awarded a prize but any cat displaying two or more faults shall neither be awarded a Challenge Certificate nor a Premier Certificate.

Silver Abyssinian (Provisional)

TYPE: As for breeds 23, 23a and 23c.
Black Silver (23s, Provisional)
Sorrel Silver (23as, Provisional)
Blue Silver (23cs, Provisional)

Abyssinian (Preliminary)

Chocolate (23b, Preliminary)
Lilac (Dilute Chocolate 23d, Preliminary)
Fawn (Dilute Sorrel 23e, Preliminary)
Red (23f, Preliminary)
Cream (23g, Preliminary)

Preliminary (Tortie Abyssinian)

Usual Tortie (23t, Preliminary)
Sorrel Tortie (23at, Preliminary)
Blue Tortie (23ct, Preliminary)
Chocolate Tortie (23bt, Preliminary)
Lilac Tortie (23dt, Preliminary)
Fawn Tortie (23et, Preliminary)

Preliminary (Silver Abyssinian)

Chocolate Silver (23bs, Preliminary)
Lilac Silver (23ds, Preliminary)
Fawn Silver (23es, Premliniary)

Abyssinian allowable outcross breeds:[12] none.

American Shorthair

ORIGIN

Shorthaired cats arrived in North America with the early settlers. In fact, some historians believe there was at least one cat aboard the Mayflower when it landed in 1620. As they had for centuries before whenever they made their way from one land to another, cats earned their passage aboard ship by protecting stores of food and grain from rats and mice. After arriving in the New World, cats were expected to continue paying their own way and making their own breeding arrangements.

By 1900, domestic cats had begun to attract some notice from cat fanciers, but that attraction was minimal. Until then the Maine Coon Cat was the favourite son (and daughter) of cat fanciers in North America, and after the turn of the century most fanciers became interested in the more unusual and exotic foreign breeds. Not surprisingly, the first shorthaired 'domestic' cat registered in the United States was from Great Britain: an orange tabby male with an unusual name, Champion Belle of Bradford, who had been imported around 1901. Belle was registered in a breed that was simply called 'Shorthair.' Some time later, after American-born cats had been incorporated into breeding programmes there, 'Domestic' was added to the breed's designation.

Brown Classic Tabby American Shorthair

DEVELOPMENT

For many years there were few requirements that had to be met for registering Domestic Shorthairs. Most were of unknown origin, and they were frequently entered in household pet classes, which had been created for all cats that did not appear to be purebred or to have registered parents. When Domestics did compete in championship classes, they were not always treated kindly. American Cat Fanciers' Association judge Kay McQuillen, who began showing cats in 1938, has written that there were often no cages provided for Domestic Shorthairs at shows and no trophies or rosettes for the winners in Domestic classes.

Once breeders began to realize the unusual colours and patterns they could develop by selectively breeding Domestic Shorthairs, they began to demand more respect for their breed. They voted to change the breed's name to American Shorthair beginning with the 1966 show season. What gained the breed even more respect, however, was the success of two silver tabbies. In 1964 a silver tabby male named Shawnee Sixth Son was CFA's Kitten of the Year, and in 1965 a silver tabby male named Shawnee Trademark was CFA's Best Cat. These were the first of their breed to achieve such status.

Over the years, the open registration of American Shorthairs has been an on-again-off-again practice. Open registration means that a person can register any shorthaired cat as an American Shorthair. Some

Silver Classic Tabby American Shorthair

breeders used this opportunity to introduce new colours to the American breed or new vigour to its gene pool by breeding street cats or farm cats to their registered Americans. Other breeders took advantage of the rule to introduce new breeds as outcrosses—mainly Persians, and the occasional Burmese. There is no question that a little Persian blood enhances the American Shorthair, producing a more stylized, rounded head and adding substance to bone and body. The silver tabby Americans competing today would not exist if it were not for outcrosses that have been made to chinchilla Persians under the generous terms of open registration. Indeed, the silver tabby is the most highly regarded American Shorthair and has enjoyed great popularity for many years.

American Shorthairs have made valuable contributions to other breeds as well. They were crossed with Siamese to lend new colours to the Colourpoint Shorthair. They were crossed clandestinely with Burmese to improve Burmese type and vigour. And thus the Bombay was born. Covert crosses between Americans and Persians produced the Exotic Shorthair. Americans also played a part in the foundation crosses that produced the Ocicat, Snowshoe, and Scottish Fold. And they were used to reintroduce calicos and bicolours to the Persian breed. What's more, American Shorthairs are still allowable outcrosses for the American Wirehair, Bombay, Devon Rex (until May 1, 1993), and Scottish Fold. The endless supply of American Shorthairs and their adaptability have benefited many breeds in need of new blood, variety, strength, or vigour.

AMERICAN SHORTHAIR

Not recognized by the GCCF

Standard, courtesy of the Cat Fanciers' Association of America. Differences in the Standards of other registries are indicated at the end of the text.

HEAD: 30 (includes eye shape and size; ear shape and set; nose structure)

TYPE: 25 (includes shape, size, bone, and length of tail)

COAT: 15

COLOUR: 20 (tabby pattern = 10 points; colour = 10 points)

EYE COLOUR: 10

GENERAL: The American Shorthair is a true breed of working cat. The conformation should be adapted for this with no part of the anatomy so exaggerated as to foster weakness. The general effect should be that of a strongly built, well-balanced, symmetrical cat with conformation indicating power, endurance, and agility.
SIZE: Medium to large. No sacrifice of quality for sake of size. Females may be less massive in all respects than males.
PROPORTIONS: Slightly longer than tall. (Height is profile measure from top of shoulder blades to ground. Length is profile measure from tip of breastbone to rear tip of buttocks.) Viewed from side, body can be divided into three equal parts: from tip of breastbone to elbow, from elbow to front of hind leg, and from front of hind leg to rear tip of buttocks. Length of tail is equal to distance from shoulder blades to base of tail.
HEAD: Large, with full-cheeked face giving the impression of an oblong just slightly longer than wide.[1] Sweet, open expression. Viewed from front, head can be divided in two equal parts: from base of ears to middle of eyes, and from middle of eyes to chin tip.
EARS: Medium size, slightly rounded at tips and not unduly open at base. Distance between ears, measured from lower inner corners, twice distance between eyes.
FOREHEAD: Viewed in profile, forehead forms smooth, moderately convex, continuous curve flowing over top of head into neck. Viewed from front, there is no dome between ears.
EYES: Large[2] and wide with upper lid shaped like half an almond (cut lengthwise) and lower lid shaped in a fully rounded curve.[3,4] At least width of one eye between eyes. Outer corners set very slightly higher than inner corners. Bright, clear, and alert.[5]
NOSE: Medium length,[6] same width for entire length. Viewed in profile, gentle concavely curved rise from bridge of nose to forehead.
MUZZLE: Squared. Definite jowls in mature males.

JAWS: Strong and long enough to grasp prey successfully. Both level and scissors bites considered equally correct. (In level bite, top and bottom front teeth meet evenly. In scissors bite, inside edge of top front teeth touch outside edge of lower front teeth.)
CHIN: Firm and well developed, forming perpendicular line with upper lip.
NECK: Medium in length, muscular and strong.
BODY: Solidly built, powerful, and muscular with well-developed shoulders, chest, and hindquarters. Back broad, straight, and level. Viewed in profile, slight slope down from hip bone to base of tail. Viewed from above, outer lines of body parallel.
LEGS: Medium in length and bone, heavily muscled. Viewed from rear, all four legs straight and parallel with paws facing forward.
PAWS: Firm, full, and rounded, with heavy pads. Toes: five in front, four behind.
TAIL: Medium long, heavy at base, tapering to abrupt blunt end in appearance but with normal tapering final vertebrae.
COAT: Short,[7] thick, even, and hard in texture. Regional and seasonal variation in coat thickness allowed.[8] Coat dense enough to protect from moisture, cold, and superficial skin injuries.
PENALIZE: Excessive cobbiness or ranginess. Very short tail.
DISQUALIFY: Any appearance of hybridization with any other breed—including long or fluffy fur, deep nose break, bulging eye set, brow ridge. Kinked or abnormal tail. Locket or button (white spots on colours not specifying same). Incorrect number of toes. Undershot or overshot bite. Obesity or emaciation. Any feature so exaggerated as to foster weakness.

AMERICAN SHORTHAIR COLOURS

(See page 170 for a full description of the colours listed below.)

Particolour colours: bicolour (white with unbrindled patches of black, white with unbrindled patches of blue, white with unbrindled patches of red, or white with unbrindled patches of cream), blue cream, calico, dilute calico, van bicolour (black and white, red and white, blue and white, or cream and white), van blue cream and white, van calico. **Shaded colours:** chinchilla silver, shaded cameo, shaded silver, shell cameo. **Smoke colours:** black smoke, blue smoke, cameo smoke, tortoiseshell smoke. **Solid colours:** black, blue, cream, red, white. **Tabby colours:** blue patched tabby, blue tabby (classic, mackerel), brown patched tabby, brown tabby (classic, mackerel), cameo tabby (classic, mackerel), cream tabby (classic, mackerel), red tabby (classic, mackerel), silver patched tabby, silver tabby (classic, mackerel).

American Shorthair allowable outcross breeds:[9] none.

1 TICA: 'Broad, rounded.'
2 TICA: 'Medium to large.'
3 ACFA, CFF: 'Eyes should be round.' TICA: 'Rounded.'
4 ACA: 'Oval.'
5 ACFA, CFF, TICA: '[Eye] colour must conform to requirements listed in coat-colour descriptions.'
6 ACA, ACFA, TICA: 'Medium short.'
7 CFF: 'Medium length.'
8 CFF: 'Allowance to be made for lack of lustre in blues.'
9 In all associations where the breed is recognized.

American Wirehair

ORIGIN

The American Wirehair grew out of a spontaneous mutation. The first wirehaired kitten appeared in a litter of barn cats that was born on March 5, 1966, in Verona, New York. Five of the kittens in that litter had ordinary coats. The sixth one, a red-and-white male, had sparse, wiry hair. When Joan O'Shea, a cat breeder living near Verona, heard about this kitten—whose every hair was crimped, coiled, and springy, even its whiskers—she went to visit the farmer who owned it. The farmer was not inclined to part with the kitten, but after its littermates had been killed by a weasel, he agreed to sell the red-and-white male for fifty dollars to O'Shea, who named the kitten Adam.

One day when Adam was fourteen months old, O'Shea noticed a calico cat wandering in her yard. The cat, who belonged to the neighbours' daughter, appeared to be in season. O'Shea 'invited the cat in' to meet Adam. This meeting produced four kittens, much to the neighbours' surprise. O'Shea offered to buy the kittens—two of which were red-and-white, wirehaired females. The others had normal coats.

By the time Adam became a father, O'Shea had mailed samples of his coat to the British geneticists Roy Robinson and AG Searle. Robinson replied that Adam's coat was unique, and that it was not related to either of the Rex mutations. All three types of Adam's hairs—down, awn, and guard—were twisted. In addition, the awn hairs were hooked at the tip. Though the Devon Rex possesses all three types of hairs, they are so foreshortened that they resemble down hairs (the shortest kind), while the Cornish Rex lacks guard hairs entirely (the longest type). Eventually, great variance developed among Wirehair coats. Some are sparse; some are close lying and tight; others are thick and springy—the most desirable kind. These variations occur because Wirehairs are crossed with American Shorthairs, many of which carry a recessive longhair gene that can influence coat texture.

DEVELOPMENT

Adam sired only three litters before dying of cystitis in 1970. Shortly after that Joan O'Shea stopped working with American Wirehairs. Fortunately, other breeders had taken up the cause. Mr and Mrs William Beck, who had worked with O'Shea in breeding Rex, owned one of Adam's daughters. William Beck, a Cat Fanciers' Association judge, helped to secure registration status for Wirehairs. Rosemonde S Peltz, M.D., at one time a CFA board member and a genetics consultant to the association, also became involved with the breed. The most active Wirehair advocate was CFA judge Bob Bradshaw. Most of today's breed stock descends from his Fesenbrad line.

CFA accepted Wirehairs for registration in September 1967, and the breed advanced to championship status on May 1, 1978. Although this breed is as truly American as the American Shorthair, from which the coat mutation sprang, American Wirehairs are registered as a separate breed. It would make more sense to consider the breed a variety of the American Shorthair, especially since the Shorthair is an allowable outcross breed for the Wirehair. This classification would allow straight-coated Wirehairs to be shown as American Shorthairs.

The Wirehair mutation is the work of a dominant gene. If a kitten inherits one gene for a wirehaired coat and another gene for a normal coat, the kitten will be a Wirehair. Breeding one Wire to another may produce a litter of all Wires, or some Wires and some straight-coated kittens, or all straight coats. The latter will only produce a Wire if they are bred to a Wire. One of the most disheartening experiences a Wirehair breeder must contend with is the surplus of straight-coated kittens. They are beautiful, normal kittens, and persons interested in breeding Wirehairs must be prepared to find good homes for them. Experienced breeders should inform prospective Wirehair fanciers about this responsibility.

RIGHT: Tortie and White (Calico) American Wirehair

BELOW: Tortie and White (Calico) American Wirehair (left) and Red and White American Wirehair (right)

AMERICAN WIREHAIR

Not recognized by the GCCF

Standard, courtesy of the Cat Fanciers' Association of America. Differences in the Standards of other registries are indicated at the end of the text.

HEAD: 25 (including size and shape of eyes, ear shape and set)

TYPE: 20 (including shape, size, bone, and length of tail)

COAT: 45

COLOUR and EYE COLOUR: 10

GENERAL: The American Wirehair is a spontaneous mutation. The coat, which is not only springy, dense, and resilient, but also coarse and hard to the touch, distinguishes the American Wirehair from all other breeds. Characteristic is activity, agility, and keen interest in its surroundings.

HEAD: In proportion to the body. Underlying bone structure is round with prominent cheekbones and well-developed muzzle and chin. There is a slight whisker break.

NOSE: In profile the nose shows a gentle, concave curve.[1]

MUZZLE: Well developed. Allowance for jowls in adult males.

CHIN: Firm and well developed[2] with no apparent malocclusion.

EARS: Medium, slightly rounded at tips, set wide and not unduly open at the base.

EYES: Large,[3] round, bright, and clear. Set well apart.[4] Aperture has slight upward tilt.

BODY: Medium to large.[5] Back level, shoulders and hips same width, torso well rounded and in proportion. Males larger than females.

LEGS: Medium in length and bone, well muscled and proportionate to body.

PAWS: Oval and compact. Toes, five in front and four behind.

TAIL: In proportion to body, tapering from the well-rounded rump to a rounded tip, neither blunt nor pointed.

COAT: Springy, tight, medium in length.[6] Individual hairs are crimped, hooked, or bent, including hair within the ears. The overall appearance of wiring and the coarseness and resilience of the coat are more important than the crimping of each hair. The density of the wired coat leads to ringlet formation rather than waves. That coat which is very dense, resilient, crimped, and coarse is most desirable, as are curly whiskers.

PENALIZE: Deep nose break. Long or fluffy fur.

DISQUALIFY: Incorrect coat. Kinked or abnormal tail. Incorrect number of toes. Evidence of hybridization resulting in the colours chocolate, lavender, the Himalayan pattern, or these combinations with white.

AMERICAN WIREHAIR COLOURS

(See page 170 for a full description of the colours listed below.)

Particolours: bicolours (black and white, blue and white, red and white, cream and white), blue cream, calico, dilute calico, tortoiseshell. **Shadeds:** chinchilla silver, shaded cameo, shaded silver, shell cameo. **Smokes:** black smoke, blue smoke, cameo smoke. **Solids:** black, blue, cream, red, white. **Tabbies:** (classic and mackerel patterns): blue tabby, brown tabby, cameo tabby, cream tabby, red tabby, silver tabby. **Other Wirehair colours:** any other colour or pattern with the exception of those showing evidence of hybridization resulting in the colours chocolate, lavender, the Himalayan pattern, or these combinations with white.

American Wirehair allowable outcross breeds:[7] American Shorthair.

[1] TICA: 'The nose and face are medium short.'
[2] TICA: Chin is 'moderately developed.'
[3] TICA: 'Medium to large.'
[4] TICA: Set 'moderately apart.'
[5] TICA: 'Medium size' body.
[6] TICA: 'Short to medium short in length.'
[7] In all associations where the breed is recognized.

Balinese

ORIGIN

The Balinese first appeared in the United States in the nonchampionship AOV class (Any Other Variety) at the Empire Show in New York City in 1961. For at least fifteen years before that, however, semi-longhaired kittens had been appearing in litters produced from Siamese parents. In the 1930s and 1940s there had been many attempts to produce a longhaired, pointed cat. Among the byproducts of these experiments were shorthaired, pointed cats. Most of these were placed in pet homes, but some were registered as Siamese—deliberately or unintentionally—because rules permitted the registration of cats of unknown origin at the time.

Blue Point Balinese

Thus, a number of Siamese-Persian hybrids that carried a recessive gene for long hair made their way into Siamese breeding programmes. Whenever two of these longhair carriers were bred together, the chances of producing semi-longhaired Siamese kittens were one out of four on the average, and on the average this happened frequently. Another possible source of the longhair gene in Siamese was the use of longhaired outcrosses, particularly the Turkish Angora, by Siamese breeders in England when they were trying to rejuvenate the breed after World Wars I and II.

DEVELOPMENT

Most Siamese breeders treated semi-longhaired kittens as if they didn't exist. 'They were discarded or quietly given away as undesirables,' one breeder reported. One hesitates to imagine what this person meant by 'discarded', but a few breeders thought their semi-longhaired kittens were desirable enough to make a breed out of them. Perhaps these breeders were unfamiliar with basic genetics. Perhaps they were unable to admit that their longhaired Siamese were hybrids. Perhaps they feared the frenzy of Siamese breeders, who were even less able to admit that *their* breed was not entirely pure. But for whatever reasons, many Balinese breeders have always insisted—as one American association's current breed brochure declares—that the semi-long coats on their cats are the result of a natural mutation.

The animosity of the Siamese breeders and the unromantic sound of Longhaired Siamese led Helen Smith of Merry Mews cattery, an early champion of the breed, to propose the name Balinese instead. Smith maintained that the graceful way her cats moved reminded her of the dancers on the island of Bali.

Such a leap of the imagination may have been possible when the breed was first developed, but the use of Siamese outcrosses in Balinese breeding programmes has shortened the Balinese coat considerably since the breed was first accepted for championship competition by the Cat Fanciers' Federation in 1963. Ruffs and britches disappeared long ago, and there is not much to distinguish a Balinese from a Siamese today except a wispy fringe on the underbelly and a meek plume of the tail. This is the Balinese dilemma: Breeding Bali to Bali to secure fullness of the coat spoils type. Breeding Bali to Siamese to refine type reduces coat. In fact, Balinese coats are so short—and the breed is so far removed from the original man-made source of its semi-long hair—that it would seem logical for Balies to become a variety of Siamese instead of remaining a separate entity.

BALINESE

(Breed 61) (Long Hair)
General Type Standard

The Balinese Cat should be a beautifully balanced animal with head, ears and neck carried on a lithe and graceful body, supported on slim legs and feet, with a tail in proportion and with a medium long coat, fine and silky in texture. The head and profile should be wedge-shaped, neither round nor pointed; the mask complete, connected by tracings with the ears (except in kittens); the eyes a clear brilliant blue; expression alert and intelligent.

BODY AND TAIL: Medium in size, Body lithe and graceful, legs proportionately slim, hind legs slightly higher than front legs, feet small and oval, tail long and tapering and free from any kink. The body, legs, feet and tail should all be in proportion giving the whole a well-balanced appearance.
HEAD AND EARS: Head long and well proportioned, carried upon an elegant neck, with width between the ears, narrowing in perfectly straight lines to a fine muzzle, with straight profile, strong chin and level bite. Ears rather large and pricked, with width at base.
EYES: Oriental in shape and slanting towards the nose, but with width between. Colour bright, clear blue; and complementary to points colour.
POINTS: Mask, ears, legs, feet and tail dense with colour clearly defined, matching on all points, showing

clear contrast between points and body colour. Mask complete and (except in kittens) connected by tracings with the ears.

REMARKS: As coat length tends to disguise tail markings on tabby point and tortie point cats, the tail should be held by the tip, shaken and viewed from the rear.

COAT: Medium long, fine and silky in texture, without woolly undercoat, lying mainly flat along the body. The ears may be tufted, the tail plume-like. Colour shading on coat (if any) should be pale and matching the points colour.

REMARKS: i) Coat lies flat along the body, with the exception of the areas around the chin, neck and tail, where there may be a tendency to frill, thereby disguising the underlying bone structure. By smoothing back the coat it is possible to study the lines of the bone. Absence of a frill is to be preferred. ii) Balinese do not normally achieve full coat until they are adults and allowance should be made for this.

BALINESE COLOURS

COLOURS: Seal, Blue, Chocolate, Lilac, Red, Cream, Tortie and Tabby in all colours.

The Balinese registration policy allows outcrosses to Siamese but all shorthaired kittens are registered as Balinese Variants and may not be shown.

Birman

ORIGIN

This fabled breed is veiled in the kind of legend that enthrals cat fanciers. This particular legend says that long before the birth of Christ, the Khmer civilisation of Asia built beautiful temples in which to pay homage to their gods. In Western Burma, an area situated between China and India, Khmers worshipped a golden goddess with sapphire blue eyes at a magnificent temple on the slopes of Mount Lugh. The Khmers' faith in reincarnation required that they keep one hundred white temple cats, for it was believed that after death the priests of the temple would return in the form of the sacred cats of Burma. These yellow-eyed cats were white in colour, except for their brown ears, nose, tail and paws—the parts of the body which came in contact with the impurities of the earth.

One moonlight night, it is said, raiders attacked the temple, murdering one of the priests as he kept vigil over the goddess. One of the faithful white temple cats was found standing on the head of his dying master and gazing sadly into the sapphire eyes of the goddess

Blue Point Birman

so continuing his master's vigil. As the priest died, the cat's white fur turned into gold and his yellow eyes became as blue as those of the goddess herself. And, where his feet touched the priest's body, the fur became white, a symbol of purity. The eyes of the remaining ninety nine cats were also turned blue; their coats became gold and their feet white. It was believed that whenever one of the temple cats died, the soul of the priest who had returned in feline form was carried into Paradise.

Such a tale befits the Sacred Cat of Burma, adding to the stature of this breed. Unfortunately, it adds nothing to the explanation of the Birman's origin. Siamese and longhaired, bicoloured Angoras are likely participants in that mysterious beginning. It is futile, however, to speculate whether this combination—if it was the one that produced the Birman—was intentional or whether it simply resulted from those cats interbreeding freely in an isolated setting. But whatever the parent breeds might have been—and wherever they might have joined forces—they had to have been carrying genes for point colour, low-grade white spotting, and long hair.

DEVELOPMENT

Accounts of the arrival of the first Birmans in western Europe are scarcely less fantastic than the temple legend. In one account, a male named Maldapour and a female named Sita were shipped from Burma to France in 1919. Maldapour did not survive the journey according to either report. Sita, who was pregnant, did. Another account attributes the introduction of the Burmese breed to Europe to an event during the first World War. British troops stationed in Burma under the command of a Major Russell Gordon successfully halted an enemy invasion, so saving one of the temples and its cats. Later, as a token of gratitude, the Birman High Priest sent a pair of the sacred temple cats to the Major who was then residing in France.

In yet another account, 'a Mr Vanderbilt' obtained the sacred cats 'for a price of gold' from a greedy servant who had stolen them from the temple. In all accounts, Sita's fate is unknown; but it is reasonable to assume that her kittens—including a perfectly marked daughter named Poupee—were the foundation stock used to create the Birman breed in France.

There is another interesting account of the Birman's arrival in France, contained in an article in the 1969 Cat Fanciers' Association Yearbook. Verner E Clum, the author of that article, claimed to have 'a magazine dated 1927 'Le Monde Felin,' in which there is a picture of a Mme Marcelle Adam, first importer of [the Birman] breed in France in 1925.' Mme Adam's cattery name, incidentally, was Maldapour, and she was president of the Federation Feline Francaise. This seemed to have settled the issue, but in her next paragraph Clum recounted the Major Russell story without bothering to say which of the two individuals—Mme Adam or Major Russell—she believed was truly the first Birman importer.

By 1925 the Sacred Cat of Burma was established well enough to be recognized for championship competition in France. Though its numbers were small, the Sacred Cat prospered until World War II. After the war there was a time when all that stood between the breed and extinction was one pair of cats. Through selective outcrossing the breed was reconstructed. The process was speeded up, no doubt, by the introduction of colourpoint longhairs with pedestrian type to Birman breeding programmes.

The Sacred Cat of Burma was re-established in France by 1955. Four years later the first pair of Sacred Cats arrived in the United States. By the mid 1960s the breed began to be accepted for championship competition in North America. At about the same time its name was changed—to Burman and then to Birman—and it was also accepted for championship competition in England.

In 1965, Mrs L C Fisher introduced the breed to Great Britain. Mrs Fisher and her close friend Mrs Margaret Richards began the Birman breeding programme under the jointly-held prefix 'Paranjoli'. Mrs Fisher's first cat was Ch Nouky De Mons Reve, a seal-point which carried the dilution factor. Two blue-point females were also imported from France and later the well known blue-point Ch Ghandi van Assindia was brought in from Germany. The breed soon became extremely popular. In 1983 at the Suffolk and Norfolk cat show the first Birman Grand Champions were made up; the male was Gr Ch Tamandria Truffles, bred by Mrs Joyce Price and the female was Gr Ch Belleview Francesca, bred and owned by Mr David Redtfeldt. Both cats were seal-point. Birmans of other colours began to appear on the show bench in the mid seventies when the red series Birmans were introduced by Mr Ken Clarke of 'Hilken' prefix and Mrs Brigliadori and Mrs Wilson-Smith started a breeding programme to produce chocolate and lilac point Birmans at approximately the same time. The Birman classes are well filled at all cat shows today and most of the cats show excellent temperament and are very popular pets.

BIRMAN

(SEAL POINT 13c1)
(BLUE POINT 13c2)

BODY: Long and massive; legs of medium length and thick-set. Paws short and strong.
HEAD: Skull strong, broad and rounded. Ears medium in size and spaced well apart. Nose medium in length (no 'stop' but with slight dip in profile). Cheeks full and round. Chin full and well developed, slightly tapered but not receding.
NOSE LEATHER: Dark seal brown in the Seals and slate-grey in the Blues
FUR: Long, silken in texture; full ruff around neck; slightly curled on the stomach.
EYES: Almost round but not bold. Blue in colour; the deeper the blue the better.
TAIL: Bushy. Medium in length and in proportion to the body.
COLOUR AND CONDITION: The distinguishing colours of the Birman are those of the Siamese (Seal Point and Blue Point), but mask (face), ears, legs and tail are dark brown in the Seals, blue- grey in the Blues. Mask, ears, legs and tail dense and clearly defined (except in kittens). On reaching maturity, the mask covers the entire face including whisker pads and is connected to the ears by tracings. The body colour in each variety is as follows: **SEAL POINT:** Clear pale beige with a slightly golden hue. **BLUE POINT:** Bluish white, cold in tone.
THE WHITE FEET ARE CHARACTERISTIC OF THE BIRMAN: Front paws—to have pure white symmetrical gloves ending in an even line across the paw and not passing beyond the angle formed by the paw and leg. Colour of the paw pads irrelevant. Back paws—have pure white gloves (gauntlets) covering the entire paw and tapering up the back of the leg to finish just below the point of the hock. Colour of the paw pads irrelevant.
Condition: The cat should be well grown, the frame (skeleton) should be strong, well covered and muscular, Eyes bright and temperament good.

Solid Point Birmans

Chocolate Point (13c3, Preliminary)
Lilac Point (13c4, Preliminary)
Red Point (13c5, Preliminary)
Cream Point (13c7, Preliminary)

Tortie Point Birmans

The colour on the points should be seal brown or chocolate intermingled with shades of light and dark red, or blue or lilac intermingled with shades of light and dark cream. The presence or absence of a blaze is immaterial. The points need not be evenly broken but each point must show some intermingling of the colours.
Seal Tortie Point (13c6, Preliminary)
Blue Tortie Point (13c8, Preliminary)
Chocolate Tabby Point (13c9, Preliminary)
Lilac Tortie Point (13c10, Preliminary)

Tabby Pointed Birmans

There should be a clearly defined 'M' marking on the forehead, light coloured 'spectacle' markings round the eyes with spotted whisker pads. Ears solid with no stripes. Clear 'thumb marks' which are less apparent in dilute colours and mottled in the Tortie Tabby Point Birmans. The legs should have clearly defined, varied sized broken stripes and/or rings with solid markings on the back of the hind legs above the gauntlets. The tail should have many varied sized, clearly defined rings ending in a solid coloured tip.
NOTES: 1. The nose leather should be pinkish outlined in pigment or to tone with the points. 2. Markings in kittens are less well defined. 3. A ringed tail is desirable but a solid top-tail, ringed on the underside, is not a fault.

Tabby Point Birmans (excluding Tortie Tabby)

These colours show distinct tabby markings, although

they are more diffuse in the dilute colours.
Seal Tabby Point (13c11, Preliminary)
Blue Tortie Point (13c12, Preliminary)
Chocolate Tortie tabby Point (13c13, Preliminary)
Lilac Tabby Point (13c14, Preliminary)
Red Tabby Point (13c15, Preliminary)
Cream Tabby Point (13c17, Preliminary)

Tortie Tabby Pointed Birmans

These colours show the normal tabby pattern which has been overlaid with shades of light and dark red or cream. The extent and distribution of the tortie areas are not important providing that both elements, tortie and tabby, are clearly visible.
NOTE: The nose leather should be mottled pink and pigmented or to tone with the points.

Seal Tortie Tabby Point (13c16, Preliminary)
Blue Tortie Tabby Point (13c18, Preliminary)
Chocolate Tortie Tabby Point (13c19, Preliminary)
Lilac Tortie Tabby Point (13c20, Preliminary)

Bombay

ORIGIN

Everyone enjoys the wonderful fantasies and myths that have developed about the origins of cat breeds, but there are still many people who know the difference between fact and fantasy. The Bombay is a case in point. It is a manufactured breed if ever there was one, but it was not manufactured in quite the way its legend would have us believe.

During the late 1950s and early 1960s, Burmese breeders realized that they needed to outcross in order to produce a more compact body while retaining the dark, even coat their breed Standard required. Crossing to a Siamese would have lengthened the Burmese body, could have resulted in blue eye colour, and would have eventually restored the darker points found on the original Burmese, which were themselves hybrid cats. Crossing to other breeds would have produced other unacceptable results. The logical candidate for an outcross, therefore, was the black American Shorthair. Many such crosses were made behind cattery doors. The kittens from these breedings were either black or brown.

Since there are no *allowable* outcrosses for the Burmese breed, anybody who wanted to use one of these non-pedigreed American-Burmese kittens in a breeding programme (or in the show ring) had to falsify its pedigree. This was accomplished in several ways. Brown hybrids were added to legitimate sable Burmese litters, and black hybrids were registered as American Shorthairs in the same manner. In addition, there was open registration of American Shorthairs at the time—i.e., registries issued papers on American Shorthairs of unknown origin. Thus, black, hybrid kittens could also be registered as American Shorthairs, 'particulars unknown.'

There were several top-winning Burmese during the late 1950s and early 1960s that carried the resilient, thicker coats resulting from the Burmese-American cross. This was, indeed, a serious matter, causing much discussion among judges, breeders, and exhibitors. Clearly the need to outcross Burmese was obvious; but the registration system, which did not allow outcrosses for this breed, actually encouraged the many frauds that breeders committed to get their hybrid cats registered and shown.

DEVELOPMENT

Nikki Shuttleworth Horner of Shawnee cattery in Louisville, Kentucky, worked with the Burmese-black American cross, eventually breeding black kittens to black kittens only. She was highly successful in establishing a truly black Burmese with excellent type and conformation. Everything about these cats was Burmese except their colour. She realized, however, that it would be years before there could be any hope of adding a new colour to the Burmese breed because of the strong position taken by Burmese breeders, who believed that sable was the only true Burmese.

Horner decided to request separate recognition for her black 'Burmese,' called the Bombays after the black leopard of India and the city of Bombay. By seeking recognition for a separate breed, she hoped to avoid hostility from Burmese fanciers who viewed the addition of a new colour as a threat to their breed. In 1976 the American Cat Fanciers' Association accepted the Bombay for championship competition. CFA still allows Bombay breeders to outcross their cats to sable Burmese for type and to black American Shorthairs for colour. The problem of nonshowable kittens is still with us because all kittens from Bombay-to-Burmese crosses are considered Bombays—whether they are black or brown—by the majority of associations. The black kittens are no problem for if good enough, they can be shown as Bombays. The brown ones can be used in Bombay breeding programmes, but cannot be shown, unless their breeders create bogus pedigrees for them, as some breeders do. The realistic approach to this situation—followed by The International Cat Association—is to show black kittens from Bombay-to-Burmese crosses as Bombays and brown kittens as Burmese. The Bombay was recognised by the GCCF in autumn 1990 as part of the Asian Group.

Bombay

BOMBAY

(Breed 72)
General Type Standard
for all Asian Shorthairs and Semi-Longhairs

The cats of the Asian Group are elegant cats of medium foreign type; the overall type should be similar to the Burmese cat (Breed 27). A tendency to Siamese type or the cobbiness of the British should be regarded as a fault.

BODY, LEGS AND TAIL: The body should be of medium length and thickness with firm muscle, and the back should be straight from shoulder to rump. The chest should be generous but not disproportionately broad. The legs should be of medium length with the hind legs slightly longer than the front legs, paws tending to be oval in shape. The tail should be medium to long, elegant, carried proud and should be of medium thickness, tapering slightly to a rounded tip.

HEAD, EARS AND EYE-SET: The head should be wide at the jaw-hinge, with a good width between the ears and with a gently rounded top. The wedge should be short and in profile a distinct nose break should be apparent. The ears should be medium to large in size with a rounded tip and set well apart, continuing the angle of the upper part of the face to produce a butterfly-wing outline from the front. In profile the ears should have a slight forward tilt. Very slight ear tufts are acceptable in Asian Shorthairs and longer tufts in the Asian Semi-Longhair (Tiffanie). The eyes should be full and expressive, set well apart, and although they should be slightly oriental in set they should be neither almond nor round. The chin should be firm and the bite should be even, in accordance with the GCCF veterinary recommendation.

EYE COLOUR: The eyes may be any colour from yellow through chartreuse to green, depending on the variety. In the silvers green is preferred.

NOSE LEATHER , PAW PADS AND EYE RIMS: The pigmentation of the eye rims, nose leather and pads should be appropriate to the coat colour.

COAT LENGTH AND TEXTURE: The coat of the Asian Shorthair should be short, fine and lying close to the body. The Asian Semi-Longhair (Tiffanie) should have a silky semi-longhair coat.

CONDITION AND TEMPERAMENT: In the Asians the condition and temperament of the cat are important considerations.

NOTE 1: We are looking for an even tempered cat and it is hoped that judges will distinguish between a balanced but temporarily upset or frightened cat and a cat with an extreme or aggressive temperament. The latter is most undesirable in the breed and should not be encouraged.

NOTE 2: In Asians the females are smaller and much daintier than the males.

BOMBAY COLOUR

One of the chief characteristics of the Bombay is a coat that looks like black shimmering patent leather. The coat must be very close lying to produce this effect, as well as jet black to the roots in the adult cat. N.B. Kitten coats sometimes need time to develop full pigmentation and the patent leather effect. The eye colour may range from gold to yellow, with deep gold preferred. The greater the depth of colour and brilliance the better. Nose leather and eye rims solid black. Paw pads solid black or very dark brown.

Bombay allowable outcross breeds: all colours of Burmese, other patterns within the Asian Group.

British Shorthair

ORIGIN

The ancestors of the British Shorthair were brought to northern Europe and then to Great Britain by Roman soldiers almost two thousand years ago. Despite these hardy cats' humble circumstances—they were called mongrel or street cats, and they bred freely without control—British Shorthairs appeared in great numbers in cat shows at London's Crystal Palace during the last quarter of the nineteenth century. Harrison Weir—the founder of the cat fancy, and the author of the first judging standards—'deemed it advisable ... to give special prizes' to blue British Shorthairs because of their beauty and popularity. As a result, British Blues were—and still are—listed separately from the other nonforeign shorthairs in Great Britain; and some people in the United States consider the British Blue a separate breed. It is not. It is one of a large variety of colours occurring among the British Shorthair breed.

DEVELOPMENT

When longhaired cats began to appear at shows in England, they attracted a great deal of interest. 'With the majority of fanciers, the long-haired cats are the most popular,' wrote English breeder and judge Frances Simpson in 1903. By that time Persians and other longhaired cats—namely the Angora and the Russian—outnumbered shorthairs four-to-one at shows. After spending four and a half pages on longhairs, Simpson begins a two-page discussion of shorthairs with a less-than-enthusiastic 'And now to consider ...' When she does consider black-and-white and tabby-and-white shorthairs, Simpson declares, 'It seems almost a pity to so far encourage these cats as to give classes for them at our shows.'

Bad came to worse for the British Shorthair during World Wars I and II. These had a ruinous effect on the cat fancy in England, and the British Shorthair suffered a devastating setback. Breeders had difficulty finding suitable studs for their females, and there is no doubt that in the interest of convenience and survival, they employed various outcrosses to keep their breeds alive. Some like to pretend that this never happened, but others admit that British Shorthairs were outcrossed to Persians, especially blues, in order to maintain eye colour, type, and coat texture.

As happened with Domestic Shorthairs in the United States, the longhaired cross seemed to enhance many an otherwise unappealing British Shorthair. What's more, judges rewarded these hybrid cats for their unusual beauty. Eventually a rule was instituted listing 'any evidence of hybridization' as a cause for disqualification in British Shorthair classes; but by then so much hybridization had occurred that the regulation made little impact. Finally, the Persian was accepted as an allowable outcross for the British Shorthair in Great Britain. This caused problems for Americans who wanted to import British Shorthairs because registries in North America required at least three generations of British-to-British matings on a pedigree before they would register the cat it described.

Though a few shorthaired cats from Great Britain had been imported by American breeders not long after 1900, cat fanciers in the United States had enough trouble gaining championship status for their own shorthairs without bothering about imports. For this reason, there was little American interest in pedigreed shorthairs from Great Britain until the mid-1960s. In 1970 the American Cat Fanciers' Association became the first American registry to recognize British Shorthairs—in blue and black only. Eventually all other colours of the breed were accepted by all associations. Today, more British colours are being seen on the show bench than ever before, and the solid—or blue self colour—is not as dominant as it once was. Because they have been developed out of such strong stock, British Shorthairs are free of known genetic defects. They require grooming as all cats do, and gentle brushing and bathing are necessary in showing a British Shorthair.

RIGHT: Blue and White Van British Shorthair

BELOW: Blue British Shorthair

In the United Kingdom a wide range of colours exist in the British breed including Tipped, Smoke, Spotted Tabby and Colourpointed (Himalayan) British Shorthairs. Until October 1971, all cats with unregistered as unknown parents were allowed to be shown. This situation seldom arose except in the British and when the rules were changed an exception was made to allow cats with such backgrounds to continue to be shown and their progeny for three generations. This was done to protect the British breed after strong protestations by Miss Kit Wilson and Mrs Elizabeth Towe, leading breeders and judges of the time, that the change in rules would decimate the British Shorthair.

BRITISH SHORTHAIRS

(General Type Standard)

The British cat is compact,well balanced and powerful, showing good depth of body, a full broad chest, short strong legs, rounded paws, tail thick at base with rounded tip. The head is round with a good width between the ears, round cheeks, firm chin, small ears, large round and well-opened eyes and a short broad nose. The coat is short and dense.

HEAD: Round face with full cheeks and good breadth of skull with round underlying bone structure. The head should be set on a short thick neck.

NOSE: The nose itself should be short, broad and straight. In profile, a rounded forehead should lead to a short, straight nose with a nose break which is neither too pronounced nor too shallow.

CHIN: A strong, firm and deep chin is essential. Any deviation from this to be considered a fault. The bite MUST be level, the tip of the chin to line up with the tip of the nose in the same vertical plane.

EARS: Small rounded at the tips. Set far apart fitting into (without distorting) the rounded contour of the head. External ear to be well covered with fur, internal furnishings not to be excessive.

EYES: Large, round and well-opened. Set wide apart with no tendency to oriental shape. No squint.

BODY: Cobby type with short level back. Low on legs with broad deep chest. Equally massive across the shoulders and the rump. Medium to large, but not rangy.

PAWS: Round and firm. Toes carried close, five on each forefoot (including dew claw) and four on each back foot.

TAIL: Should be thick and of medium length, thicker at the base with rounded tip.

COAT: Must be short, dense and crisp. A soft and/or over-long and fluffy coat is incorrect.

CONDITION: Perfect physical condition, muscular with alert appearance.

BRITISH SHORTHAIR COLOURS

(See page 170 for a full description of the colours listed below.)

Particolours: bicolours (black and white, blue and white, red and white, cream and white), blue cream, calico, dilute calico, tortoiseshell. **Smokes:** black smoke, blue smoke. **Solids:** black, blue, cream, white. **Tabbies:** (classic, mackerel, and spotted tabby patterns): blue tabby, brown tabby, cream tabby, red tabby, silver tabby.

These additional colours are recognized by the GCCF:
Smokes: red, cream, tortoiseshell and blue tortie.
Tipped: all recognised self and tortie colours.
Colourpointed: all self and tabby colours including chocolate and lilac.

British Shorthair allowable outcross breeds: Persian Longhairs, but offspring will be placed on the Supplementary Register.

Burmese

ORIGIN

Probably no other breed has endured so much controversy and political conflict as the Burmese, which first arrived in the United States in 1930 in the form of a small brown cat. The cat's name was Wong Mau. She had accompanied a sailor, whose name has not been recorded, on a journey from Rangoon to San Francisco. There she was purchased by Dr Joseph Thompson, a Navy psychiatrist. Wong Mau had a dark-brown body with still darker points—i.e., markings—on her face, ears, legs, and tail. She also had a somewhat rounded head and eyes. She was mated first to a seal point Siamese in an effort to establish her type. She produced typically pointed Siamese kittens and pointed kittens with darker-than-Siamese bodies like her own. When the darker-bodied cats were bred together—or when darker-bodied males were bred back to Wong Mau—they produced even-coloured, dark-all-over kittens. All of which proved that Wong Mau was a hybrid with Siamese in her background.

DEVELOPMENT

Burmese were first registered in 1936 in the United States. Their standard called for an 'even, sable brown [colour] shading to a trifle lighter on chest and abdomen [with] mask, ears, legs, and tail clearly defined and a darker brown than the body.' The American Cat Fanciers' Association, ever the purist among registries, required three generations of like-to-like breeding before it would enrol kittens as Burmese. There was no way this condition could be met because the Burmese gene pool was too small, and many breeders were still using seal point Siamese from Siamese-Burmese crosses in their breeding programmes. The difference between Siamese and Burmese then was not so pronounced as it is today.

By 1940 Burmese had been accepted for championship competition by the three registries that existed in the United States at the time: CFA, the American Cat Association, and the Cat Fanciers' Federation. But on May 8, 1947, the CFA board of directors passed a motion which declared that 'the recognition of the so-called Burmese breed ... is indefinitely suspended.' CFA took this step because there weren't many Burmese that could meet its strict, three-generation breeding requirement. During their suspension Burmese were denied access to CFA shows, foundation records, and stud books. All existing registrations were suspended, and registration fees were returned. ACA and CFF continued to recognize Burmese during that time, which probably helped to save the breed from extinction. The CFA decision had been prompted by Siamese breeders, who claimed that Wong Mau had been nothing more than a Siamese with bad type and poor colour, and who feared that the results of crosses between Burmese and Siamese cats would filter into their lines.

It was not until the 1956-57 show season that a Burmese met the requirements for stud book listing and the breed was reinstated by CFA. With the return of the Burmese a new standard was developed. It called for a solid, sable colour without darker points on the extremities, and for a short, cobby body—surprisingly heavy for its size—a round head, and round, gold eyes. Theoretically, these requirements should have eliminated any interest in crossing Burmese with Siamese. Outcrosses were still needed, however, and the next logical choice was a black Domestic Shorthair. Some Burmese from this period reveal evidence of this practice, and, of course, many such clandestine matings were not recorded at all.

The new look in Burmese became popular. So did new, dilute colours—champagne, platinum, and blue—but only after bitter, life-and-death battles had been fought among Burmese breeders. Their resistance is puzzling because new colours add interest and vigour to a breed. This truth has been repeatedly demonstrated in the history of the Cat Fancy.

Today's Burmese are of top quality, but classes are not large considering the age of the breed. This is largely the result of problems that have developed within many Burmese lines. The 'contemporary' look with its extreme head type which became popular during the 1980s has, in some cases, carried with it certain deformities.

Cleft palates, skulls that do not close, and other abnormalities occur frequently in contemporary Burmese kittens, along with improvements in type

Brown (Sable) Burmese

The British Burmese, seen here, has a longer head and a longer body than the American version of this breed.

such as a shorter nose, more prominent eyes, and rounder muzzle. Some breeders claim that these defects, nonexistent in 'traditional' Burmese, can be bred away or minimized through judicious outcrossing. Others are not so optimistic.

These difficulties have not occurred in England. Because of the six-month quarantine regulation, there were few Burmese imported, and breeders were obliged to outcross in order to preserve the breed. They chose Siamese and British Shorthairs, which produced more colours than the few that exist in American Burmese, and a style of cat that is much more foreign-bodied and less extreme than the American version.

The GCCF recognized the Burmese in 1952 and until 1955 it had only appeared as a brown cat, but when Champion Chinki Golden Gay was mated to her father Champion Casa Gatos Darkee a kitten was produced which was a blue colour and it was confirmed that it was the blue dilute form of the brown Burmese. This colour was recognized in 1960. In the late 1960s and early 70s Chocolate Burmese were imported from the United States, and during the early seventies both Chocolate and Lilac kittens resulted from matings between the imported cats, and in 1972 Chocolate and Lilac were given breed recognition.

In early 1964 a group of breeders led by Mrs Pocock of Pussinboots prefix had been developing the red and cream lines of Burmese and these were also given breed recognition in 1971 and 1972.

The Burmese cat has become extremely popular in the United Kingdom and accounts for about one seventh of all pedigree cats registered. The breed produces very lively and inquisitive cats which cannot be allowed to roam too widely for fear of mishap.

The first Burmese to become a Supreme Show winner was Grand Champion Bambino Bluebelle who won the Supreme Adult award at the 1990 Supreme Show.

BURMESE SECTION BURMESE

General Type Standard

The Burmese is an elegant Cat of a foreign type, which is positive and quite individual to the breed. Any suggestion of either Siamese type, or the cobbiness of a British cat, must be regarded as a fault.

BODY LEGS AND TAIL: The body should be of medium length and size, feeling hard and muscular, and heavier than its appearance indicates. The chest should be strong, and rounded in profile, the back straight from shoulder to rump. Legs should be slender and in proportion to the body: hind legs slightly longer than front; paws neat and oval in shape. The tail should be straight and of medium length, not heavy at base, and tapering only slightly to a rounded tip without bone defect. A visible kink or other bone defect in the tail is a fault, precluding the award of a Challenge Certificate, but an invisible defect at the extreme tip may be overlooked in an otherwise excellent specimen.

HEAD EARS AND EYE-SET: The head should be slightly rounded on top, with good breadth between the ears, having wide cheek bones and tapering to a short blunt wedge. The jaw should be wide at the hinge and the chin firm. A muzzle pinch is a bad fault. Ears should be medium in size, set well apart on the skull, broad at the base, with slightly rounded tips, the outer line of the ears continuing the shape of the upper part of the face. This may not be possible in mature males who develop a fullness of cheek. In profile the ears should be seen to have a slight forward tilt. There should be a distinct nose break, and in profile the chin should show a strong lower jaw. The eyes, which must be set well apart, should be large and lustrous, the top line of the eye showing a straight oriental slant towards the nose, the lower line being rounded. Either round or oriental eyes are a fault.

EYE COLOUR: Eyes should be any shade of yellow from chartreuse to amber, with golden yellow preferred. Green eyes are a serious fault in Brown Burmese, but Blue Burmese may show a slight fading of colour. Green eyes with more blue than yellow pigmentation must preclude the award of a Challenge Certificate in Burmese of all colours.

COAT: The coat should be short, fine, satin-like in texture lying close to the body. The glossy coat is a distinctive feature of Burmese and is indicative of good health.

CONDITION: Cats should be well-muscled, with good weight for size; lively and alert.

BURMESE COLOURS

In all colours, the underparts will be lighter than the back. In kittens and adolescents, allowances should be made for faint tabby barring and, overall, a lighter colour than adults. The presence of a few white hairs may be overlooked in an otherwise excellent cat, but a noticeable number of white hairs, or a white patch, is a serious fault, precluding the award of a Challenge Certificate.

BROWN (27): In maturity the adult should be a rich warm Seal brown.

BLUE (27a): The adult should be a soft silver grey only very slightly darker on the back and tail.

CHOCOLATE (27b): The overall colour should be a warm milk chocolate.

LILAC (27c): In maturity the coat colour should be a pale, delicate dove-grey.

RED (27d): In maturity the coat colour should be light tangerine. Slight Tabby markings may be found on the face, and small indeterminate markings elsewhere (except on sides and belly) are permissible in an otherwise excellent cat.

BROWN TORTIE (27e) (Normal Tortie): Coat should be a mix of brown and red with no obvious barring.

CREAM (27f): In maturity the coat colour should be rich cream. Slight tabby markings may be found on the face, and small indeterminate markings elsewhere.

BLUE TORTIE (27g) (Blue-Cream): Coat should be a mix of blue and cream without any obvious barring.

CHOCOLATE TORTIE (27h): Coat should be a mix of chocolate and red without any obvious barring.

LILAC TORTIE (27j) (Lilac-Cream): The coat should be a mixture of lilac and cream without any obvious barring.

Burmese allowable outcross breeds:[8] none.

Chartreux

ORIGIN

The Chartreux has been called 'something of a national treasure' in France, where the breed was developed. References to blue, grey, or blue-grey cats can be found throughout French literature. The earliest recorded use of the name *Chartreux* to describe cats with blue fur has been found in the 1723 edition of the *Universal Dictionary of Commerce*, but we know from the work of the French poet Joachim du Bellay that 'entirely grey' cats were common in France as early as 1558.

Legend, which often passes for fact in the cat fancy, credits the Carthusian monks with the development of the Chartreux. Members of this nine-hundred-year-old order, whose Le Grande Chartreux monastery is located near Grenoble, were known long ago as talented steel workers; and they also forged a potent,

Chartreux

green liqueur. There is no evidence, however, that they were cat breeders, that they obtained cats from monastic knights returning from the Crusades, or that they brought cats back to France from the Cape of Good Hope in the seventeenth century. Nor is there any evidence that the monks named the Chartreux. In fact, Carthusian archives do not mention cats at all.

DEVELOPMENT

The first Chartreux breeders of record are two sisters, whose surname was Leger. They lived on the small Brittany island of Belle-Ile-sur-Mere off the northwest coast of France, where they originally bred Persians and Siamese in their de Guerveur cattery. The Legers became acquainted with the Chartreux in the late 1920s when they moved from the mainland to Belle-Ile-sur-Mere. Shortly after they arrived on the island, they discovered a large population of blue-grey cats in Le Palais, the island's principal city. No one knows how or when the blue-grey cats migrated from the French mainland to Belle-Ile-sur-Mere, but show records indicate that in 1931 at a show held in Paris, a Mlle Leger became the first person to exhibit a Chartreux in France.

More than sixty years after making its debut, the Chartreux remains one of the cat fancy's rarest breeds, with a worldwide population scarcely more than one thousand. The principal reasons for this scarcity are World Wars I and II. Hostilities in France left many cats homeless, obliging them to fend for themselves and to arrange their own breedings in the streets. In addition, cats were sometimes killed for food when provisions were scarce, and several French observers have reported that Chartreux were also killed for their plush coats.

When breeders finally determined to preserve the Chartreux in the early 1950s, they attempted to strengthen the breed by outcrossing to other blue cats—Persians, British Shorthairs, and whatever non-pedigreed cats they could find in France that approximated the Chartreux Standard. Fortunately, there is no lack of blue cats in the world. Chartreux fanciers had many breeds and varieties to choose from in their effort to revitalize the breed. Unfortunately, breed characteristics are compromised and the distinctions between breeds are erased by any but the most carefully planned and controlled outcrossing. By 1970, there was so little difference between the British Blue and the Chartreux that the Feline International Federation declared they had to be judged in the same category. This situation lasted for seven years until European breeders insisted that the Chartreux was a separate breed and deserved to be cultivated and judged as such. In England, however, there is still no distinction made between the two cats.

The Chartreux came to the United States in 1970 when a cat fancier from La Jolla, California, named Helen Gamon brought the first Chartreux to America. Three of the first ten imports by American breeders came from the Leger sisters, who had begun working with Chartreux more than forty years before. In the years since the breed arrived in the United States, the Chartreux has developed a style of its own that distinguishes it from the many breeds and varieties of blue cats.

CHARTREUX

Not recognized by the GCCF

Standard, courtesy of the Cat Fanciers' Association of America. Differences in the Standards of other registries are indicated at the end of the text.

HEAD: (15)
Shape 4
Size 3
Profile/nose 5
Muzzle 3

NECK: (4)
Length 2
Size 2

EARS: (10)
Shape 3
Size 2
Placement 5

EYES: (10)
Shape 3
Size 3
Colour 4

BODY: (20)
Shape 5
Size 5
Boning 5
Musculature 5

TAIL: (4)
Shape 2
Size 2

LEGS: (6)
Length 2
Boning 2
Musculature 2

FEET: (2)
Shape 1
Size 1

COAT: (14)
Length 4
Texture 10

COLOUR: (15)
Uniformity 8
Brilliance 7

GENERAL: The Chartreux is a sturdy French breed coveted since antiquity for its hunting prowess and its dense, water repellent fur. Its husky, robust type is sometimes termed primitive, neither cobby nor classic. Though amply built, Chartreux are extremely supple and agile cats; refined, never coarse nor clumsy. Males are much larger than females and slower to mature. Coat texture, coat colour, and eye colour are affected by sex, age, and natural factors which should not penalize. The qualities of strength, intelligence, and amenability, which have enabled the Chartreux to survive the centuries unaided, should be evident in all exhibition animals and preserved through careful selection.
HEAD AND NECK: Rounded and broad but not a sphere.[1] Powerful jaw; full cheeks, with mature males having larger jowls. High, softly contoured forehead; nose straight and of medium length/width;[2] with a slight stop at eye level. Muzzle comparatively small, narrow, and tapered with slight pads.[3] Sweet, smiling expression. Neck short and heavyset.
EARS: Medium in height and width;[4] set fairly high on the head;[5] very erect posture.
EYES: Rounded and open; alert and expressive.[6,7] Colour range is copper to gold; a clear, deep, brilliant orange is preferred.
BODY AND TAIL: Robust physique; medium long with broad shoulders and deep chest. Strong boning; muscle mass is solid and dense. Females are medium; males are large. Tail of moderate length; heavy at base; tapering to oval tip. Lively and flexible.
LEGS AND FEET: Legs of medium length; straight and sturdy; comparatively fine boned. Feet are round and medium in size (may appear almost dainty compared to body mass).
COAT: Medium short[8,9] and slightly woolly in texture (should break like a sheepskin at neck and flanks). Resilient undercoat; longer, protective topcoat. *Note*: degree of woolliness depends on age, sex, and habitat, mature males exhibiting the heaviest coats. Silkier, thinner coat permitted on females and cats under two years.
PENALIZE: Severe nose break, snubbed or upturned nose, broad, heavy muzzle, palpable tail defect, eyes too close together giving angry look.
DISQUALIFY: White locket, visible tail kink, green eyes.

CHARTREUX COLOUR

Any shade of blue grey from ash to slate; tips lightly brushed with silver. Emphasis on colour clarity and uniformity rather than shade. Preferred tone is a bright, unblemished blue with an overall iridescent sheen. Nose leather is slate grey; lips blue; paw pads are rose taupe. Allowance made for ghost barring in kittens and for tail rings in juveniles under two years of age.

Chartreux allowable outcross breeds:[10] none.

[1] ACA, ACFA, CFF, TICA: The head is 'large and broad but not round.'
[2] ACA, ACFA, CFF: 'Nose short and straight.'
[3] TICA: ' ... but is not to be pointed.'
[4] ACA, ACFA, CFF, TICA: 'Small to medium in size.'
[5] ACA, CFF: ' ... with slightly rounded tips.'
[6] TICA: 'Large and set moderately wide apart.'
[7] ACA: 'At least the width of an eye between the eyes.'
[8] ACA, TICA: 'May be longer than that of other domestic shorthaired cats.'
[9] ACFA, CFF: 'Medium.'
[10] In all associations where the breed is recognized.

Colourpoint Shorthair

ORIGIN

Years before the orthodox Siamese colours (seal, chocolate, lilac, and blue) had been granted championship status, breeders were producing the occasional odd-pointed variety. John Jennings, a British cat fancier, judge, and author wrote in 1893, that 'experiments have been tried with a view to introducing another colour other than the characteristic dun (to the Siamese).' A genticicist in Sweden created tabby pointed Siamese in 1924; two red points were shown at a Siamese Cat Club show in England in 1934; and a few tabby pointed Siamese were bred in Scotland in 1940. Serious work on expanding the Siamese colour scheme and gene pool began, in the late 1940s. Naturally, this infuriated the steadfast purist because additional colours could be produced only by outcrossing to other breeds—British or American shorthairs or Abyssinians, for example. As Jennings had warned fifty years earlier, 'Any deviation from the pure, typical breed will, I opine, not be generally cared for, if for no other reason than its being incorrect.' Then, as now, as always: the only thing more certain than change in the cat fancy is resistance to change.

DEVELOPMENT

Red and cream point Siamese were the first new colours to gain recognition. Along with the red and cream came the tortie points, and before long the tabby points followed. Indeed it was possible to produce any colour and confine it to point restriction. In a short time breeders were producing remarkable Siamese type and deep blue eye colour in hybrid Siamese.

In Great Britain the Governing Council of the Cat Fancy offered to recognize red and cream pointed Siamese as Pointed Foreign Shorthairs, but the breeders of these cats would not accept this designation. Meanwhile, in 1963 the American Cat Fanciers Association voted to deny these cats recognition as Siamese. The following year, they were accepted as a separate breed called the Colourpoint Shorthair. England solved this what's-in-a-name problem by registering non traditional Siamese under a different breed number from the four original colours.

To this day CFA and the Canadian Cat Association treat the Colourpoints as a separate breed, even though there is no longer a need to cross these cats to anything but other Colourpoints or Siamese, and the percentage of non Siamese blood in today's Colourpoints is minuscule. This backward thinking classification system is a lingering consequence of the early Colourpoint breeders' belief that their cats resulted from a solemn and spontaneous mutation—despite written, genetic, and common-sense evidence to the contrary. Unfortunately, this unrealistic attitude led to the adaption of unrealistic rules which demand that any seal, chocolate, lilac, or blue point kittens born from Siamese-Colourpoint crosses be registered as Colourpoints. Such non Siamese Siamese cannot be shown legally, but the quality and type of these Colourpoints is so outstanding that many are being registered illegally with Siamese litters, a process known as paperhanging. This temptation does not exist in the four associations that recognize a wider variety of Siamese colours.

Associations that enforce artificial distinctions in any breed are creating a climate for fraud by not adopting registration rules based on genetics rather than exclusiveness. In registries that are genetically based, pedigrees are more likely to reflect the true background of a kitten, and buyers are free to accept or reject that kitten on the basis of an accurate pedigree. It is impossible to legislate morality, and the cat fancy must come to accept the fact that it is dealing with pedigreed, not purebred, cats.

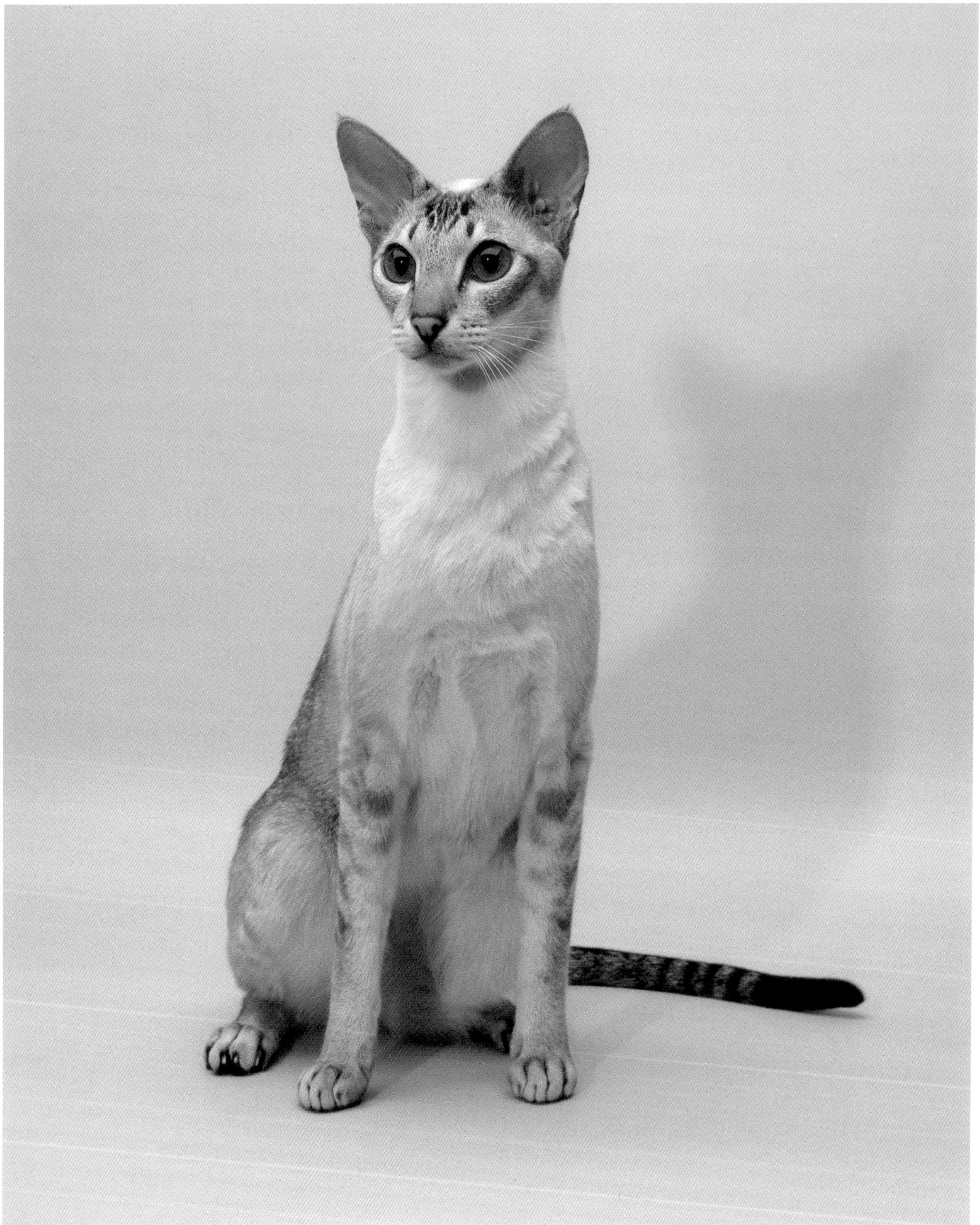

Tabby (Lynx) Point Colourpoint Shorthair

Cornish Rex

ORIGIN

The Rex cat is one of those rare developments that often result for some strange reason following a war or other period of massive change. On July 21, 1950, a curly coated, cream male kitten was born in a litter of five barn cats in Cornwall, England. The litter belonged to Nina Ennismore, who named the curly coated male Kallibunker. Since she had formerly bred Rex rabbits, Ennismore assumed that Kallibunker's coat was the work of a spontaneous mutation, one that had also occurred in rats, mice, and horses.

Encouraged by cat fancier Brian Stirling-Webb and geneticist A C Jude, Ennismore bred Kallibunker to his mother—a tortie-and-white straighthaired cat named Serena—whom she also owned. This breeding produced two males and a female in August 1952. The female was normal coated, the males were both Rex. One of those died at seven months; the other, named Poldhu, was eventually used to propagate Ennismore's new breed, called the Cornish Rex after its place of origin.

Meanwhile, in East Germany in 1951, a wavy-haired, black female cat—which had been observed on the grounds and in the basement of the Hufeland Hospital for five years—had been adopted by a cat lover named Dr Rose Sheuer-Karpin. For the next seven years this German Rex, named Lammchen, produced numerous straighthaired kittens sired by local toms. When she was bred finally to one of her sons, two of their four kittens had wavy hair. This suggested that the gene behind the German Rex was recessive: that is to say the Rex coat pattern would be expressed only when a kitten inherited two copies of the gene for that trait, one from each parent.

Black and White Cornish Rex

In the United Kingdom, considerable outcrossing had taken place and Cornish Rex were beginning to lose the original foreign type. Mrs Alison Ashford imported a Cornish Rex from Canada. This cat was the great great grandson of Lamorna Cove, one of the first Cornish Rexs, and was named Rio Vista Kismet. Kismet grew to be a lovely male of extremely good foreign type and was mated to various queens, producing excellent Cornish Rex type. Enthusiasts then embarked on a carefully controlled breeding programme to improve the coat of the Cornish Rex and to maintain the improved type.

DEVELOPMENT

After Nina Ennismore had inbred her strain of Rex as far as possible, she began to outcross to ordinary shorthaired cats so as not to risk her cats' health or reproductive ability. Though it would have been possible to introduce the Rex coat to any breed, she and other Rex fanciers chose to confine the gene to shorthairs. Longhaired Rex were most unappealing, and their coats were difficult to keep from matting.

As Ennismore's cat population grew—she had more than forty cats at one point—she was unable to sell enough kittens to defray expenses. She felt that she had no choice but to put a number of cats to sleep—Kallibunker and his mother Serena among them. Their son Poldhu came to grief of another sort when two veterinarians performed a testicular biopsy on him. The vets wanted to determine whether Poldhu was simply a blue-tabby-and-white stud or a rare, siring blue-cream-and-white. The latter is a sex-linked colour that appears virtually always in females. Males of this colour are rare, and non sterile ones are more rare yet. The vets had assured Ennismore that this 'slight operation would in no way affect' Poldhu's reproductive vigour, but after the biopsy he never sired again. Ironically, the tissue sample that had been taken from Poldhu was lost in the laboratory along with his virility.

By the late 1950s Ennismore had stopped working with Rex cats entirely, but Brian Stirling-Webb was determined to see the breed through. In 1961 he learned that a male Rex kitten had been born in Devon, one county east of Cornwall, the preceding year. The dam of this kitten was a tortie-and-white stray who had taken up with Beryl Cox. The sire was a feral, Rex-coated male who lived in a derelict tin mine near Cox's home.

When she learned of Stirling-Webb's interest in Rex, Cox offered to send her male kitten, whom she had named Kirlee, to live with Stirling-Webb so that Kirlee might provide some new blood for the new breed. Kirlee was bred to several Rex females from Cornwall, but every kitten from these matings had straight hair. Thus, Stirling-Webb concluded that Cornish Rex and the Rex from Devon were carrying separate mutation genes, and that the children of Kallibunker belonged to a different breed of cat than Kirlee did. Since, as Stirling-Webb knew, the Rex gene is recessive, all kittens born from Cornish Rex females bred to Kirlee would have been wavy coated had the gene responsible for Kirlee's mutation been the same one responsible for Kallibunker's. Subsequent test matings between Cornish and German Rex in the United States proved that those two strains were compatible.

Before she was obliged to give up her cats in the late 1950s, Nina Ennismore had sent several Rex to American breeders. Most of these were Siamese breeders who used their own stock as outcrosses for the new Rex breed. This provided the fine bone, unusual head type, large ears, and racy, greyhound look that characterizes the best Cornish Rex today.

The Cornish Rex has been a straightforward success in the cat world. It is accepted for championship competition by the GCCF and by all North American registries.

CORNISH REX

(Breed 33)
General Type Standard

COAT: Short and plushy, without guard hairs, and should curl, wave or ripple particularly on back and tail. Whiskers and eyebrows crinkled and of good length. All coat colours acceptable. Asymmetrical white marking to be allowed for Cornish Rex. White marking, however, not allowed on Siamese pattern.
HEAD: Medium wedge. Head length about one-third greater than the maximum width, narrowing to a

strong chin. The skull to be flat. In profile a straight line to be seen from the centre of forehead to end of nose.
EYES: Oval shaped, medium in size, colour in keeping with coat colour or, except in the case of Si-Rex, chartreuse, green or yellow.
EARS: Large, set rather high on head, wide at base, tapering to rounded tips and well covered with fine fur.
BODY AND LEGS: Body hard and muscular, slender and of medium length. Legs long and straight, giving an overall appearance of being high on the legs. Paws small and oval.
TAIL: Long, fine and tapering, but also well covered with curly fur.

CORNISH REX COLOURS

Particolour colours: bicolour (solid colour and white, smoke and white, tabby and white, etc.), blue cream, calico, dilute calico, tortoiseshell, van bicolour, van blue cream and white, van calico. **Shaded colours:** chinchilla silver, shaded silver. **Smoke colours:** black smoke, blue smoke. **Solid colours:** black, blue, cream, red, white. **Tabby colours:** blue (classic, patched, and mackerel), brown (classic, patched, and mackerel), cream (classic and mackerel), red (classic and mackerel), silver (classic, patched, and mackerel). **Other Rex colours:** any other colour or pattern.

Cornish Rex allowable outcross breeds: Cornish Rex breeders outcross to other shorthair breeds including Siamese, Burmese and Abyssinians. The resulting straight-coated kittens are called variants and are only of value for the production of rex-coated cats.

Cymric

ORIGIN

The longhaired Manx or Cymric (*kim* rick) has appeared in Manx litters for as long as the breed has existed. There is no doubt that on the Isle of Man, where Manx originated, cats with long hair bred freely with the indigenous short-coated, tailless cats. The longhairs are thought to have arrived when the Vikings colonized this tiny island.

Red Classic Tabby and White Cymric

DEVELOPMENT

Beginning in the late 1930s and continuing for several decades, Manx breeders began to use Persians in their breeding programmes, not from any deep desire to produce longhaired Manx, but in order to improve conformation and thickness of coat in their shorthairs. This was a convenient strategy because owners of stud Manx were few. It also served, though unintentionally, to increase the Manx gene pool. Cat fanciers, being what they are, will frequently seek recognition for

anything new or different that appears in their litters. Just as frequently they will attempt to explain the unique in terms of a rare mutation, and some people tried to use this as an explanation for the appearance of longhaired Manx kittens. Such was not the case.

Nor was it necessarily a good idea to promote the longhaired Manx as a championship breed. There are enough problems with Manx, and adding long hair to the picture—which could impede the cats' toilet duties, and become severely matted as a result—should not be encouraged. With more and more of the longhaired Manx kittens appearing, however, some breeders began to campaign to have them recognized as a breed. The Canadian Cat Association was the first to do so, granting championship status to Cymrics in the mid 1970s.

Cymrics tend to have a personality quite similar to that of the Manx. They are clownlike in behaviour and really are true companions. Like other cats that are longhaired variants of what were originally short-haired breeds, the Cymrics' coat does not seem to carry the fullness, thickness, or length exhibited by those breeds where longhair-to-longhair breeding is done repeatedly.

CYMRIC

Not recognized by the GCCF

Standard, courtesy of the Cat Fanciers' Association of America. Differences in the Standards of other registries are indicated at the end of the text.

HEAD and EARS:	25	**LEGS and FEET:**	15
EYES:	5	**COAT LENGTH:**	10
BODY:	25	**COAT TEXTURE:**	10
TAILLESSNESS:	5	**COLOUR:**	5

GENERAL: The overall impression of the tailless Cymric is that of roundness; round head with firm, round muzzle and prominent cheeks; broad chest; substantial, short front legs; short back, which arches from shoulders to a round rump; great depth of flank; and rounded, muscular thighs. The heavy, glossy double coat of medium length is the main differentiating factor of the Cymric from its parent breed—the Manx. The Cymric should be alert, clear of eye, with a glistening, clean, well-groomed coat. It should have a healthy physical appearance, feeling firm and muscular, neither too fat nor too lean. It should be surprisingly heavy when lifted. Cymrics are slow to mature and allowance should be made in young cats.

HEAD AND EARS: Round head with prominent cheeks and a jowly appearance. Head is slightly longer than it is broad. Moderately rounded forehead, pronounced cheekbones, and jowliness (more evident in adult males) enhance the round appearance. Short, thick neck. Definite whisker break, with large, round whisker pads. In profile there is a gentle nose dip.[1] Well-developed muzzle, slightly longer than broad, with a strong chin. Ears are wide at the base, tapering gradually to a rounded tip, with full interior furnishings. Medium in size in proportion to the head, widely spaced, and set slightly outward. When viewed from behind, the ear set resembles that of the rocker of a cradle.

EYES: Large, round,[2] and full. Set at a slight angle toward the nose (outer corners slightly higher than inner corners). Ideal colour conforms to requirements of coat colour.[3,4]

BODY: Solidly muscled, compact, and well balanced, medium in size with sturdy bone structure. The Cymric is stout in appearance, with broad chest and well-sprung ribs; surprisingly heavy when lifted. The constant repetition of curves and circles gives the Cymric the appearance of great substance and durability, a cat that is powerful without the slightest hint of coarseness. Males may be somewhat larger than females. Flank (fleshy area of the side between the ribs and hip) has greater depth than in other breeds, causing considerable depth to the body when viewed from the side. The short back forms a smooth, continuous arch from shoulders to rump, curving at the rump to form the desirable round look. Shortness of back is unique to the Cymric (and Manx), but is in proportion to the entire cat and may be somewhat longer in the male. Because of the Cymric's longer coat over the rump area, the body may appear longer.

TAILLESSNESS: Absolute in the perfect specimen, with a decided hollow at the end of the backbone where, in the tailed cat, a tail would begin. A rise of the bone at the end of the spine is allowed and should not be penalized unless it is such that it stops the judge's hand, thereby spoiling the tailless appearance of the cat. The rump is extremely broad and round.
LEGS AND FEET: Heavily boned, forelegs short and set well apart to emphasize the broad, deep chest. Hind legs much longer than forelegs, with heavy, muscular thighs and substantial lower legs. Longer hind legs cause the rump to be considerably higher than the shoulders. Hind legs are straight when viewed from behind. Paws are neat and round, with five toes in front and four behind.
COAT LENGTH: The double coat is of medium length,[5] dense and well padded over the main body, gradually lengthening from the shoulders to the rump. Breeches, abdomen, and neck ruff are longer than on the main body. Cheek coat is thick and full. The collarlike neck ruff extends from the shoulders, being biblike around the chest. Breeches should be full and thick to the hocks in the mature cat. Lower leg and head coat (except for cheeks) should be shorter than on the main body and neck ruff, but dense and full in appearance. Toe tufts and ear tufts are desirable. Preference should be given to the cat showing full coating.[6]
COAT TEXTURE: Coat is soft and silky, falling smoothly on the body yet being full and plush due to the double coat. Coat should have a healthy, glossy appearance. Allowance to be made for seasonal and age variations.
TRANSFER TO AOV: Definite, visible tail joint. Short coat.
PENALIZE: Coat that lacks density, has a cottony texture, or one that is of an overall even length.
SEVERELY PENALIZE: If the judge is unable to make the cat stand or walk properly.
DISQUALIFY: Evidence of poor physical condition; incorrect number of toes; evidence of hybridization.

CYMRIC COLOURS

(See page 170 for a full description of the colours listed below.)

Particolour colours: bicolours (black and white, red and white, blue and white, cream and white), blue cream, calico, dilute calico, tortoiseshell. **Shaded colours:** chinchilla silver, shaded silver. **Smoke colours:** black smoke, blue smoke. **Solid colours:** black, blue, cream, red, white. **Tabby colours:** blue tabby (classic, mackerel), blue patched tabby, brown tabby (classic, mackerel), brown patched tabby, cream tabby (classic, mackerel), red tabby (classic, mackerel), silver tabby (classic, mackerel), silver patched tabby. **Other Cymric colours:** any other colour or pattern with the exception of those showing hybridization resulting in the colours chocolate, lavender, the Himalayan pattern, or these combinations with white.

Cymric allowable outcross breeds:[7] Manx.

[1] ACA: 'Nose longer and broader than the American Shorthair's.'
[2] ACA: 'Almost' round.
[3] ACA: 'Any eye colour allowed and of secondary importance.'
[4] TICA: Eye colour should 'conform to coat colour, but should only be considered if all other points are equal.'
[5] ACA: 'Medium long.'
[6] ACA: 'Seasonal variation should not be penalized.'
[7] In all associations where the breed is recognized.

Devon Rex

ORIGIN

In 1960 a kitten with wavy hair was discovered in a litter of straight-coated feral kittens in Devonshire, England. The father of this litter was believed to have been a tomcat with a similar wavy coat who lived in an abandoned tin mine near Buckfastleigh in Devonshire. The mother of the litter was a tortie-and-white, normal-coated stray that raised her kittens in a field at the foot of a garden belonging to Beryl Cox, who lived not far from the mine. Since the gene responsible for the Devon Rex coat is recessive—i.e., kittens will not develop this coat unless they inherit one copy of the curly-coated gene from each parent—many people assume that the tortie and white who produced the curly-coated youngster was herself an offspring of the tin-mine tomcat.

Beryl Cox named the wavy-haired kitten Kirlee, and he soon became her great favourite. She delighted in

White Devon Rex

his unique appearance, intelligence, and warmth and—it has been reported—his ability to walk a tightrope and to wag his tail like a dog when he was praised for this feat. For all Kirlee's charm, however, Cox had no inclination to create an entire curly-coated breed. Yet when she heard that a cat fancier named Brian Stirling-Webb was working to establish a curly-coated strain whose patriarch had been born in Cornwall, one county west of Devonshire, she offered to send Stirling-Webb her beloved Kirlee. After several breedings between Kirlee and the Cornish Rex produced nothing but normal-coated kittens, breeders concluded that the Devon and Cornish Rex were not compatible. These were separate breeds caused by separate gene mutations. Thenceforward the two breeds were cultivated separately.

DEVELOPMENT

Since the Devon would not mix with the Cornish—and since there were not many Devons with which to mix—their gene pool was established with the help of other breeds. These outcrosses were chosen to produce as many colours and patterns as possible, including the restricted colourpoint pattern of the Siamese. The kittens that were retained from these initial outcrosses were used to establish, refine and set Devon Rex type were selected for coat quality and conformation. Kirlee, whom Cox had generously given to Stirling-Webb, was used throughout the early establishment of the breed. He was eventually neutered and sent to live as a pet with friends of Stirling-Webb.

By the late 1960s the Devon Rex had arrived in the United States, where it was first accepted for championship competition in 1972 by the American Cat Fanciers Association. The small gene pool encouraged breeders to outcross to British Shorthairs initially but over the years outcrosses have been made to Siamese, Burmese and Abyssinians so producing Si-Rex with a Siamese coat pattern, a few Burmese patterned Rex and a large number with the Tonkinese coat pattern. The resulting straight coated kittens are known as variants and, in addition to having straight coats, resemble ordinary household pets, which leads breeders to theorize that the Devon gene controls type and conformation as well as coat.

The Devon Rex can be distinguished from its next door neighbour from Cornwall in several ways: the Devon has a shorter coat that is less plush and less wavy than the Cornish coat, even though Cornish lacks guard hairs—the coarse, outer layer of a cat's coat. The Devon Rex has a decided stop to its nose; the Cornish has a Roman nose. Finally, the Cornish has a noticeable tuck up to its abdomen, and the Devon Rex does not.

DEVON REX

(Breed 33a)
General Type Standard

COAT: Very short and fine, wavy, curly and soft, can have a rippled effect. Whiskers and eyebrows crinkled, rather coarse, and of medium length. All coat colours acceptable.

HEAD: Wedge shaped with face full cheeked. Short muzzle with strong chin and whisker break. Nose with a strongly marked stop. Forehead curving back to a flat skull.

EYES: Wide set, large, oval shaped and sloping towards outer edges of ears. Colour in keeping with coat colour or, except in Si-Rex, chartreuse, green or yellow.

EARS: Large, set rather low, very wide at base, tapering to rounded tops and well covered with fine fur. With or without ear muffs.

BODY, LEGS AND NECK: Body hard and muscular, slender and of medium length, broad in chest, carried high on slim legs, with length of hind legs emphasized. Paws small and oval. Neck slender.

TAIL: Long, fine and tapering, well covered with short fur.

DEVON REX COLOURS

(See page 170 for a full description of the colours listed below.)

Particolour colours: bicolours (solid colour and white, tabby and white, tortoiseshell and white, etc), blue cream, calico, fawn cream calico, lilac cream calico, cinnamon cream calico, chocolate tortoiseshell, cinnamon tortoiseshell, dilute tortie and white including van pattern, fawn cream, lilac cream, tortoiseshell, van bicolour, tricoloured, cinnamon cream van calico. **Shaded colours:** blue cream shaded, blue shaded, cameo shaded, chinchilla, chocolate shaded, chocolate tortoiseshell shaded, cinnamon shaded, cinnamon tortoiseshell shaded, fawn cream shaded, fawn shaded, lilac cream shaded, lilac shaded, shaded silver, tortoiseshell shaded. **Smoke colours:** black smoke, blue smoke, blue cream smoke, chocolate smoke, chocolate tortoiseshell smoke, cinnamon smoke, cinnamon tortoiseshell smoke, cream smoke, fawn smoke, fawn cream smoke, lilac smoke, lilac cream smoke, red smoke cameo, tortoiseshell smoke. **Solid colours:** black, blue, cinnamon, chocolate, cream, fawn, lilac, red, white. **Tabby colours:** blue brown, cameo, chocolate, chocolate silver, cinnamon, cinnamon silver, cream, fawn, lilac, lilac silver, red tabby, silver tabby, blue silver, cream silver, fawn silver. **Other Devon Rex colours:** any other colour or pattern. Examples: any colour with one, two, three, or four white feet. Ticked tabbies. All point restricted colours such as seal point, chocolate point, blue point, lilac point, cream point, tabby points, cinnamon point, etc. Burmese, Tonkinese coat patterns in all colours.

Devon Rex allowable outcross breeds: Devon Rex breeders outcross to other shorthair breeds including Siamese, Burmese and Abyssinians. The resulting straight-coated kittens are called variants and are only of value for the production of rex-coated cats.

Egyptian Mau

ORIGIN

The Egyptian Mau gained recognition because of the efforts of Princess Nathalie Troubetskoy, one of the most accomplished and extraordinary persons ever associated with the cat fancy. A member of one of the oldest Russian families, the princess was born in Poland in 1897. She studied at the art theatre and the medical school in Moscow, and served throughout World War I on Russian battle fronts. After living in England for twenty years, she went to Italy; and when the allied armies arrived, she served as chief nurse to the U.S. 2675th Regiment.

While the princess was living in Rome, a youngster whom she knew gave her a spotted silver, female kitten. The kitten had been given to him by a member of the diplomatic corps in one of the Mideast embassies. The princess named the kitten Baba, and realizing that she had unique qualities, sought to learn more about the kitten's background. After consulting with a veterinarian and several professors, the princess concluded that Baba was descended from Egyptian stock.

DEVELOPMENT

In December 1956 Princess Troubetskoy arrived in the United States with Baba and two other Egyptian Maus. Had she been able, as she had planned, to book passage on the Andrea Doria, which sank in the Atlantic off the coast of North America, the breed might never have been established. The cats that the princess brought to America were the first and only Egyptian Maus imported to this country.

When Baba was brought to the United States, the four-year-old Mau was a tall, elegant queen. Clear silver in colour, she had black spotting, vivid necklaces and bracelets, and large eyes outlined in black. Another of the three Maus was Baba's three-year-old son Giorgio, called Jo-Jo, who was a larger, stronger-looking bronze cat. An eleven-month-old female named Liza, ochre in colour, completed the group. She was exhibited at the Empire Cat Show in 1957. Eleven years later the Cat Fanciers' Federation granted championship status to the Mau, which is now accepted in all associations in America.

Baba's offspring were, of course, the result of domestic crossing and much inbreeding. Like their mother they were most unpredictable, fiery, and wild natured. They did not accept other cats easily and were comfortable only on their own home territory. They would literally climb the walls in strange homes or at shows. Through selective breeding, those who pioneered the Mau have produced more docile cats—active and intelligent and great companions.

This cat is not recognized in the UK; its nearest equivalent is the Oriental Spotted Tabby.

EGYPTIAN MAU

Not recognized by the GCCF

GENERAL: The Egyptian Mau is the only natural domesticated breed of spotted cat. The Egyptian's impression should be one of an active, colourful cat of medium size with well-developed muscles. Perfect physical condition with an alert appearance. Well balanced physically and temperamentally. Males tend to be larger than females.

HEAD: A slightly rounded wedge without flat planes, medium in length. Not full cheeked. Profile showing a gentle contour with slight rise from the bridge of the nose to the forehead. Entire length of nose even in width when viewed from the front.

Silver Egyptian Mau

MUZZLE: Neither short nor pointed. Allowance to be made for jowls in adult males.
EARS: Medium to large,[1,2] alert and moderately pointed, continuing the planes of the head. Broad at base. Upstanding with ample width between ears. Hair in ears short and close lying. Inner ear a delicate, almost transparent, shell pink. May be tufted.
EYES: Large[3] and alert, almond shaped,[4] with a slight slant towards the ears. Skull apertures neither round nor oriental.
BODY: Medium long and graceful, showing well-developed, muscular strength. Loose skin flap extending from flank to hind leg knee. General balance is more to be desired than size alone. Allowance to be made for muscular necks and shoulders in adult males.[5]
LEGS AND FEET: In proportion to body. Hind legs proportionately longer, giving the appearance of being on tiptoe when standing upright. Feet small and dainty, slightly oval, almost round in shape. Toes: five in front and four behind.
TAIL: Medium long, thick at base, with slight taper.
COAT: Hair is medium in length with a lustrous sheen. In the smoke colour the hair is silky and fine in texture. In the silver and bronze colours, the hair is dense and resilient in texture and accommodates two or more bands of ticking separated by lighter bands.
PENALIZE: Short or round head. Pointed muzzle. Small, round, or oriental eyes. Cobby or oriental body. Short or whip tail. If no broken necklaces. Pencillings in spotting pattern on torso. Poor condition. Amber cast in eye colour in cats over the age of $1\frac{1}{2}$ years.
DISQUALIFY: Lack of spots. Blue eyes. Kinked or abnormal tail. Incorrect number of toes. White locket or button distinctive from other acceptable white-coloured areas in colour sections of standard.

MAU PATTERN
(Common to all colours)

PATTERN: Markings on torso are to be randomly spotted with variance in size and shape. The spots can be small or large, round, oblong, or irregular shaped. Any of these are of equal merit, but the spots, however shaped or whatever size, shall be distinct. Good contrast between pale ground colour and deeper markings. Forehead barred with characteristic 'M' and frown marks, forming lines between the ears which continue down the back of the neck, ideally breaking into elongated spots along the spine. The spinal lines, as they reach the rear haunches, meld together to form a dorsal stripe that continues along the top of the tail to its tip. The tail is heavily banded and has a dark tip. The cheeks are barred with 'mascara' lines; the first starts at the outer corner of the eye and continues along the contour of the cheek, with a second line, which starts at the centre of the cheek and curves upwards, almost meeting below the base of the ear. On the upper chest there are one or more broken necklaces. The shoulder markings are a transition between stripes and spots. The upper front legs are heavily barred but do not necessarily match. Spotting patterns on each side of the torso need not match. Haunches and upper hind legs to be a transition between stripes and spots, breaking into bars on the lower leg. Underside of body to have 'vest buttons' spots; dark in colour against the correspondingly pale ground colour.

EGYPTIAN MAU COLOURS

EYE COLOUR: Light green, 'gooseberry green.' Amber cast is acceptable only in young adults up to $1^1/_2$ years of age.
BRONZE: Warm, coppery-brown ground colour across head, shoulders, outer legs, back, and tail, being darkest on the saddle and lightening to a tawny buff on the sides. Underside fades to a creamy ivory. All markings dark brown-black with a warm, coppery-brown undercoat, showing good contrast against the lighter ground colour. Back of ears tawny pink and tipped in dark brown-black. Nose, lips, and eyes outlined in dark brown, with bridge of nose brown. Upper throat area, chin, and around nostrils pale, creamy white. Nose leather: brick red. Paw pads: black or dark brown, with same colour between toes and extending beyond the paws of the hind legs.
SILVER: Pale silver ground colour across the head, shoulders, outer legs, back, and tail. Underside fades to a brilliant pale silver. All markings charcoal colour with a white to pale silver undercoat, showing good contrast against lighter ground colours. Back of ears greyish pink and tipped in black. Nose, lips, and eyes outlined in black. Upper throat area, chin, and around nostrils pale clear silver, appearing white. Nose leather: brick red. Paw pads: black with black between the toes and extending beyond the paws of the hind legs.
SMOKE: Pale silver ground colour across head, shoulders, legs, tail, and underside. All markings jet black with a white to pale silver undercoat, with sufficient contrast against ground colour for pattern to be plainly visible. Nose, lips, and eyes outlined in jet black. Upper throat area, chin, and around nostrils lightest in colour. Nose leather: black. Paw pads: black with black between the toes and extending beyond the paws of the hind legs.
PEWTER (as described in the American Cat Association Standard): Ground colour suggesting pale fawn. Each hair to be composed of bands of pale silver and beige with black tipping. Loses ticking and lightens to cream on undersides. Chin, upper throat, and nose outlined in cream. Markings are charcoal to dark brown, with good contrast between ground colour and markings. Paw pads: charcoal to dark brown. Nose leather: brick red. Eyes, nose, and lips outlined in charcoal to dark brown.

Egyptian Mau allowable outcross breeds:[6] none.

[1] TICA: 'Medium to medium large.'
[2] ACA, CFF: 'Large.'
[3] ACA, CFF: 'Very large.'
[4] TICA: 'Rounded almond.'
[5] ACA: 'Neck is arched, proportionately long in relation to body.'
[6] In all associations where the breed is recognized.

Exotic Shorthair

ORIGIN

Although it officially became eligible for championship competition on May 1, 1967, the Exotic Shorthair had been competing *sub rosa* as an American Shorthair for some time before that. In the days when American Shorthairs were still known as Domestic Shorthairs — i.e., prior to May 1, 1966—persons looking for an edge with this breed began crossing Persians to their Domestic Shorthair stock. The cats produced through this illegal scheme were far more pleasing than the Domestic Shorthairs with legitimate pedigrees. They were also far more successful in the show ring, where judges did not overlook them, even though the Domestic Shorthair Standard warned that 'any evidence of hybridizing' was grounds for disqualification. Since evidence is in the eye of the beholder, judges always found a way to justify giving awards to these cats.

DEVELOPMENT

The American Cat Fanciers' Association tried to stop people from using Persian-Domestic crosses by closing the Domestic Shorthair registry. When the modified Domestic Shorthairs had first appeared, breeders were allowed to register any domestic, non-pedigreed cat—real or imagined—for the price of a registration fee and a brief description of the cat. These foundation Domestics, spelled with an uppercase *D* once the registration fee had been accepted, could then be used in breeding programmes. Or they could be used on paper as the nominal sires or dams of litters, while Persians capable of producing the same colours in a litter were doing the actual breeding. Obviously, closing the Domestic Shorthair registry was not going to put an end to this practice. If a breeder with a red tabby Domestic Shorthair male owned a red tabby Persian male also, that breeder could still use the Persian for mating and claim on the application for litter registration that the Domestic cat was the father of the litter. Instead of putting a stop to hybridization, closing the Domestic Shorthair registry served only to make pedigrees less reliable. Before the registry was closed, anyone who saw 'unknown' on a Domestic Shorthair pedigree generally assumed that 'unknown' was code for 'Persian.'

Matters became more difficult with the appearance of silver American Shorthairs. Not only was their type and conformation suspect, their colour was one that didn't exist in the Domestic Shorthair population. Silver had to have come from chinchilla or shaded silver Persians. Worse yet, some of these silver Domestic Shorthairs had no Domestic ancestors at all, having been produced from silver Persian-Abyssinian crosses. Judges of conscience withheld awards on silver Americans because the evidence of hybridization was as plain as the colour of the cats. The American CFA, however, chose to deal with the problem by returning to open registration, thereby flinging open the barn doors to outside influences once again.

In 1966 two co-chairs of CFA's breed programme suggested that CFA establish a new breed to accommodate the cats being produced and shown illegally as American Shorthairs. This proposed new breed was called the Exotic Shorthair because *Exotic* accurately reflected the use of Abyssinians, Burmese, and other non-American breeds in its development. Breeders with hybrid Americans had the option of transferring their cats to this newly created breed, which was given championship status as of May 1, 1967. At that point the breeds that could be used legally to produce Exotics were limited to Persians and American Shorthairs.

The Exotic Shorthair has gained immense popularity with those who love Persian type but not the grooming required to maintain the Persian coat. In fact, the success of this breed, which ought to be called the Shortcoated Persian, has been so great that Exotics can now compete evenly with their longhaired counterparts, which was not always the case.

Once breeders had crossed an American Shorthair to a Persian to achieve a short coat, there was no reason to continue using Americans in Exotic Shorthair breeding programmes. Nor is it advisable to breed Exotic to Exotic for more than one generation—two at most. Doing so invariably results in a loss of the desired Persian type and conformation. With so many Persians being used to produce Exotics—and with the longhaired gene being recessive—it is possible to produce longhaired kittens from two Exotics or from an Exotic-Persian cross. There is no difference between these longhaired Exotic Shorthairs and the so-called purebred Persians.

The development of the Exotic Shorthair in the United Kingdom has depended largely on the out-crossing of the British Shorthair to the Persian Longhair. The resulting kittens were normally registered as British Shorthair but in recent years a group of Exotic Shorthair breeders began to register the Persian type shorthair kittens as Exotics. By selecting from the shorthair kittens for Persian type, an improving type had begun to evolve. At this time all longhair kittens resulting from such matings were allowed to be registered as Persian Longhairs, except in the case of colourpointed cats. It was unnecessary to place any restriction on the registration because there had always been out-crossing of British Shorthairs to Persian Longhairs; this only resulted in the kittens being placed on the Supplementary rather than the Full register.

Brown Classic Tabby Exotic Shorthair

Exotic Shorthair breeders, desirous of improving the quality of the breed, decided to import from both Europe and the United States. One of these imported cats, a male, Purrfun My Main Man from America, was used extensively shortly after his arrival in the United Kingdom in a well designed breeding policy to improve the type of the Exotics. Breeders were very pleased with the results of such matings, except that on one or two occasions the colour of the cats produced seemed to be difficult to identify. When one such kitten appeared at the Surrey and Sussex cat show registered as a Chocolate Smoke, judges were dubious about the accuracy of this registration and called upon two members of the Genetics Committee of the GCCF, Lesley Pring and Julia May, who happened to be present at the show to look at the cat in question. Both went independently to examine the kitten and both came to the conclusion that it showed a Tonkinese coat pattern. This was very disturbing as the Burmese coat restriction gene had not been introduced into the Longhair breed. The Executive Committee considered the situation carefully and reluctantly decided that the registration policy for the Persian Longhairs resulting from Exotic matings would have to be modified and all such longhairs are now registered as Exotic Variants. Obviously, many such cats do not carry the Burmese gene but it was felt that by isolating all possible carriers, at a later stage programmes could be developed to clear lines of Exotic Shorthairs of being carriers of the Burmese coat restriction gene. However, this work has not yet started and so the longhair kittens have to be registered as Exotic Variants.

EXOTIC SHORTHAIR

Preliminary
General Type Standard

HEAD: Round and massive with good breadth of skull. Round face with round underlying bone structure. Well set on a short, thick neck. Firm chin.
NOSE: Short, snub and broad with definite 'break'.
CHEEKS: Full
JAWS: Broad and powerful with level bite.
EARS: Small and rounded. Slight forward tilt. Not unduly open at base. Set far apart and low on the head, fitting into (without distorting) the rounded contour of the head.
EYES: Large, round and wide open. Set far apart and lustrous, giving a sweet expression to the face. Colour corresponding to the coat colour.
BODY: Of cobby type, low on the legs, deep in the chest, equally massive across shoulders and rump with with a short well rounded trunk. Large or medium in size.
BACK: Level
LEGS: Short, thick and strong. Forelegs straight.
PAWS: Large, round and firm. Toes carried close, five on front feet, including one dew claw, and four on back feet.
TAIL: Short, but in proportion to body length. A kink to be considered to be a fault.
COAT: Dense, plush, soft in texture, full of life. Stands out from the body due to density, not flat or close lying. Medium in length, slightly longer than shorthairs, but not long enough to flow.

EXOTIC SHORTHAIR COLOURS

(See page 170 for a full description of the colours listed below.)

Particolour colours: bicolours (black and white, blue and white, red and white, or cream and white), blue cream, calico, dilute calico, tabby and white, tortoiseshell, van bicolour, van calico, van dilute calico. **Pointed colours:** blue lynx point, blue point, blue-cream point, chocolate point, chocolate-tortie point, cream point, flame (red) point, lilac point, lilac-cream point, seal lynx point, seal point, tortie point. **Shaded colours:** chinchilla golden, chinchilla silver, shaded cameo, shaded golden, shaded silver, shaded tortoiseshell, shell cameo, shell tortoiseshell. **Smoke colours:** black smoke, blue smoke, blue-cream smoke, cameo smoke, smoke tortoiseshell. **Solid colours:** black, blue, chocolate, cream, lilac, peke-face red, red, white. **Tabby colours:** blue (classic, patched, and mackerel), brown (classic, patched, and mackerel), cameo (classic and mackerel), cream (classic and mackerel), peke-face red, red (classic and mackerel), silver (classic, patched, and mackerel).

Exotic Shorthair allowable outcross breeds: Persian.

Havana Brown

ORIGIN

The Havana Brown was created in Great Britain during the 1950s, but brown cats first appeared at cat shows more than one hundred years ago. Some of the earliest cats imported from Siam by English cat fanciers were solid brown. An all-brown cat won first prize at a show in England in 1888. Six years later a brown cat said to belong to a breed called the Swiss Mountain Cat was exhibited in England. And in 1928 the Siamese Cat Club of Britain presented a special award to the cat with the best chocolate body in show.

By 1930, however, the Siamese Cat Club had decided that it was 'unable to encourage the breeding of any but blue-eyed Siamese.' Therefore, brown cats were not seen in England again until 1954, when photographs of two chestnut-coloured kittens appeared in the August edition of the journal *Our Cats.* These kittens were called Bronze Leaf and Bronze Wing. They were from the Craigiehilloch cattery of Mrs R Clarke in Reading, in Berkshire. The mother of the kittens was a seal point Siamese named Our Miss Smith. Their father was Elmtower Bronze Idol, a brown hybrid who was the first Havana registered in England. Bronze Idol's mother was a black domestic shorthair by a seal point Siamese. Idol's father was also a seal point Siamese.

DEVELOPMENT

At first, chestnut-brown kittens with green eye colour were called Havanas, though there is some disagreement about the origin of that name. Some people declare that the breed was named after the rabbit of the same colour. Others say that Havana tobacco was the inspiration. When the Governing Council of the Cat Fancy in England recognized Havanas for championship competition in 1958, it assigned the name Chestnut Brown Foreign to the breed. A dozen years later GCCF reverted to calling the cats by their original name, Havana.

The first Chestnut Brown Foreigns arrived in the United States during the mid 1950s. By the end of the decade the United Cat Federation accepted the breed for championship competition under the name Havana Brown. While the American and the English versions of this breed ultimately shared the same name, they do not share the same conformation. In the United States the general conformation is midway between the short-coupled, thickset breeds and the elongated, svelte ones but in England the Havana is a cat of Siamese type and is exhibited with all the other Siamese type shorthairs in an Oriental Shorthair section at cat shows.

The British Havana is a chocolate cat of Siamese type and is not the same as an American Havana Brown.

Havana Brown

HAVANA BROWN COLOURS

General Type Standard

GENERAL: The Havana should be a beautifully balanced animal with head and ears carried on a slender neck and with a long svelte body supported on fine legs and feet with a slender, whipped tail, free from abnormalities. The body, legs, feet, head and tail should all be in proportion giving a well-balanced appearance. The expression should be alert and intelligent. The cat should be in excellent physical condition.

HEAD, NECK AND EARS: Head long and well-proportioned with width between the ears and narrowing in perfectly straight lines to a fine muzzle and forming a balanced triangle with no break or pinch at the whiskers. The head and profile should be wedge shaped, neither round nor pointed, avoiding exaggerated type. In profile the nose should be straight, free from any stop or dip and the chin should be strong with a level bite. The tip of the chin should line up with the tip of the nose in the same vertical plane. The neck should be long and slender. The ears should be large, pricked and wide at the base with their setting continuing the lines of the wedge.

EYE SHAPE AND SETTING: Oriental in shape and slanting towards the nose with good width between. No tendency to squint.

BODY, LEGS AND PAWS: Medium in size. Long and svelte with a tight abdomen. Legs long and slim. Hind legs higher than the front legs. The body and legs to be firm and well muscled throughout. Paws small and oval.

TAIL: Long and tapering. Not blunt ended and free from any abnormality of the bone structure.

COAT: Very short and fine in texture. Glossy and close lying. Even and sound throughout in adults and free from any flakes of dead skin.

CONDITION: Excellent physical condition.

EYE COLOUR: Clear bright vivid green with no flecks of contrasting colour.

COAT COLOUR: Rich warm chestnut brown. Not dark or cold toned.

NOSE LEATHER: Brown or pinkish-brown.

PAW PADS: Solid brown or solid pinkish-brown.

Havana Brown allowable outcross breeds: Havana cats may be bred from any of the oriental breeds except the Foreign White and with Siamese. Outcrosses to Siamese will appear on the supplementary register.

Japanese Bobtail

ORIGIN

The earliest written evidence of cats in Japan indicates that they arrived, most likely from China or Korea, at least one thousand years ago. Unfortunately, we cannot tell from records whether these immigrants had bobbed tails or whether the mutation that produces these tails first appeared in Japan. For hundreds of years bobtailed cats were highly valued and guarded, but in 1602 Japanese authorities decreed that all cats should be set free to cope with vermin which were threatening silk worms. Buying or selling cats was forbidden, and from that time forward bobtailed cats lived in the streets and on farms.

Red and White Japanese Bobtail

DEVELOPMENT

After World War II, United States military personnel stationed in Japan brought their families and their family pets with them. Some of these pets were pedigreed cats, and where there are pedigreed cats, there are eventually cat shows. At first, there was no interest, however, in registering the bobtailed cats of Japan. Ego, social structure, and pride of ownership among the Japanese dictated that foreign cats (as they generally are, no matter what the country) were the most prized. American-bred Persians, Siamese, or Abyssinians were much sought after, and Japanese brokers had a field day buying cats in the United States for resale at inflated prices back home.

There was no thought of registering the bobtailed cats of Japan until the early 1960s when American judges began officiating at Japanese shows. By the end of the decade there were a handful of bobtails in the United States. In 1971 the American Cat Fanciers' Association awarded the breed provisional status. Five years later Japanese Bobtails became eligible for championship competition in CFA, and they are now recognized in all associations.

There is a distinct difference between the Japanese Bobtail and the Manx. The Bobtail gene is recessive, and the cats, therefore, breed true. Furthermore, Bobtails are not plagued by the birth defects that occur in the Manx. In order to ensure the separation of these breeds, the Japanese Bobtail Breed Committee developed a Standard that would offer no advantage to anyone crossbreeding the two. Since the tail is not a physical structure that can be controlled by breeding, there is no set type required by the Standard—as long as the tail is present and is not more than three inches in length.

Long-coated kittens have appeared occasionally in some Bobtail litters, the result of deliberate or accidental crossing to other shorthaired cats carrying the recessive longhair gene. Half-tailed kittens have begun to appear, too. This demonstrates the truth of one of the oldest maxims in the cat fancy: In breeding cats it is wise to remember that what goes up, comes down. What you put in, you get out.

JAPANESE BOBTAIL

Not recognized by the GCCF

Standard, courtesy of the
Cat Fanciers' Association of America.
Differences in the Standards of other registries are indicated at the end of the text.

HEAD: 20

TYPE: 30

TAIL: 20

COLOUR and MARKINGS: 20

COAT: 10

GENERAL: The Japanese Bobtail should present the overall impression of a medium-sized cat with clean lines and bone structure, well muscled but straight and slender rather than massive in build. The unique set of its eyes, combined with high cheek bones and a long parallel nose, lend a distinctive Japanese cast to the face, especially in profile, quite different from the other oriental breeds. Its short tail should resemble a bunny tail with the hair fanning out to create a pom-pom appearance which effectively camouflages the underlying bone structure of the tail.

HEAD: Although the head appears long and finely chiselled, it forms almost a perfect equilateral triangle with gentle curving lines, high cheekbones, and a noticeable whisker break, the nose long and well defined by two parallel lines from tip to brow with a gentle dip at, or just below, eye level. Allowance must be made for jowls in the stud cat.

EARS: Large, upright, and expressive, set wide apart but at right angles to the head rather than flaring outward, and giving the impression of being tilted forward in repose.

MUZZLE: Fairly broad and rounding into the whisker break; neither pointed nor blunt.

EYES: Large, oval rather than round, but wide and alert; set into the skull at a rather pronounced slant when viewed in profile. The eyeball shows a shallow curvature and should not bulge out beyond the cheekbone or the forehead.

BODY: Medium in size, males proportionately larger

than females. Torso long, lean, and elegant, not tubular, showing well-developed muscular strength without coarseness. No inclination toward flabbiness or cobbiness. General balance of utmost importance.
LEGS: In keeping with the body, long, slender, and high, but not dainty or fragile in appearance. The hind legs noticeably longer than the forelegs, but deeply angled to bend when the cat is standing relaxed so that the torso remains nearly level rather than rising toward the rear. When standing, the cat's forelegs and shoulders form two continuous straight lines, close together.
PAWS: Oval. Toes: five in front and four behind.
COAT: Medium length, soft and silky, but without a noticeable undercoat. Relatively non-shedding.
TAIL: The tail is unique not only to the breed, but to each individual cat. This is to be used as a guideline, rather than promoting one specific type of tail out of the many that occur within the breed. The tail must be clearly visible and is composed of one or more curves, angles, or kinks, or any combination thereof. The furthest extension of the tail bone from the body should be no longer than three inches. The direction in which the tail is carried is not important. The tail may be flexible or rigid and should be of a size and shape that harmonizes with the rest of the cat.[1]
PENALIZE: Short, round head, cobby build.
DISQUALIFY: Tail bone absent or extending too far beyond body. Tail lacking in pom-pom or fluffy appearance. Delayed bobtail effect (i.e., the pom-pom being preceded by an inch or two of normal tail with close-lying hair rather than appearing to commence at the base of the spine).

JAPANESE BOBTAIL COLOURS

COLOUR: In the bicolours and tricolours (mi-ke) any colour may predominate with preference given to bold, dramatic markings and vividly contrasting colours. In the solid-colour cat the coat colour should be of uniform density and colour from the tip to the root of each hair and from the nose of the cat to the tail. Nose leather, paw pads, and eye colour should harmonize generally with coat colour. Blue eyes and odd eyes are allowed.

PARTICOLOUR COLOURS

Black and white; mi-ke (tricolour): black, red, and white; red and white; tortoiseshell: black, red, and cream.

SOLID COLOURS

BLACK: dense, coal black, sound from roots to tip of fur. Shiny and free from any tinge of rust on tips. **RED:** deep, rich, clear, brilliant red, the deeper and more glowing in tone the better. **WHITE:** pure glistening white.

OTHER COLOURS

These include the following categories and any other colour or pattern or combination thereof except colouring that is point restricted (i.e., Siamese markings) or unpatterned agouti (i.e., Abyssinian colouring). 'Patterned' categories denote and include any variety of tabby striping or spotting with or without areas of solid (unmarked) colour, with preference given to bold, dramatic markings and rich, vivid colouring. **Other solid colours:** blue or cream. **Patterned self colours:** red, black, blue, cream, silver, or brown. **Other bicolours:** blue and white or cream and white. **Patterned bicolours:** red, black, blue, cream, silver, or brown combined with white. **Patterned tortoiseshell:** blue cream. Patterned blue cream. **Dilute tricolours:** blue, cream, and white. **Patterned dilute tricolours:** patterned mi-ke (tricolour), tortoiseshell with white.

Japanese Bobtail allowable outcross breeds:[2] none.

[1] CFF: 'It should be noted that the tail of the Japanese Bobtail is very sensitive and should be handled very gently. No attempt should be made to straighten out the tail.'
[2] In all associations where the breed is recognized.

Korat

ORIGIN

The first representation of the cat believed to be the ancestor of the modern-day Korat appears in the *Cat-Book Poems,* a manuscript preserved in the Thai National Library in Bangkok. This anonymous work contains verses that describe several kinds of cats. Among them is a solid blue presumed to be the ancestor of the Korat. Since the *Cat-Book Poems* was rescued from the Siamese city of Ayudha, which was 417 years old when it was levelled by Burmese invaders in 1767, we can assume that the Korat is more than two centuries old, and quite possibly older. Yet even though it is the namesake of the Siamese province of Korat, this silver-blue cat with the heart-shaped face and luminous green eyes can be found in most of the other provinces of Thailand (formerly Siam) as well.

In 1896 a blue cat was entered in the Siamese class at the National Cat Club Show in England. The judge disqualified the cat because it did not look like the other Siamese. Its body was blue instead of biscuit coloured. The cat's owner, who had recently returned from Siam, protested that his entry was indeed from that country, and that he had seen other cats like it on his journey. Whether this cat was a Korat or a blue point Siamese is not certain, but it has been established that the seal point Siamese, which is also common to Siam, carries the gene for blue colour; and there surely had to have been some crossbreedings between Siamese and the self-coloured blue cats in Siam, for it has also been reported that blue point kittens appeared in the litters born to the earliest Korats imported to the United States. Thus it is safe to assume that the Korat began life in the United States as an established hybrid, which is how the American Cat Fanciers' Association classified the breed when it was first recognized.

DEVELOPMENT

Although a Mr Robins living in New York City in 1906 asserted that blue cats then existed in the province of Korat, little else was known about the breed in the United States until a pair of cats from Thailand arrived at Portland, Oregon, on June 12, 1959. These cats—a brother and sister named Nara and Darra—were a gift to Mrs Jean Johnson of Gresham, Oregon, from a friend in Thailand. Jean and her husband Robert had lived in Thailand from 1947 to 1953. During their stay, Jean Johnson asked her Thai friends where she might find a Siamese cat, but she discovered that her friends had a different cat in mind than the Siamese she described.

As any American would have, Jean Johnson was referring to a buff-coloured cat with dark-brown points: a seal point Siamese. When she eventually obtained one, her Thai friends informed her that while this was a Siamese cat, it was not *the* cat of the Siamese people: the Korat or *Si-Sawat* (see-sah-what) cat. In the Thai language the compound *Si-Sawat* means *a mingled colour, with a smooth glossy shell*—a definition probably inspired by the silver sheen of the Korat's fur. And among *Sawat*'s several meanings are *good fortune* and *prosperity*. Thus, the Korat is also known as the good-luck cat.

Following its importation, the Korat attracted the attention of several cat fanciers in the United States. In September 1964 *The New York Times* reported the appearance of two Korats at the Empire Cat Club Show, and the following year the Korat Cat Fanciers Association was formed. KCFA's preliminary membership list included twenty-six breeders and/or owners in North America. These Korat fanciers submitted a proposed Standard to various registries, and in 1966 Korats were accepted by the American Cat Association, the now defunct National Cat Fanciers' Association, and the United Cat Federation. By the end of the decade, all other registries had followed suit.

This universal acceptance had been preceded by much discussion about whether the Korat might actually be a blue Burmese. There was a great similarity in body type between the two breeds at the time, and both had overly large eyes and close-lying fur. Consideration was given to registering the Korat as a Burmese colour, not as a separate breed, but Burmese breeders would have rather died than accept any colour other than sable into their breed. In fact, they would not even acknowledge the existence of the dilute colours of sable for a long time.

The Korat has been a cat of good fortune indeed. There are no genetic deficiencies attached to this breed. Although some outcrosses were made to blue point Siamese in order to enlarge the Korat gene pool after it had first been brought to the United States, the overriding concern of the Korat breed club has been to keep this cat as pure—and as true to its original look—as possible. The breed club further requires that anyone wishing to register a Korat must show proof that the cat originated in Thailand.

Korat

The Korats were granted Championship status by the GCCF in 1977 and 11 males and 40 females appeared in the 1977-80 stud book, with the Abbotsbrook prefix of Mrs and Miss Champneys being prominent. However the breed has not increased very much since the late seventies and in 1990 only 130 Korats were registered.

KORAT

(Breed 34)
General Type Standard

HEAD AND EARS: When viewed from the front, the head is heart shaped, with breadth between and across the eyes, gently curving to a well developed but neither sharply pointed nor squared muzzle. Forehead large, flat. Ears are large and with a rounded tip and large

flare at base, set high on head, giving an alert expression. Inside ears sparsely furnished.
EYES, COLOUR AND SHAPE: Large and luminous, particularly prominent. Wide open and oversized for the face; eye aperture, which appears as well rounded when fully open but has Asian slant when closed or partially closed. Colour: brilliant green, but amber cast acceptable. Kittens and adolescents up to two years have yellow or amber to amber-green eyes.
NOSE: Short and with slight downward curve. In profile there is a slight stop between forehead and nose.
CHIN AND JAW: Strong.
BODY AND TAIL: Medium sized body, strong, muscular and semi-cobby. Medium bone structure, males powerful, females should be smaller and dainty. Back carried in a curve. Tail medium in length, heavier at the base, tapering to a rounded tip.
COAT: Single. Hair is short to medium in length, glossy and fine and lying close to body. The coat over the spine is inclined to break as the cat moves.
LEGS AND PAWS: Legs should be well-proportioned to body and paws oval. Five toes in front, four at back.
CONDITION: Perfect physical condition, muscular, alert appearance.

KORAT COLOUR

Any shade of blue all over, tipped with silver, the more silver tipping the better. Without shading or tabby markings. When the coat is short the silver sheen is intensified. Silver tipping develops throughout kittenhood and adolescence to full intensity at about two years old. Nose leather and lips dark blue or lavender. Paw pads, dark blue ranging to lavender with pinkish tinge.

Korat allowable outcross breeds: none.

Maine Coon Cat

ORIGIN

The Maine Coon Cat is a naturally occurring breed whose origins have been described in fantasies and legends that greatly add to its charm. According to some observers the Maine Coon descended from cats that had been sent to the United States from France by Marie Antoinette. Others believe that a sea captain named Coon brought Persian and Angora cats to the United States, and Coon's cats, after jumping ship, introduced the longhair gene to the New World.

Persons knowing little about cat behaviour and reproduction used the term Coon cats for another reason: they believed the Maine Coon resulted from a cross between a racoon and a cat. This is genetically impossible, even though many of the first longhaired domestic cats were brown ticked or seal brown in colour and had tabby rings on their tails—much like the racoon.

Legends notwithstanding, early settlers undoubtedly brought the ancestors of the Maine Coon to America, and these were very likely the first domestic cats to arrive on the North American continent. They existed, no doubt, in much of the settled northeastern coast and on some coastal islands. It has not been established that Maine Coon Cats were more or less popular in Maine than they were anywhere else. Like most new breeds, they excelled in numbers and recognition where there were interested fanciers to promote them, and Maine seems to have been the first place where this occurred.

DEVELOPMENT

Maine Coon Cats were exhibited in shows as early as the 1860s. They were apparently very popular, and were frequent winners. In the 1895 Madison Square Garden Show, a brown tabby Maine Coon owned by Mrs E N Baker was best cat. But as cat shows became more sophisticated and as more imported varieties came to the United States, cats with long pedigrees and generations of like-to-like breeding gained preference with fanciers. Their goal was to produce cats of uniform colour, without white markings or lockets. This new vogue caused the Maine Coon to take a back seat at shows and, eventually, to disappear from the show bench altogether.

Persian breeders continued to use Maine Coons for a time as outcrosses because they were especially strong and vigorous. In those days registries accepted cats of unknown parentage if they conformed to the colours recognized for a breed and if the person registering the cat provided a sworn affidavit testifying that it was a longhair or whatever else a breed Standard might require. Since Persian type then was very similar to the Maine Coon's, any solid white, blue, black, or red Coon Cats were quite acceptable in Persian breeding programmes. The American Cat Fanciers' Association registration form allowed longhairs to be of Persian or Angora 'type.' Persian type was preferred, but there was no distinction made between the two for registration purposes.

During the years when the Maine Coon was in decline, loyal fanciers attempted to gain recognition for the breed. Their efforts were always defeated by the snobbery of other breeders and the Coon fanciers' inability to develop a fitting Standard. Should it be a man-made, progressive Standard: the kind that allows a cat room to grow like the Persian and the Siamese? Or should it be designed to describe and preserve an existing cat? And if so, whose cats would be used to set the Standard to which all other breeders would have to conform? Furthermore, other opponents of Maine Coon recognition insisted that these cats did not possess desirable conformation and that the many colours occurring in the breed could not be controlled through selective breeding. No one would have dared to request recognition of any and all colours that appeared in litters. That would have made the breed appear too common.

Time and again the question arose: is the Maine Coon Cat simply the longhaired variety of the domestic, or American Shorthair? Experience suggested that Maine Coons were originally the true Angora cats, and some books mention that New Englanders reported seeing Angora cats in the northeastern woods. In any case, the liberty to breed at random did produce a natural breed that is hail, hearty, and prolific. A breed whose wide variety of colours and markings appeals to everyone.

Many of the top-winning Maine Coons are a far cry from those still living on farms or in a semi wild condition. Today's show cats are much larger, longer, and in many cases too fine in bone and sparse in coat. The vast number of entries at the shows will result, in time, in a much more uniform cat; and it will, as with all other breeds, come together.

Though it is a longhair, the Coon Cat has a different texture and coat quality from the Persian. Maine Coons will mat if they are neglected totally, but they remain mat-free with little effort. A good metal comb and a bath will produce a strikingly handsome cat.

The GCCF gave the breed preliminary recognition in 1989 and the Maine Coon is becoming increasingly popular, with very large entries appearing in assessment classes at shows.

MAINE COON

(64) (Preliminary)
General Type Standard

The Maine Coon evolved as a working domesticated cat in a rural environment; this role is reflected in a muscular cat of rugged outdoor appearance with a characteristic weatherproof coat on the demeanour of an alert capable hunter.

HEAD: Medium in length, the nasal bridge being

Brown Classic Tabby Maine Coon

equidistant from the ear line and the tip of the nose, with the width being slightly less than the length of the head. Allowance should be made for additional breadth or jowls in mature males. The muzzle should be square with a firm chin: chin, upper lip and nose leather should fall in a perpendicular line. Cheeks fairly full, with high cheek bones. Bite level. Nose of uniform width with a shallow concave curve at the nasal bridge when viewed in profile and without a sharp break or stop. Large, tall ears, wide at the base and tapering to appear pointed at the tip; set high but well apart.
EYES: Full and round, spaced wide apart with a slightly oblique aperture and set. Shades of green, gold or copper; coat and eye colour may be unrelated. Odd or blue eyes are permissible in White cats.
BODY: Large to medium size, solid and muscular with breadth of chest. Long back with proportionate limbs to create the characteristic rectangular appearance; square rump. Neck moderately long; particularly thick and muscular in mature males. Substantial legs with large round paws; toes carried close, five in front, four behind. Tail long, at least the length of the back, wide at the base and tapering towards the the tip.
COAT: Waterproof and virtually self-maintaining, consisting of an undercoat covered by a more substantial glossy top coat. Fur shorter on the head, neck and shoulders increasing in length down the back, flanks and tail. A fluffy appearance is undesirable. Breeches and belly fur full and shaggy. Frontal ruff beginning at the base of the ears; heavier in males than females. Tail fur long, profuse and flowing; not bushy. Ears feathered and preferably tufted at the tips; the ear feathering should extend beyond the outer edges of the ear. Paws tufted, with long tufts emanating from under the paws extending backwards to create snowshoe effect.

MAINE COON CAT COLOURS

(See page 170 for a full description of the colours listed below.)

Solid colours: white, black, blue, red, cream. **Tabby colours:** silver tabby (classic, mackerel, patched), red tabby (classic, mackerel), brown tabby (classic, mackerel, patched), blue tabby (classic, mackerel, patched), cream tabby (classic, mackerel), cameo tabby. **Tabby-with-white colours:** colours accepted are silver, red, brown, blue, or cream. **Patched-tabby-with-white colours:** colours accepted are silver, brown, or blue. **Particolours:** tortoiseshell, tortoiseshell with white, calico, dilute calico, blue cream, blue cream with white, bicolour (red and white, black and white, blue and white, cream and white. **Other Main Coon colours:** chinchilla silver, shaded silver, shell cameo (red chinchilla), shaded cameo (red shaded), black smoke, blue smoke, cameo smoke (red smoke), blue-cream smoke, tortie smoke.
SOLID COLOURS: The fur should be sound in colour and free from any shadings, markings or hair of any colour other than the basic colour. Nose leather, paw pads and eye rims to tone with the body colour.
TORTOISESHELLS: The patterning should extend throughout the coat including the limbs, tail and face; blaze desirable.
TABBY COLOURS: The coat pattern may be Classic or Mackerel pattern.
SHADED AND SMOKE COLOURS: Any solid or tortoiseshell colour accepted. The under-colour should be as white as possible with tips shading to the basic colour; the dark points being most clearly defined on the back, head and feet and the lighter points on the flanks and ear tufts. In a smoke cat the white undercoat should not be clearly visible until the coat is parted. Whereas in the shaded cat the coloured fur should give the overall appearance of a mantle on the back.
BICOLOUR AND PARTICOLOUR: Any solid tabby, tortoiseshell, shaded or smoke colour and white.

Maine Coon Cat allowable outcross breeds: none.

Manx

ORIGIN

It is difficult to think of the Isle of Man, located in the Irish Sea off the coast of Britain, without being reminded of the tailless cat so closely identified with this scenic place. Fanciful theories about the origin of the Manx run rampant, adding to the mystique of this unusual cat, which is so revered that it appears on a British coin. Yet no one knows how or when the Manx arrived on the Isle of Man. A logical explanation is that a Spanish ship with tailless cats on board foundered on Spanish Rock, which is close to the Manx shore. The cats swam to the rock and from there to the island at low tide.

DEVELOPMENT

The Manx was a popular, established breed in England long before the birth of the cat fancy in the 1870s, and Manx-type cats may have existed in other places as early as the 1500s. The spontaneous mutation that results in taillessness in cats can appear at any time in any location, but the size of the Isle of Man–221 square miles—ensured that the gene responsible for taillessness was easily propagated. This gene is an incomplete dominant. If a kitten inherits one gene for taillessness and another for a normal tail, the kitten will for certain be tailless.

While taillessness is the Manx trademark, the breed produces a variety of kittens: *rumpies*, which are completely tailless, with a hollow or dimple where the tail would normally be; *risers*, which have enough tail vertebrae to form a small knob at the end of the spine; *stumpies*, which have a definite, visible tail stump that is usually movable but is often curved or kinked; and *longies*, or cats with a fully developed tail. A Manx is at its very finest, of course, when it is absolutely tailless. This is perfection highly prized, but risers may also be shown if the rise does not impede the progress of a judge's hand as it moves along the cat's back and over the spine.

Breeding two rumpy Manx together does not result in a complete litter of rumpies. This variety occurs because all Manx possess one gene for taillessness and another for full tails. Manx kittens that inherit two genes for taillessness—a lethal condition—die in the womb at an early stage of development. Genetic modifiers account for the differences in length on tailed Manx.

Manx are a very discouraging breed. It would be an injustice to the cat and to the new fancier not to mention the disappointments the prospective breeder should be prepared to cope with. Only those fanciers with a deep concern for the Manx' well-being should be involved with them, for heartaches most frequently exceed triumphs.

There is good reason to argue that the Manx should not be a natural breed. True, it produces tailless kittens quite naturally, but a pure breed should not produce defects from like-to-like breedings. This happens all too often with Manx. Kittens may be born with a variety of spinal problems and weak hindquarters that lead to crippling. For as long as Manx have been recognized the genetic defects have never been bred out of these cats, but the gene pool can be increased by mating to British Shorthair.

A healthy Manx is a joy to own, and anyone who does becomes totally devoted to the breed. Its rabbitlike gait and amusing antics bring endless pleasure and entertainment. It is important, therefore, to select for breeding those Manx that have the proper back and spine line. Too often Manx are seen on the show circuit that are swaybacked instead of possessing a rounded arch and a nice, high rump. Because of the potential for lameness in Manx, the conscientious judge will not place a win on a Manx that will not stand up. The cat should not rest on its hocks like a rabbit. It must be able to stand on all four paws.

There were many Manx taking prizes in British shows more than a century ago and a black and white Manx was pronounced Supreme adult at the 1979 GCCF Supreme show.

White Manx

MANX

Breed 25

HEAD: Fairly round and large with prominent cheeks. Nose broad and straight, of medium length without break. Strong muzzle without any hint of snipyness. Firm chin and even bite.
EARS: Fairly tall, set rather high on the head and angled slightly outwards. Open at base tapering to a narrow, rounded tip.
EYES: Large and round. Colour preferably in keeping with coat colour.
BODY: Solid, compact, with good breadth of chest and short back ending in a definite round rump. The rump to be higher than the shoulder. Flanks of great depth.
LEGS: Of good substance with front legs short and well set to show good breadth of chest. Back legs longer than the front with powerful, deep thighs.
COAT: Double coated showing a well padded quality arising from a short, very thick undercoat and a slightly longer overcoat. The double quality of the coat is of far more importance than colour or markings, which should only be taken into account if all other points are equal. All colours and patterns are acceptable with the exception of the 'Siamese' pattern.

TAILLESSNESS: Absolute taillessness is essential. The rump should be felt to be completely rounded with no definite rise of bone or cartilage interfering with the roundness of the rump.

MANX COLOURS

(See page 170 for a full description of the colours listed below.)

Particolour colours: bicolours (white with unbrindled patches of black, white with unbrindled patches of blue, white with unbrindled patches of red, or white with unbrindled patches of cream); blue cream, calico, dilute calico, tortoiseshell. **Shaded colours:** chinchilla silver, shaded silver. **Smoke colours:** black smoke, blue smoke. **Solid colours:** black, blue, cream, red, white. **Tabby colours:** blue patched tabby, blue tabby (classic, mackerel), brown patched tabby, brown tabby (classic, mackerel), cream tabby (classic, mackerel), red tabby (classic, mackerel), silver patched tabby, silver tabby (classic, mackerel). **Other Manx colours:** any other colour or pattern with the exception of those showing hybridization resulting in the colours chocolate, lavender, the Himalayan pattern, or these combinations with white.

Manx allowable outcross breeds: British Shorthair.

Norwegian Forest Cat

ORIGIN

According to Norse legend, Freya, the goddess of beauty, love and fertility travelled often in a chariot drawn by two large cats. Norwegian Forest Cat fanciers like to believe that these two large cats who pulled Freya's chariot—and possibly a third cat who was so heavy the mighty Thor could not lift him—were the mythological ancestors of today's Wegies, as these cats are known by their fanciers.

The Norwegian Forest Cat is an old, naturally occurring breed that has lived for hundreds of years in the woods of Norway. The earliest references to cats that resemble today's Wegies are found in Norwegian folk tales that were catalogued between 1837 and 1852. Some observers believe that Forest Cats may be the descendants of shorthaired cats brought to Norway from Great Britain by the Vikings and longhaired cats imported by the crusaders.

DEVELOPMENT

Whatever its origin, the Forest Cat owes its vitality, resourcefulness, and sensible, water-repellent coat to

Brown Mackerel Tabby and White Norwegian Forest Cat

the extremely harsh winters of its native country. The Wegie's natural habitat are the farmlands and woodlands of central Norway, which lies roughly between the 59th and 62nd parallels of latitude. Thus, unlike many show cats, the Wegie has a diehard constitution and a tremendous resilience forged in a harsh, wet climate. These characteristics, so valuable to the Norwegian Forest Cat throughout its development, still serve to make this breed a sturdy indoor show cat or pet.

Until the 1930's, no one except the farmers of Norway, who prized the cat's superior hunting ability, paid much attention to the Forest Cat. The very first Norwegian Forest Cat to be shown was a red-and-white male called Petten, exhibited in 1930 by Mrs Holdis Rohlss, who, in 1938 founded a club to promote the cat, which is known as the *Norsk Skaukatt* in its native land.

In the years after the second World War (which had halted the development of the breed) the Norwegian Forest Cat faced the threat of extinction because of continued interbreeding with free-ranging domestic cats. However, in the early 1970s Carl-Fredrik Nordane, the past president of the Norwegian Cat Association, began lobbying on the Wegie's behalf. He organized the first Norwegian Forest Cat breeding programme, and he helped to charter the *Norskskogkattering*, a Wegie breed club which held its first meeting in February 1975.

Two and a half years later, in 1977, Nordane travelled to Paris, where he made a presentation about Forest Cats to the general assembly of the Feline International Federation of Europe (FIFe). Norway's quarantine laws made it impossible for Nordane to bring live cats with him, but he showed the FIFe assembly slides of two Wegies with winning names: Trules and Pippi Skogpus.

Because of Nordane's work, the general assembly of the Feline International Federation of Europe voted in late November 1977 to accept the Forest Cat for championship competition. When Nordane returned to Oslo from Paris the next day, he was greeted with music, flags, and a parade of grateful members of NORAK Norwegian Cat Fancy Council.

Two years to the month after its acceptance in Europe, by FIFe the Norwegian Forest Cat arrived in the United States. The first Norwegian litter born in the States appeared on March 21, 1981.

The breed is not yet accepted for championship competition by every association in the United States. Part of the reason is its resemblance to the Maine Coon, but Norwegian Forest Cat breeders insist that there are important differences between the two cats.

There are many differences between these two breeds The Maine Coon is long and rectangular; the Norwegian is boxy. The Maine Coon has a slight curve in its nose; the Norwegian, especially the male, has a straight nose. The Maine Coon has a prominent, squared-off muzzle; the Norwegian's muzzle fits neatly into its triangular face. The Maine Coon's ears sit upright on top of its head; the Norwegian's ears are wide spaced and tilted forward.

The Norwegian Forest Cat was granted preliminary recognition by the GCCF in 1990. The registration policy does not allow outcrosses to other breeds and no interbreeding is allowed within two generations and so parent/offspring and brother/sister matings are unacceptable.

Though Forest Cats take time to mature—not reaching full maturity until they are five—they are particularly affectionate. 'Their purr boxes are constantly working,' says one breeder, 'and they continuously exhibit their love for people.'

NORWEGIAN FOREST

(Breed 67)
(Preliminary) General Type Standard

TYPE: Big and strongly built, long body, high on the legs, the hind legs higher than the front ones. Solid bone structure.
HEAD: Triangular, long straight profile without break in line. Strong chin.
EYES: Large, well-opened, slightly oblique. All colours allowed, regardless of coat colour.
EARS: High and open, with good width at the base (width between ears being less than the width on one ear), high set so that the lines of the ears follow the line of the head down to the chin. With lynx-like tufts and long hair out of the ears.
TAIL: Long and bushy, should reach to the neck.
COAT: Semi-long. The woolly undercoat is covered by a smooth, water-repellent overcoat. This glossy hair covers the back and the sides. A fully coated cat has shirt-front, a full ruff and knickerbockers. (During summer months the coat is considerably shorter.)

NORWEGIAN FOREST CAT COLOURS

All listed colours are allowed (except chocolate, lilac and Siamese pattern).

Allowable Norwegian Forest Cat outcross breeds: none.

Ocicat

ORIGIN

The Ocicat was developed in the early 1960s by Virginia Daly, a Michigan breeder. Daly worked with several breeds and was known to experiment with 'rare, unusual, newly developed varieties.' Her experiments were a source of concern for other breeders, one of whom said to Daly one day, 'The next thing you'll be making will be an Abyssinian-pointed Siamese.' 'Until then', said Daly, 'I had never dreamed of such a thing, but I decided to take up the challenge.'

Daly bred a seal point Siamese female to a ruddy Abyssinian male. The resulting kittens looked like Abyssinians, but they carried the recessive gene for the Siamese pattern. When Daly bred one of them—a female named She—to a Siamese, She produced the Aby-pointed Siamese for which Daly had been hoping. She also produced a large, ivory cat with bright, golden spots and copper eyes. Daly named the cat Tonga. It was Daly's daughter who named this new breed Ocicat, because of Tonga's resemblance to an Ocelot.

Tonga was sold for ten dollars, with the agreement that he be neutered. Shortly afterwards, Daly read an article in the *Journal of Cat Genetics* in which the author suggested that somebody ought to try to recreate the long-extinct Egyptian spotted fishing cat. Daly wrote to the author saying that she had and that the cat had just been sold. The author wrote back suggesting Tonga should be bred to his mother, but Tonga was never available when She was in season. Tonga's father was, and that mating produced a second Ocicat. At this point, Daly gave up on the Aby-pointed Siamese. 'There are enough Siamese in the world,' she said. 'So why continue with bread when you can make cake?'

DEVELOPMENT

At the 1966 Detroit Persian Society Show, Tonga caught the eye of a Cat Fanciers' Association judge. CFA soon announced that the Ocicat would be accepted for registration. Yet by October 15, 1970, only two Ocicats had been registered. Personal obligations in the Daly family and a pet-limitation ordinance in Berkeley, Michigan, delayed the further development of the Ocicat, and the breed did not advance from registration to provisional status until February 1986. The following year it was accepted for championship competition by CFA and The International Cat Association. At that point the Ocicat became an overnight sensation.

Between 1986 and 1989, annual Ocicat registrations jumped 292 percent. In fact, three out of four Ocicats registered between 1958 and 1990 in CFA were registered in the last five years of the 1980s.

'For a long time the Ocicat just didn't have the right sort of promotion,' says Bill McKee, who was instrumental in getting the breed accepted. But once a new breed club was started, 'a lot of people came out of the woodwork who had had Ocicats but weren't doing anything with them.'

Ocicats have recently been imported to Britain and are being registered by GCCF but the breed is not yet well enough established for recognition to be granted.

OCICAT

Not recognized by the GCCF

Standard, courtesy of the
Cat Fanciers' Association of America.
Differences in the Standards of other registries are indicated at the end of the text.

HEAD: (25)
Skull 5
Muzzle 10
Ears 5
Eyes 5

BODY: (25)
Size 5
Torso 10
Legs and feet 5
Tail 5

COAT and COLOUR: (25)
Texture 5
Coat colour 5
Contrast 10
Eye colour 5

PATTERN: 25

Cinnamon Ocicat

GENERAL: The Ocicat is a medium to large, well-spotted, agouti cat of moderate type. It displays the look of an athletic animal: well muscled and solid, graceful and lithe, yet with a fullness of body and chest. It is alert to its surroundings and shows great vitality. The Ocicat is found in many colours with darker spots appearing on a lighter background. Each hair (except on the tip of tail) has several bands of colour. It is where these bands fall together that a thumb-print-shaped spot is formed. This powerful, athletic, yet graceful, spotted cat is particularly noted for its 'wild' appearance.
HEAD: The skull is a modified wedge showing a slight curve from muzzle to cheek, with a visible, but gentle, rise from the bridge of the nose to the brow. The muzzle is broad and well defined with a suggestion of squareness, and in profile shows good length. The chin is strong, and the jaw firm with a proper bite. The moderate whisker pinch is not too severe. The head is carried gracefully on an arching neck. An allowance is made for jowls on mature males.
EARS: Alert, moderately large, and set so as to corner the upper, outside dimensions of the head. If an imaginary horizontal line is drawn across the brow, the ears should be set at a 45-degree angle, i.e., neither too high nor too low. When they occur, ear tufts extending vertically from the tips of the ears are a bonus.
EYES: Large, almond shaped, and angling slightly upwards toward the ears with more than the length of an eye between the eyes.
SIZE: Medium to large.[1] The Ocicat should have a surprising weight for its size. It should be noted that females are generally smaller than males. The overall structure and quality of this cat should be of greater consideration than mere size alone.
TORSO: Solid, rather long bodied, with depth and fullness but never coarse. Substantial bone and muscle development, yet with an athletic appearance. There should be some depth of chest with ribs slightly sprung, the back is level to slightly higher in the rear, and the flank reasonably level. Preference is given to the athletic, powerful, and lithe, and objection taken to the bulky or coarse.
LEGS AND FEET: Legs should be of good substance and well muscled, medium long, powerful and in good proportion to the body. Feet should be oval and compact with five toes in front and four in back, with size in proportion to legs.
TAIL: Fairly long, medium slim with only a slight taper and with a dark tip.
COAT TEXTURE: Short, smooth, and satiny in texture with a lustrous sheen. Tight, close lying, and sleek, yet long enough to accommodate the necessary bands of colour. There should be no suggestion of woolliness.
TICKING: All hairs except the tip of the tail are banded. Within the markings, hairs are tipped with a darker colour, while hairs in the ground colour are tipped with a lighter colour.
COAT COLOUR: All colours should be clear and pleasing. The lightest colour is usually found on the face around the eyes, and on the chin and lower jaw. The darkest colour is found on the tip of the tail. Contrast is scored separately.
CONTRAST: Distinctive markings should be clearly seen from any orientation. Those on the face, legs, and tail may be darker than those on the torso. Ground colour may be darker on the saddle and lighter on the underside, chin, and lower jaw. Penalties should be given if spotting is faint or blurred, though it must be remembered that pale colours will show less contrast than darker ones.
EYE COLOUR: All eye colours except blue are allowed. There is no correspondence between eye colour and coat colour. Depth of colour is preferred.
PATTERN: There is an intricate tabby 'M' on the forehead, with markings extending up over the head between the ears and breaking into small spots on the lower neck and shoulders. Mascara markings are found around the eyes and on cheeks. Rows of round spots run along the spine from shoulder blades to tail. The tail has horizontal brush strokes down the top, ideally alternating with spots, and a dark tip. Spots are scattered across the shoulders and hindquarters, extending as far as possible down the legs. There are broken bracelets on the lower legs and broken necklaces at the throat–the more broken the better. Large well-scattered, thumb-print-shaped spots appear on the sides of the torso, with a subtle suggestion of a classic tabby pattern–a spot circled by spots in place of the bull's eye. The belly is also well-spotted. The eyes are rimmed with the darkest coat colour and surrounded by the lightest colour. Penalties should be given for elongated spots following a mackerel pattern.
DISQUALIFY: White locket or spotting, or white anywhere other than around eyes, nostrils, chin, and upper throat (except white agouti ground in silvered

colours). Kinked or otherwise deformed tail. Blue eyes. Incorrect number of toes. Due to the spotted, patched-tabby (torbie) cats resulting from the sex-linked O gene, no reds, creams, or torbies are allowed. Very rufous cinnamons and fawns may resemble red or cream, but never produce female torbies.

OCICAT COLOURS

BLUE: Blue spotting on a pale blue or buff agouti ground. Nose leather: blue rimmed with dark blue. Paw pads: blue.

BLUE SILVER: Blue spotting on a white agouti ground. Nose leather: blue rimmed with dark blue. Paw pads: blue.

CHOCOLATE: Chocolate spotting on a warm-ivory, agouti ground. Nose leather: pink rimmed with chocolate. Paw pads: chocolate pink.

CHOCOLATE SILVER: Chocolate spotting on a white agouti ground. Nose leather: pink rimmed with chocolate. Paw pads: chocolate pink.

CINNAMON: Cinnamon spotting on a warm-ivory, agouti ground. Nose leather: pink rimmed with cinnamon. Paw pads: pink or rose.

CINNAMON SILVER: Cinnamon spotting on a white agouti ground. Nose leather: pink rimmed with cinnamon. Paw pads: pink or rose.

FAWN: Fawn spotting on a pale-ivory, agouti ground. Nose leather: pink rimmed in fawn. Paw pads: pink.

FAWN SILVER: Fawn spotting on a white agouti ground. Nose leather: pink rimmed in fawn. Paw pads: pink.

LAVENDER:[2] Lavender spotting on a pale-buff or ivory agouti ground. Nose leather: pink rimmed with dark lavender. Paw pads: lavender pink.

LAVENDER SILVER:[3] Lavender spotting on a white agouti ground. Nose leather: pink rimmed with dark lavender. Paw pads: lavender pink.

SILVER: Black spotting on a pale, silver/white agouti ground. Nose leather: brick red rimmed with black. Paw pads: black.

TAWNY (BROWN SPOTTED TABBY):[4] Black or dark-brown spotting on a ruddy or bronze agouti ground. Nose leather: brick red rimmed with black. Paw pads: black or seal.

Ocicat allowable outcross breeds:[5] Abyssinian for litters born before January 1, 1995.

[1] ACA, TICA: 'Large.'
[2] TICA does not recognize this colour.
[3] TICA does not recognize this colour.
[4] TICA calls this colour brown.
[5] In all associations where the breed is recognized.

Oriental Shorthair

ORIGIN

The Oriental Shorthair was born on a winter's night in 1950 when a British cat fancier named Baroness von Ullman decided to create a new variety of cat: a brown shorthair with green eyes and Siamese body type. Nearly four years later photographs of two kittens answering to this description appeared in the August 1954 issue of the British journal *Our Cats*. The kittens were called Bronze Leaf and Bronze Wing, and even though they had not been produced by the baroness, their colour and conformation met her original design. The mother of these kittens was a seal point Siamese named Our Miss Smith. Their father was a brown hybrid called Elmtower Bronze Idol. He was by a seal point Siamese male out of a black domestic shorthair female who had a seal point Siamese father. At first the chestnut-brown kittens were called Havanas after the rabbit of the same colour, according to some authorities; after Havana tobacco, according to others. For some reason, when the Governing Council of the Cat Fancy in England recognized the rabbit/tobacco-coloured cats for championship competition in 1958, it issued the name Chestnut Brown Foreign to this breed instead.

DEVELOPMENT

Four years after Chestnut Browns had been accepted, a British cat breeder and geneticist named Patricia Turner began working to produce a blue-eyed white cat of the same foreign type. Two other breeders started similar programmes at about that time, and they began pooling their resources in 1964. The preliminary result of their work was exhibited at a cat show in York, England, the following year. Before long these sound-hearing, blue-eyed white cats became 'the talk of the cat fancy,' wrote one observer. They were eventually accorded championship status under the name Foreign White in England, where individual colours are often registered as separate breeds.

Persons working with Foreign Whites combined Siamese with a variety of shorthaired breeds to achieve their goal. In addition to the blue-eyed whites they sought, they also produced cats of Siamese conformation whose colour was not restricted to their points—i.e., face, ears, legs, and tail. In 1972 Peter and Vicky Markstein, two of the United States' better-known Siamese breeders, went to England in search of new Siamese lines. To the Marksteins' surprise they found the Siamese type they wanted in the newly emerging Foreign Whites and associated, non-pointed colours. The Marksteins were so taken with these cats that after returning home, they decided to seek the acceptance of all Foreign shorthairs as one breed that would be called the Oriental Shorthair in the United States.

Meanwhile, in the United Kingdom the first of the Foreign Lilac cats had appeared as a result of matings of Havanas to Siamese. Shortly after this the Foreign Blacks and Foreign Blues appeared, so completing the quartet of the four original Siamese colours. Further development work resulted in the introduction of the Foreign Red and Foreign Cream. At this time it was decided that all the self colour cats, apart from the Havana, would use the description of 'Foreign' and all patterned cats would have the description 'Oriental.' However, very recently the GCCF has decided that all colours in the Oriental group, apart from the Havana and the Foreign White, will be known as 'Oriental' in future.

The Oriental Tortoiseshells have received Championship status but the other non-tabby patterns, such as the Smoke, Shaded and Tipped Orientals are still working towards this goal. The tabby pattern is recognised in Spotted, Classic, Mackerel and Ticked patterns but only the Oriental Spotted Tabby in the normal colours from brown to cream has received Championship status.

The colours of cats in the Oriental section cover the whole range from black to cinnamon and caramel, and cats of all colours are registered by the Governing

Council and have either Preliminary or Provisional status. As a result, this section potentially very large given the wide range of colours and coat patterns that are accepted into it.

ORIENTAL SHORTHAIR

(Except the Foreign White)
General Type Standard

The Oriental should be a beautifully balanced animal with head and ears carried on a slender neck and with a long svelte body supported on fine legs and feet with a slender, whipped tail· free from abnormalities. The body, legs, feet, head and tail should all be in proportion giving a well-balanced appearance. The expression should be alert and intelligent. The cat should be in excellent physical condition.

HEAD, NECK AND EARS: Head long and well-proportioned with width between the ears and narrowing in perfectly straight lines to a fine muzzle and forming a balanced triangle with no break or pinch at the whiskers. The head and profile should be wedge shaped, neither round nor pointed, avoiding exaggerated type. In profile the nose should be straight, free from any stop or dip and the chin should be strong with a level bite. The tip of the chin should line up with the tip of the nose in the same vertical plane. The neck should be long and slender. The ears should be large, pricked and wide at the base with their setting continuing the lines of the wedge.

EYE SHAPE AND SETTING: Oriental in shape and slanting towards the nose with good width between. No tendency to squint.

BODY, LEGS AND PAWS: Medium in size. Long and svelte with a tight abdomen. Legs long and slim. Hind legs higher than the front legs. The body and legs to be firm and well muscled throughout. Paws small and oval.

TAIL: Long and tapering. Not blunt ended and free from any abnormality of the bone structure.

White Oriental Shorthair

COAT: Very short and fine in texture. Glossy and close lying. Even and sound throughout in adults and free from any flakes of dead skin.
CONDITION: Excellent physical condition.

FOREIGN WHITE - 35

The Foreign White should be a beautifully balanced animal with head, ears and neck carried on a long svelte body, supported on fine legs and feet, with a tail in proportion. The head and profile should be wedge-shaped, not round or pointed, the eyes a deep clear brilliant blue. Expression alert and intelligent.
HEAD: Long and well proportioned, carried upon an elegant neck with width between the ears, narrowing in straight lines to a fine muzzle, with straight profile, strong chin and level bite.
EARS: Large and pricked set so as to follow the lines of the wedge.
EYES: Oriental in shape and slanting, clear brilliant blue.
BODY: Long and slender, the rump carried higher than the shoulders. Well muscled and elegant.
LEGS: Long and slender, paws neat and oval.
TAIL: Long and tapering, whip-like without kink.
COAT: Pure white, short and close-lying.
NOSE LEATHER, PAW PADS AND EYE RIMS: Pink.

ORIENTAL SHORTHAIR COLOURS

(See page 170 for a full description of the colours listed below.)

Particolour colours: blue cream, cinnamon tortoiseshell, chestnut tortie, fawn cream, lavender cream, tortoiseshell. **Shaded colours:** blue cream silver, blue silver, cameo, chestnut silver, chestnut tortie silver, cinnamon silver, cinnamon tortie silver, ebony silver, fawn silver, lavender cream silver, lavender silver, tortoiseshell silver. **Smoke colours:** blue smoke, cameo smoke, chestnut smoke, cinnamon smoke, ebony smoke, fawn smoke, lavender smoke, particolour smoke (white undercoat deeply tipped with ebony, chestnut, blue, or lavender with clearly defined, unbrindled patches of red and/or cream tipped hairs). **Solid colours:** blue, chestnut, cinnamon, cream, ebony, fawn, lavender, red, white. **Tabby colours:** blue silver, blue, cameo, cinnamon silver, cinnamon, chestnut silver, chestnut, cream, ebony, fawn, lavender silver, lavender, red, silver.

In addition to the above colours the GCCF recognise caramel, caramel tortie, caramel smoke, caramel tabbies, caramel tipped.

The tabby are recognised in these four tabby patterns: spotted, classic, mackerel and ticked.

Oriental Shorthair allowable outcross breeds: Siamese.

Persian

ORIGIN

The Persian is certainly the most prized—and plentiful—of all pedigreed cats. Nearly three out of four cats registered in the Cat Fancier's Association of America belong to the Persian/Himalayan family; and new registrations of a single Persian colour—black—regularly outnumber all but a handful of individual breeds. Because Persians comprise such a large entry at most major shows—and because Persians are recognized in nearly fifty colours and patterns—this

breed is grouped into seven colour divisions in the Cat Fanciers' Association of America to allow for greater mechanical ease in judging. Those divisions are: solid, tabby, shaded, smoke, particolour, bicolour, and pointed.

All this diversity may have started with a single colour more than 350 years ago. According to the Italian traveller Pietro della Valle (1586-1652), who is credited with introducing the Persian to Europe, there was in Persia 'a species of cats which properly belong to the province of Chorazan.' The beauty of these cats, said della Valle, 'consists in the colour of their hair, which is grey [and] soft as silk, and so long that, though not frizzled, it forms ringlets in some parts, and particularly under the throat.' Della Valle described these grey, longhaired cats as 'very tame,' and observed that 'the Portugese have brought them from Persia into India.'

Commenting on della Valle's description of the grey cats from Chorazan province, the French naturalist Count de Buffon (1707-1778) wrote, 'It appears that the Persian cats resemble, in colour, those we call Chartreux cats, and that, except in colour, they have a perfect resemblance to the cat of the Angora. It is probable, therefore, that the cat of Chorazan in Persia,

Tortie and White (Calico) Persian

the cat of Angora in Syria, and the Chartreux cat constitute but one race, whose beauty proceeds from the particular influence of the climate.'

What de Buffon ascribed to climate—'the most beautiful and longest hair' on the Persians and Angoras—is actually the result of a spontaneous mutation preserved through interbreeding in the confined mountain areas of Turkey and Persia. Eventually, through the efforts of della Valle, who wrote that he planned to bring home 'four couple' of these cats, longhairs were imported from Chorazan province to Italy. Other travellers then brought other longhaired cats to France and, finally, to England, where they were known as French cats until the middle of the nineteenth century.

Though de Buffon wrote that the Persian had 'a perfect resemblance' to the Angora, by the time the cat fancy was founded in Great Britain in the 1870s, there were noticeable differences between the two types. The Angora had a smaller, more narrow, less rounded

Orange (Copper) Eyed White Persian kitten

Red Classic Tabby Persian

head, less rounded eyes, and finer bone than the Persian. The Angora's tail was more fanlike and pointed at the tip; and the Angora's coat—frilly on the chest and longer on the underparts—was not so heavy nor immense as the Persian's.

Despite these differences, no fancier cared to separate the two types, and they were used interchangeably to breed cats that were classified generically as longhairs and judged according to that classification. When the Points of Excellence, the first Standards by which cats were judged, were drawn up by Harrison Weir in England, they contained descriptions of Abyssinians, Manx, Siamese, 'long-haired' cats, and 'short-haired' cats. Neither the Persian nor the Angora was mentioned by name. Nevertheless, in his seminal work *Our Cats and All About Them*, published in 1889, Weir included a short chapter on Angoras and another on Persians, and in these chapters he described the differences between the two.

He also included a chapter about longhaired cats from Russia, which 'differed from the Angora and the Persian in many respects, [being] larger in the body with shorter legs' and having eyes that were 'large and prominent, of a bright orange, slightly tinted with green.' The tail was short and woolly. Weir had little experience of breeding Russians, but C H Lane, writing in 1903, warned against crossing Persians with Russians because any increase in size obtained by this cross, 'would be more than counterbalanced by coarseness and want of clearness in markings.'

Gradually the Angora began to fade from prominence (the Russians never really attained it), and by 1903 Frances Simpson, an English cat breeder, author, and judge declared, 'There are two distinctive breeds, viz., the *Long-haired* or Persian Cats, and *Short-haired* or English and Foreign Cats.' Be that as it was, when the Governing Council of the Cat Fancy (GCCF) was organized in England in 1910, it was decided that Persians should continue to be called *longhairs*, a practice that survives in England to this day.

In addition, GCCF treats each longhaired colour as a separate breed: White Longhair, Blue Longhair, Black Longhair, and so forth, with blacks enjoying the status of breed Number 1 in the British registry. This classification scheme enlarges on the one started by Harrison Weir, whose *Points of Excellence* contained one Standard that applied to 'black, blue, grey, red, or any self- or solid-coloured long-haired' cats and a separate Standard for judging 'White, long-haired' cats. Weir also had a Standard for 'brown, blue, silver, light grey, and white tabby' longhairs.

One British writer has observed that classifying colours as separate breeds 'recognizes the practical fact that body type does tend to differ slightly from one colour to another' among Persians. Perhaps Weir's classification also recognizes the fact that most of the French cats imported to England before 1850 were

white. 'Coloured long-haired cats were then rare,' said Weir, 'and but little cared for or appreciated.'

By the turn of the century the cat fancy was established in the United States, and American fanciers had been importing Persians and other cats from Great Britain for several years. (As early as 1885 a brown tabby male named King Humbert was exported to America, where his new owner subsequently refused one thousand dollars for him.) Until the 1900s the Maine Coon Cat had been the dominant longhair at shows in the United States, but the Persian soon claimed that distinction.

When Frances Simpson wrote *Cats and All About Them* in 1903 (a title similar to the one Weir used for his earlier book), there were already separate Standards in the United States for blue Persians, orange Persians (both self and tabby), creams (also known as fawns), and orange-and-white cats (longhaired and short). Furthermore, white Persians were being judged in two classes—one for blue-eyed-whites, the other for golden-eyed whites. There were also separate Standards for shaded silvers, chinchillas, and tortoiseshells.

Chinchilla Persian kitten

In longhairs, as in all other breeds, imported cats set the standard in the United States during the first decades of this century. In 1930 the American Cat Fanciers' Association established the rank of Grand Champion—the highest, show-ring title a cat could attain. The first cat to achieve that designation was Eastbury Trigo, a red tabby Persian male imported from England. Not until World War II had brought devastation to the cat fancy in England did American breeders begin to assert their independence from British influence.

DEVELOPMENT

SOLID PERSIANS

While Persians have improved considerably since World War II, improvement has not been unilateral. The British writer who observed that body type differs among Persian colours might have added that facial type varies among colours as well. The first Persian colour to gain dominance was blue. Queen Victoria was a patron of blues; a Blue Persian Society was founded in England in 1901; the first entry in the first stud book published in the United States was a 'golden-eye Blue Female Longhair'; and by the middle of this century and beyond, blue Persians excelled so much in type that it was difficult to see anything other than a blue take best-in-show or best-kitten awards.

Such was the quality of blue Persians that many breeders would not consider mating anything but a blue to another blue for one generation after the next.

This Cream Cameo Longhair, bred in England, typifies the British preference for a more moderate head type.

LEFT: Known as a Blue Point Colourpoint Longhair in England, where it was bred, this cat would be called a Blue Point Himalayan/Persian in the United States.

BELOW: Blue Longhair, bred in England

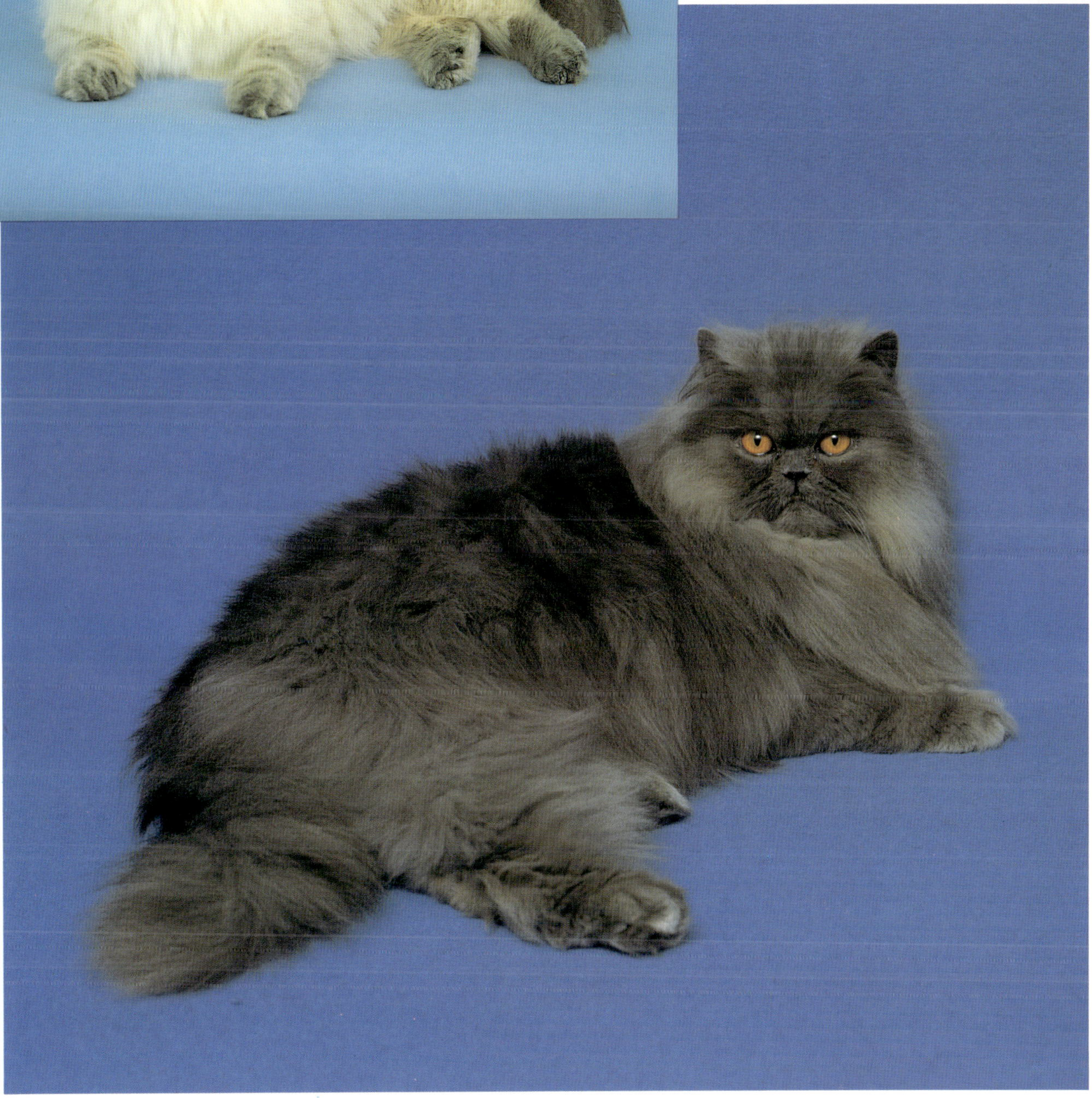

This practice was known as colour breeding, and it occasioned great debates about whether a cat was eligible to be called colourbred after three or after five generations of like-colour-to-like-colour breeding. The question was moot for all but the blues, however, because blues were the only cats for whom colour breeding resulted in an increase rather than a decrease in overall quality.

Many of the outstanding blues produced in the 1940s and 1950s eventually became the breeding stock of catteries in the United States. Breeders who could not hope to compete with blues in the ring directed their attention to other colours, often using blues to improve the type of reds, blacks, blue creams, shadeds, torties, tabbies, and smokes. Some of these colours—at first the creams and blue creams and then

Black Smoke Persian kitten

Blue Cream Longhair bred in England

others—began rivalling blues, which ultimately surrendered their dominance at shows.

TABBY PERSIANS

Though tabbies were present at the creation of the cat fancy in England and had competed at the first shows there, Harrison Weir did not believe that tabbies had been among the original longhaired cats imported to Europe and subsequently to England from the Middle East. He suggested that tabby patterns had been introduced by crossing longhairs with shorthaired tabbies in England or with the longhaired Russian cats, which were also tabbies. Judging from Weir's Standards and illustrations, the original tabbies shown were mackerel longhairs, mackerel shorthairs, or spotted shorthairs. Today the classic (or blotched) tabby pattern is the most popular. This pattern, which is recessive to the mackerel and which does not occur in the wild, was a development exclusive to the cat fancy.

It was extremely difficult from the beginning to produce tabbies of any quality. Of course, this discouraged many breeders, and it serves to explain why tabbies have never enjoyed great popularity. The most important consideration in breeding tabbies is to produce the boldest, most clearly defined markings possible. Breeding tabby to tabby, strangely enough, may result in a muddled pattern that contains too

Tortoiseshell Longhair bred in England

many markings and irregularities. To avoid this problem and to improve type in their tabbies, breeders have crossed them with blues, blacks, reds, creams, and tortoiseshells, thus producing new tabby colours, including blue and cameo, and a new tabby pattern, the patched tabby (or torbie), which is a tortoiseshell cat with the usual patches of red and cream but whose predominant colour is tabby instead of black.

Of all the tabbies, the reds have achieved type comparable to the best Persians today. Red tabbies, however, are frequently neither-nors: cats that have too many markings to qualify as solid reds but fewer and less distinct markings than the tabby Standard calls for.

The peke-faced Persian, a seldom-seen variety, competes in the regular solid and tabby divisions in some associations, but is judged as a separate class or breed by the others. The Cat Fanciers' Federation, which considers the peke a separate breed, explains in its Standard that peke-faced Persians 'resemble the Pekinese dog. There is a cascading of skin under the eyes ... an indentation or depression in the bone on each side of the nose [and] the muzzle is broad and decidedly wrinkled.' In addition, 'the eyes are large, very round, set wide apart, and very prominent and have a different expression from the standard Persian.'

SHADED PERSIANS

There has always been a great deal of confusion regarding shaded Persians. At present the colours in the shaded division are: chinchilla silver, shaded silver,

Tortoiseshell Persian kitten

chinchilla golden, shaded golden, shell cameo, shaded cameo, shell tortoiseshell, and shaded tortoiseshell. Most observers believe that the first shaded cats, a silver-coloured variety that came to be known as chinchillas, were produced in the early 1880s in Great Britain by breeders who crossed silver tabbies of unsound markings to lightly tipped smokes; and although no one knows where the name *chinchilla* originated, there may well have been some connection with the South American rodent so prized for its coat, which was similar in colour.

It is interesting that Weir's only mention of *chinchilla* in *Our Cats and All About Them* (1889) is in reference to a silver-grey Abyssinian colour. When a specialty club for silver Persians was formed in England a few years later, it included self-silvers, shaded silvers, silver tabbies, and smokes. At that time self-silvers were not supposed to have any black shadings or markings, but, as Frances Simpson observed, 'no self-silver has yet been born or bred.' Therefore, the most lightly shaded

Cream and White Persian

silvers—the cats that were called chinchillas—filled in the self-silver class; and the silvers with darker shadings went into the shaded class, which was eliminated in 1902 because judges were having too much trouble distinguishing between chinchillas and shaded silvers.

No one can deny that the chinchilla is the most glamorous of all colours. Except for the chest and belly, which are pure white, the coat should be tipped evenly in one eighth of an inch of black at the end of each hair. Though the chinchilla is finer in bone and not as extreme as other Persians, it more than meets the Standard in refinement. Massive dimensions would not enhance this cat. What's more, the large, emerald-green eyes with their black eye lining and the black-lined nose and lips produce a very theatrical look that sets the chinchilla apart from all other Persians.

Though CFA recognizes the chinchilla and the shaded silver, the latter is nothing more than a silver cat with longer tipping and heavier shading than the chinchilla; and some shaded silvers, after they have matured, should be reclassified as chinchillas. It would probably be well to combine these colours into one class—especially since the Standard offers little help in this regard. For the chinchilla silver it reads: 'undercoat pure white. Coat on back, flanks, head, and tail sufficiently tipped with black to give the characteristic sparkling silver appearance. Legs may be slightly shaded with tipping. Chin, ear tufts, stomach, and chest, pure white.'

And for the shaded silver: 'undercoat white with a mantle of black tipping shading down from sides, face, and tail from dark on the ridge to white on the chin, chest, stomach, and under the tail. Legs to be the same tone as the face. The general effect to be much darker than a chinchilla.' But how much darker is a light shaded than a dark chinchilla?

The other shaded colours—golden, cameo, and tortoiseshell—were added to the division (as the smokes were being removed from it) during the 1960s and 1970s. These new shaded colours do not present

Cream and White Longhair bred in England

quite the same challenges in breeding as the shaded and chinchilla do. These silver challenges include: avoiding a diminution in size, maintaining the correct green or blue-green eye colour, and refining the silver personality so that the cats are as sweet as they look.

SMOKE PERSIANS

The smoke Persian was known in England as early as 1860, according to one writer, who also reports that a smoke was exhibited at a show in Brighton in 1872. By 1893 the smoke was granted its own breed classes. Smokes were originally thought to be 'a mixture of three self-coloured breeds—black, white, and blue.' (Remember, in England every Persian colour constitutes a breed.) Yet it is impossible to produce smokes no matter how many breeds or colours are combined if at least one cat that carries the smoke gene is not included in the calculation.

Seventeen years after being awarded its own colour classes, the smoke had made little progress in England, and by the time GCCF was formed in 1910, there were only eighteen smokes recorded in the first stud book. Worse yet, during the years following the Second World War, the smoke just about disappeared in England. Fortunately that situation did not occur in the United States, where the smoke classes, though small, were consistently high in quality.

The same cannot be said for smokes today. Even the best seem to fall short in overall quality compared to other Persians.

For many years smokes were part of the silver or shaded division, but since the smokes had better bone and head type, they won frequently over the silvers. Silver breeders eventually petitioned CFA to remove the smokes from the shaded division because smokes had copper eyes and were not compatible to the breeding of silvers. As a result there is now a smoke

Red (Flame) Point Himalayan/Persian

division, which includes black, blue, blue cream, cameo, and tortoiseshell smokes.

Like the shaded colours, smokes belong to the *tipped* category, a general name that indicates a pattern of coloured tipping overlying a pale undercolour. This effect is produced because each hair on a smoke is white at the roots, and every hair should display the white frill as well as the white undercoat. Even if you spread the fur on a smoke's legs or head, it should be white at the base. Never should a smoke's coat anywhere be solid in colour.

PARTICOLOUR PERSIANS

Tortoiseshells have existed—in shorthaired classes at least—since the earliest days of the cat fancy, but it wasn't until the turn of the century that longhaired classes for torties were established. Many of the first torties probably did not endear themselves to the general public. Even today torties always seem to have a cross look and a temper to match. In addition, their muddled markings of red, black, and cream do not seem to give off the sweet expressions desired in the Persian. Perhaps this is why there were only eleven grand champion tortoiseshells during the first sixty-five years that CFA sponsored shows.

The tortie is a naturally occurring colour achieved by combining black and red, which are both dominant colours, or by combining one of these dominants with the dilute of the other one—a black female with a cream male, for example. It is also possible, among other ways, to obtain torties by crossing tortoiseshell females with black, red, blue, or cream males, or by crossing blue-cream females with black or red males.

Tortoiseshell and blue cream are sex-linked colours. It is theoretically impossible to obtain males in these colours. Though such anomalies do occur infrequently, they are able to breed even more infrequently.

BICOLOUR PERSIANS

For many years tortoiseshells and their dilute sisters the blue creams were the only particoloured Persians in the fancy. Then in the early 1950s a New Jersey breeder of red and tabby Persians became interested in calico American Shorthairs, which were still called Domestic Shorthairs at the time. Calico was not then a recognized colour in Domestic Shorthairs. Like many other Domestic breeders of her day, this woman used Persians to improve type in her calicos while she was waiting for them to gain championship recognition without documenting the fact. In the meantime she came up with a few calico longhairs, which she registered as such according to the prevailing rules of open registration. Other breeders liked the old-fashioned, picture-postcard look of these cats and began crossing them to Persians. This interest eventually resulted in the acceptance of calico Persians in June of 1955, the same month that calico Domestic Shorthairs were accepted.

For the next fifteen years, however, bicolour males produced by the now-acceptable calico Persians were not eligible for registration. Many breeders were convinced that the acceptance of bicolours and their subsequent crossing with solid-colour Persians would lead to a return of the buttons and lockets that breeders had worked for decades to eliminate from their solid-coloured Persians. Eventually reason prevailed among most breeders who realized that it was absurd to recognize the female of a sex-linked colour—i.e., the calico—but not the male. Bicoloured males were duly accepted, and they have not ruined the Persian breed in the meantime.

POINTED PERSIANS

On February 20, 1984, CFA incorporated the Himalayan breed into the Persian breed, making the former a colour division of the latter. Absorbing one major breed into another forced many breeders and judges to rethink their ideas of what constitutes a breed.

Over the years there have been several attempts to produce Siamese cats with long hair. Or Persian cats with Siamese markings, if you will. This had been tried on the continent in the 1920s and in the United States in 1932. The attempt in the United States was successful, but the accomplishment did not inspire any sense of obligation in the cat fancy; and the idea went nowhere. In 1950 Margaret Goforth in the United States and Brian Stirling-Webb in England began working with Siamese-Persian crosses. They, along with Ben and Ann Borrett in Canada and Mrs. Harding in England, were the successful pioneers in developing the Persian-Siamese cross, which came to be known as the Himalayan.

When the Himalayan was accepted as a breed in

1957, CFA required four generations of like-to-like colourpoint breeding behind kittens being presented for registration. The association was very strict in its rules, and it was lucky to have one or two Himalayans at a show. As time went on and other associations passed CFA in the number of Himalayan entries they were drawing, CFA decided that since the Himalayan was already a hybrid it made no difference if Persians were used in their Himalayan breeding programmes. At once CFA began to see more and better Himalayans at shows, but the organization still refused to allow non-pointed cats from Persian-Himalayan crosses into the show ring. These cats could be used for breeding, but that was all.

Though one or two farsighted persons argued in the early 1960s that Himalayans should be recognized in the United Satates as colourpoint longhairs—as they are in England—that idea met with much debate and resistance. Interestingly enough, Siamese breeders, who are responsible for more experimental crosses than any other group, were the most vocal in their opposition to that move. Today, however, there should be no question that the Himalayan is indeed a Persian, for only colour and point-restricted patterns were introduced to the Persian breed. What's more, Himalayans have enjoyed incredible success at the shows and have achieved a level of quality that should keep any Persian breeder from fearing a colourpoint or a colourpoint carrier in the pedigree.

As it should have done before, CFA also allows non-pointed Himalayans, known as colourpoint carriers, to compete in any division for which their colour qualifies them. For many years before this became the rule, a number of these cats passed successfully as 'Persians,' thanks to their superior type and the creative paperhanging of their breeders and owners. As of early 1991, CFA and the American Cat Association were the only North American registries to incorporate the Himalayan breed into the Persian. All other associations still considered the Himalayan a separate breed. At least one group, the Canadian Cat Association, has separate classes for non-pointed Himalayan hybrids; and two registries, the Cat Fanciers' Federation and the Canadian Cat Association, have established a separate breed called the Kashmir for solid lilac and solid chocolate cats that result from Persian-Himalayan crosses. In Great Britain the Himalayans have always been known as Colourpoints, and are part of the Longhair sector.

EPILOGUE

Since the Persian Standard in the United States has always been very progressive, there has been little change in it over the years, but there has been a tremendous change in the cat it describes. Beginning in the early 1970s American Persians have grown increasingly overtyped compared to longhairs in Great Britain. Yet we must remember that English breeders are renowned for producing many of the finest animals in the world. Their Persians remain less extreme than American cats because that is how the British prefer them.

PERSIAN SELF LONG HAIRS

General Type Standard

HEAD: Round and massive with great breadth of skull; well balanced. Small, round-tipped ears, set wide apart and low on the head, fitting into the rounded contour of the head, with full ear furnishings but not unduly open at the base.
CHEEKS: Full cheeks; round forehead.
NOSE: Short broad nose of even width with stop (break). Nose leather fully formed.
CHIN: Strong chin and full muzzle with broad and powerful jaws, without a 'pinch'.
EYES: Large full round eyes; brilliant in colour and set well apart. Bold and not deep set.
NECK: Short thick neck.
BODY: Large or medium in size. Of cobby type; low on the legs. Broad deep chest; massive shoulders and rump; well muscled. Short thick strong legs. Large round firm paws, preferably well tufted. Toes carried close: five in front four behind.
TAIL: Tail short and bushy but in proportion to body length.
COAT: Long and thick. Fine in texture; not excessively woolly. Soft and full of life. Full frill covering the shoulders and continuing into a deep frill between the front legs. Cats should be shown in good general condition and well presented.

SMOKE LH AND TIPPED LH:

BLACK SMOKE LH (6): A Smoke is a cat of contrasts, the undercolour being as white as possible, with the tips shading to black, the darker points being most defined on the back, head and feet, and the light points on frill, flanks and ear tufts. COLOUR: Body: Black shading to silver on the sides and flanks. Mask and feet: black with no markings. Frill and ear tufts: silver. Undercolour: as nearly white as possible. COAT: Silky texture, long and dense, extra long frill. HEAD: Broad and round with width between the ears, which should be small and tufted; snub nose. BODY: Cobby, not coarse but massive; short legs. EYES: Orange or copper in colour, large and round in shape, pleasing expression. TAIL: Short and bushy.

CHINCHILLA LH (10): COLOUR: The undercoat pure white, the coat on back, flanks, head, ears, and tail being tipped with black; this tipping to be evenly distributed, thus giving the characteristic sparkling silver appearance; the legs may be very slightly shaded with the tipping, but the chin, ear tufts, stomach and chest must be pure white; any tabby markings or brown or cream tinge is a defect.The tip of the nose brick red, and the visible skin on eyelids and the pads black or dark brown. HEAD: Broad and round, with breadth between ears, which should be small and well tufted; wide at the muzzle; snub nose. SHAPE: Cobby body; short thick legs. EYES: Large, round and most expressive, emerald or blue green in colour.

TABBY LONGHAIRS

General Type Standard

HEAD: Round and broad with plenty of space between well tufted ears, which should be small, neat and well covered. Short, broad nose with a stop that is not extreme. Full cheeks and broad muzzle with no pinch. Level bite, firm chin.

BODY: Cobby, muscular with short, thick sturdy legs.

EYES: Wide open, large and round (not deep set).

COAT: Long dense, silky with a glossy sheen.

TAIL: Short, full and well furnished. (No kink allowed).

COAT PATTERN: Markings on Longhaired Tabbies should be clearly defined and dense in colour with no brindling. On the forehead there should be a letter 'M'. There should be an unbroken line running back from the corner of the eye, with pencilling on the cheek, and lines running over the back of the head extending to the shoulder markings, which should be shaped like a butterfly. On the neck and chest there should be unbroken necklaces, the more the better. There should be a line running down the spine from the butterfly to the tail with a clear line running parallel to each side of this line; these three stripes down the back to be separated by stripes of the ground colour. Each flank should have an oyster marking. The markings on each side should be identical. The abdominal area should be spotted. Legs should be identically barred with bracelets going down from the body markings to the feet, tail should be well ringed. Allowance to be made for diffusion of Classic Tabby markings in cats showing extra long or full flowing coats.

PERSIAN COLOURS

(See page 170 for a full description of the colours listed below.)

Particolour colours: bicolours (black and white, blue and white, red and white, or cream and white), blue cream, calico, dilute calico, tabby and white, tortoiseshell, van bicolours (black and white, red and white, blue and white, or cream and white), van calico, van dilute calico. **Pointed colours:** blue lynx point, blue point, blue-cream point, blue-cream lynx point, chocolate point, chocolate-tortie point, cream point, flame (red) point, lilac point, lilac-cream point, seal lynx point, seal point, tortie point, tortie lynx point. **Shaded colours:** chinchilla golden, chinchilla silver, shaded cameo (red shaded), shaded golden, shaded silver, shaded tortoiseshell, shell cameo (red chinchilla), shell tortoiseshell. **Smoke colours:** black smoke, blue smoke, blue-cream smoke, cameo smoke (red smoke), smoke tortoiseshell. **Solid colours:** black, blue, chocolate, cream, lilac, peke-face red, red, white. **Tabby colours:** blue patched tabby, blue tabby (classic, mackerel), brown patched tabby, brown tabby (classic, mackerel), cameo tabby (classic, mackerel), cream tabby (classic, mackerel), peke-face red tabby, red tabby (classic, mackerel), silver patched tabby, silver tabby (classic, mackerel).

Persian allowable outcross breeds: none.

NB Peke faced Persians are not recognised by GCCF.

Ragdoll

ORIGIN

The patriarch of the Ragdoll breed was a mitted, Seal point male named Daddy War Bucks, who was born in Riverside, California, in the mid-1960s. War Bucks' mother was a longhaired, free-running white named Josephine. His father, according to Ann Baker, who was Josephine's owner, was a Sacred Cat of Burma (Birman).

DEVELOPMENT

Baker developed the Ragdoll by crossing Daddy War Bucks' children—and their children—with one another. After naming the breed, she sought championship status for her cats. She founded the International Ragdoll Cat Association (IRCA) in 1971, but soon

Blue Mitted Ragdoll

afterwards breeders who felt that IRCA guidelines were too restrictive formed the Ragdoll Fanciers' Club (RFC). Working with the established federations, RFC has obtained championship status for Ragdolls in every organization in the United States except the Cat Fanciers' Association.

Baker and the RFC have always claimed that there are significant differences between Ragdolls and other cats. Ragdolls are bigger and more impervious to pain, and they go limp in a person's arms when held—a tendency that inspired their name. These attributes, says Baker, first appeared in Josephine's kittens after she had recovered from being hit by a car. They had not been noticeable in the kittens she bore prior to the accident.

As for the Ragdoll's size, females should range between ten and thirteen pounds, and males between fifteen and twenty. That makes the Ragdoll, the largest breed of cat in the *Guinness Book of Pet Records.*

Veterinary advice was taken about these suggested characteristics before preliminary recognition was granted by the GCCF and no abnormality of the central nervous system was found in the cats examined. The breed was granted preliminary status in March 1990.

RAGDOLL

(Preliminary)
General Type Standard

Head: Skull medium to large size, flat plane between ears. Cheeks well developed, tapering to a round well-developed muzzle and firm chin with a level bite. The nose should have a very gentle break and be of medium length.
Ears: Medium in size, broad at the the base with a slight tilt forward. Medium furnishings (tufts) in the ears. The ears should be rounded at the tip, set wide on the skull.
Eyes: Large, oval, set with a slight slant. Outer edge of the eye aperture to be level with the base of the ear. Blue in colour; the deeper blue the better.
Body: The body is long and muscular. The neck should be short, strong and heavy set. Chest should be broad and well expanded. Full maturity is achieved between three and four years of age.
Legs and Paws: Legs must be medium in length and of medium heavy bone. Hind legs to be slightly higher than the front. The paws should be large, round, firm and tufted.
Tail: The tail should be long, bushy, slightly tapered towards the tip and in proportion to the body.
Coat: Silky texture, dense, medium length, lying with the body and parting as the cat moves. Short on the face. Longer around the neck framing the face. Short over the shoulders. Medium length on the back, sides, abdomen and hindquarters. Short to medium length on the front legs. (Seasonal variations in coat shall be recognized.)

PATTERN DESCRIPTIONS

Colour Pointed Ragdoll (Breed 66): The colour of the points (mask, ears, feet and tail) to be well defined. The mask covers the cheeks, whisker pads, nose, eyes, and chin. Nose leather and paw pads should be same colour as points. White anywhere is considered a fault.
Mitted Ragdoll (Breed 66w): The colour of the points (mask, ears, legs and tail) to be well defined. A narrow white blaze on the nose is permitted. The chest, chin and bib are white as is the underbody from chest to tail. The two front paws will have white mittens that are evenly matched and not extending beyond the angle formed by the paw and the leg. The back legs will have white boots to hock. Nose leather should be the same colour as the points and paw pads should be pink.
Bicolour Ragdoll (Breed 66 31): The mask should have an inverted 'V' of white starting on the forehead, extending downwards covering the nose, whisker pads and chin. The bib, chest and entire underbody to the base of the tail should be white. The front legs should be all white. The back legs should be white to the level of the hock. The 'V' should be balanced and not extend beyond the outer aperture of the eye. A limited amount of white is permitted on the body but not on the points. The colour of the points (remainder of the mask, ears and tail) to be clearly defined. All nose leather and paws, pads will be pink.

RAGDOLL COLOURS

Good contrast is required between the points and body colour. Lack of contrast is considered a fault. Allowances should be made for incomplete masks and maturity of colour in kittens and younger cats (under 3 years). Mature cats with lighter back colouring are preferred.
SEAL POINT: The back colour should be of an even beige, lightening gradually to a cream colour on the belly and chest. Points should be a dense, deep seal brown, and all of the same shade.
BLUE POINT: The back should be bluish white in colour, shading into a lighter colour on the belly and chest. Points should be a greyish-blue and all of the same shade.
CHOCOLATE POINT: The body colour should be ivory. The points should be a milk chocolate colour and all of the same shade.
LILAC POINT: The body colour should be magnolia white. The points should be of pinkish-grey tone and all of the same shade.

Ragdoll allowable outcross breeds: none.

Russian Blue

ORIGIN

For the first forty-one years that cat shows were held in Great Britain, all shorthaired blue cats, regardless of origin, competed in the same class. Some of those cats were blue domestic shorthairs from Great Britain, others were foreign-born cats that were variously called Archangel cats, Russian blues, Spanish blues, Chartreuse blues, and even American blues. The cats from Archangel, said cat lover Harrison Weir, 'were of a deeper, purer tint than the English cross-breeds.' The Archangel cats 'had larger ears and eyes, and were larger and longer in the head.' They had been named after the city of Arkhangelsk, a port on the White Sea about 150 miles south of the Arctic Circle, from where they may have been carried by sailors to Western Europe in the 1860s.

Perhaps because the cobby, round-headed British cats dominated the blue shorthaired classes, the Russian entries were assigned to their own judging

Russian Blue

category, called the Foreign Blue, in 1912. Their fortunes improved after this, but as all other breeds did, they fell into decline during World War II. After the war, breeders in England seeking to revive their lines outcrossed to other cats whose colour and type most closely resembled the Russian Blue's. Some English breeders chose the British Blue, which contributed a plush, pale-coloured coat to the re-emerging breed. Other breeders preferred to use blue point Siamese, which produced a more extreme, foreign body type.

After World War II only three breeding Russian Blues remained in Great Britain. The survival of the breed was due to the efforts of Mrs Rochford, who had cared for them throughout the entire war. These cats formed the nucleus of a new breeding programme, which included outcrosses to British Blues and Blue-point Siamese. Unfortunately, this outcrossing was very detrimental to the breed and it took many years to re-establish the typical Russian type and plush coat. It was claimed that the extreme cold climate in Russia was responsible for the evolution of this beautiful double coat. The originator of the White Russian in the United Kingdom suggested rather whimsically that the White was natural camouflage for the cat in its native country. However, careful examination of the pedigrees and outcrosses which produced the White cat suggest that this is probably not the case.

During the late 1940s and 1950s Scandinavian cat fanciers began working to develop a Russian Blue of their own, crossing a blue cat from Finland with a blue point Siamese. And what wonderful heads they produced. Some of the Russian Blues in Scandinavia were as fierce as they were big, but they possessed a style that enhanced the breed, a look all its own, just the thing to separate the Russian from the other blue shorthairs. The coats on the Scandinavian cats, unfortunately, were short and tight as well as dark.

DEVELOPMENT

A few Russian Blues had reached the United States around 1900, but little is known about these cats beyond their names, and serious work with the breed did not begin until 1947 when a Texan named C.A. Commaire imported two Russian Blues from England. Dorothy Leck of Three Crown cattery in America imported several cats from the Swedish lines with their magnificent heads and emerald green eyes, and the subsequent combination of the English and Scandinavian lines eventually produced pale, silver-blue coats and graceful body type. Since there were no natural Russian Blues to be imported, hybridizing did not cease. Breeders did what they had to do in order to expand the gene pool and to improve temperament, for Russian Blues were not exhibited in great numbers, and their temperament left a good deal to be desired.

During the 1970s a very limited number of breeders experimented with outcrosses, one of which involved a white non pedigree. Preliminary recognition for white and black Russians was granted in 1982, but very few cats have been registered. The white cats had the dominant white gene and were bred with orange or blue eyes.

RUSSIAN BLUE

(Breed 16a)
and other colour Russian Shorthairs
General Type Standard

COAT: The texture and appearance of the coat are the truest criteria of the Russian. The coat is double, short, thick and very fine, standing up soft and silky, very different in texture from any other breed.

HEAD: Short wedge with flat appearance between ears. In profile forehead and nose should appear straight, meeting at an angle level with the upper edge of the eye; there should be no stop or break. Prominent whisker pads. Strong chin with level bite. The tip of the chin should line up with the tip of the nose in the same vertical plane.

EARS: Large and pointed, wide at base with little inside hair and set vertically to the head.

EYES: Vivid green, except in the case of kittens where allowance should be made for eye colour. Set rather wide apart, almond in shape.

BODY: Long and graceful in outline and carriage. Medium strong bone. Cobby or heavy build undesirable.

LEGS AND FEET: Long legs, feet small and oval.

TAIL: Moderately long and tapering in proportion to the body. Neither blunt ended nor whip. The tail should be free from any abnormality of bone structure.

RUSSIAN BLUE COLOUR

Clear blue and even throughout with a distinct silvery sheen. Medium blue is preferred. The coat must be sound in colour to the roots and in maturity free from tabby markings, shading, tipping or ticking. Nose leather blue. Paw pads blue but not necessarily as blue as nose leather. Pinkish-lavender pads acceptable in kittens.

Russian Shorthair (Preliminary)

Russian White (16a14c, Preliminary)
Russian Black (16a15, Preliminary)
Blues resulting from matings with Blacks or Whites are registered on the reference register and are not accepted for blue breeding.

Russian Blue allowable outcross breeds: none.

Scottish Fold

ORIGIN

All Scottish Folds are descended from a white cat named Susie, who was born near the village of Coupar Angus in east central Scotland in 1961. Susie, whose parents were both straight-eared farm cats, owed her uniquely folded ears to a spontaneous mutation. Cat fanciers, who have long been enchanted by the Fold, owe the preservation of this breed to a shepherd named William Ross and his wife, Mary.

The Rosses lived near Susie's owners, a family named McCrae. After William Ross had noticed Susie playing in the McCraes' yard, he and Mary went to visit the McCraes, who promised that if Susie ever gave birth to fold-eared kittens, they would let the Rosses know. Two years later, after giving birth to a litter by a farm cat, the McCraes gave the Rosses one of Susie's kittens, a female with a snow-white coat like her mother's. The Rosses named her Snooks.

DEVELOPMENT

When Snooks was a year old, she produced a white, fold-eared male named Snowball, whose father was a red tabby farm cat. The Rosses then bought a British Shorthair female to breed to Snowball, and began visiting cat shows to see if anyone else was interested in fold-eared cats. They were introduced to Pat Turner, a lively English woman with an interest in cats and genetics, who obtained a fold-eared male from the Rosses and began a series of experimental breedings. She concluded that the gene responsible for folded ears is an incomplete dominant: i.e., if a kitten has one gene for folded ears and one gene for straight ears, it will always develop folded ears. Turner also discovered, as the Rosses had earlier, that Folds' ears look normal at birth. Around the age of fifteen to twenty-five days, when the ears of kittens are normally beginning to straighten, Folds' ears begin growing in the opposite direction.

According to the laws of chance, half the kittens from fold-eared/straight-eared crosses will have folded ears. Some breeders try to increase the number of Folds in a litter by breeding one fold-eared cat to another. This will produce, on average, three Folds instead of two in a litter of four; but there is reason to suspect that this breeding strategy produces short, inflexible tails, and hocks that curve like the rockers on a rocking chair. Neither of these conditions is life threatening, nor is the fold-eared gene a lethal one; but there is

reason to question the existence of any breed in which you cannot mate like to like without putting kittens at risk. In fact, the GCCF does not recognize Scottish Folds in Great Britain, though the newer Cat Association of Britain does.

In 1971 it became known that several skeletally abnormal Scottish Fold cats were alive and a preliminary genetic study of the breed followed. In 1973 the investigation was undertaken by Dyte and Turner. In 1974 Oliphant F Jackson PHD MRCVS warned the Cat Fancy and the Veterinary profession that an Osteodystrophy of the cat was associated with the fold-eared breed and suggested that the breeding should be limited. The Governing Council accepted this recommendation and decided not to recognize the Scottish Fold.

By 1970 three Scottish Folds had been sent to Dr Neil Todd, a New England geneticist. Todd did not continue his Fold research very long, and one of his cats went to Salle Wolfe Peters in Pennsylvania, who bred Manx and American Shorthairs. Thanks to the work of Peters and Karen Votava, a Fold breeder from Lubbock, Texas, Scottish Folds were accepted for registration in the United States in 1973 and for championship competition five years later. Logically, the Scottish Fold should have been accepted as a variety of the British Shorthair. This would have solved the problem of nonshowable, straight-eared kittens—which could then be shown, if good enough, as British Shorthairs.

Silver Classic Tabby Scottish Fold

SCOTTISH FOLD

Not recognized by the GCCF

Standard, courtesy of the
Cat Fanciers' Association of America.
Differences in the Standards of other registries are indicated at the end of the text.

HEAD: (55)
Ears 25
Head shape, muzzle, neck, chin, profile 15
Eyes 15

BODY: (40)
Body structure of torso, legs and paws 10
Tail 20
Coat 10

COLOUR: (5)
Colour of coat and eyes 5

GENERAL: The Scottish Fold cat occurred as a spontaneous mutation in farm cats in Scotland. The breed has been established by crosses to British Shorthair and domestic cats in Scotland and England. In America, the outcross is the American and British Shorthair. All bona fide Scottish Fold cats trace their pedigree to Susie, the first fold-eared cat discovered by the founders of the breed, William and Mary Ross.
HEAD: Well rounded with a firm chin and jaw. Muzzle to have well-rounded whisker pads. Head should blend into a short neck. Prominent cheeks with a jowly appearance in males.
EYES: Wide open with a sweet expression. Large, well rounded, and separated by a broad nose.[1] Eye colour to correspond with coat colour.[2]
NOSE: Nose to be short with a gentle curve. A brief stop is permitted but a definite nose break considered a fault. Profile is moderate in appearance.
EARS: Fold forward and downward. The smaller tightly folded ear preferred to a loose fold and large ear. The ears should be set in a caplike fashion to expose a rounded cranium. Ear tips to be rounded.
BODY: Medium, rounded, and even from shoulder to pelvic girdle. The cat should stand firm on a well-padded body. There must be no hint of thickness or lack of mobility in the cat due to short, coarse legs. Toes to be neat and well rounded with five in front and four behind. Overall appearance is that of a well-rounded cat with medium bone; fault cats obviously lacking in type. Females may be slightly smaller.
TAIL: Tail should be medium to long but in proportion to the body. Tail should be flexible and tapering. Longer, tapering tail preferred.
COAT: Dense, plush, medium short,[3] soft in texture, full of life. Standing out from body due to density; not flat or close lying.[4] Coat texture may vary due to colour and/or region or seasonal changes.
DISQUALIFY: Kinked tail. Tail that is foreshortened. Tail that is lacking in flexibility due to abnormally thick vertebrae. Incorrect number of toes. Any evidence of illness or poor health.

SCOTTISH FOLD COLOURS

(See page 170 for a full description of the colours listed below.)

Particolour colours: bicolours (black and white, blue and white, red and white, cream and white), blue cream, calico, dilute calico, tortoiseshell. **Shaded colours:** chinchilla silver, shaded cameo (red shaded), shaded silver, shell cameo (red chinchilla). **Smoke colours:** black smoke, blue smoke, cameo smoke (red smoke). **Solid colours:** black, blue, cream, red, white. **Tabby colours:** (in classic, mackerel, patched, or spotted patterns): blue tabby, brown tabby, cameo tabby, cream tabby, red tabby, silver tabby. **Other Scottish Fold colours:** any other colour or pattern with the exception of those showing evidence of hybridization resulting in the colours chocolate, lavender, the Himalayan pattern, or these combinations with white.

Scottish Fold allowable outcross breeds:[5] British Shorthair, American Shorthair.

[1] CFF: 'The overall appearance should be of innocence or surprise.'
[2] ACA: 'Any eye colour allowed and of secondary importance.'
[3] ACA, ACFA, CFF, TICA: 'Short.'
[4] CFF: 'A double coat shall be penalized.'
[5] In all associations where the breed is recognized.

Scottish Fold Longhair

ORIGIN

All Scottish Folds, regardless of coat length, are descended from a white, fold-eared cat named Susie: a shorthaired kitten with curious ears born near the village of Coupar Angus in east central Scotland in 1961. The breed Susie inspired was born in the United States during the next decade when Folds were accepted for championship competition. A decade later the second breed that Susie inspired, the Scottish Fold Longhair, took its place on the show bench.

From the start, longhaired kittens had appeared in Scottish Fold litters. Indeed, Susie and her daughter Snooks produced longhairs themselves, which indicates that genotypically the Scottish Fold was a dual-coated breed from the beginning. The potential of Susie, Snooks, and their offspring to throw longhaired kittens was complemented by the British Shorthairs used in Scottish Fold breeding programmes. The British, too, carry a longhair gene because Persians are a legitimate outcross for British Shorthairs in England.

Silver Classic Tabby and White Scottish Fold Longhair

DEVELOPMENT

The decision to pursue championship status for shorthaired Folds only, was a practical, but timid one. William and Mary Ross, the breed's founders, were advised not to promote longhairs because they looked as if they didn't have any ears at all. The Rosses and other cat fanciers involved with Folds in the 1960s and early 1970s accepted this advice because they already anticipated some difficulty gaining recognition for their singular-looking breed. They were, of course, correct. The GCCF eventually rescinded the registration of Scottish Folds, though the breed is currently accepted by the Cat Association of Britain.

Though Fold breeders were not committed to promoting longhairs, no one seemed committed to stop producing them either. The first registered Fold in the United States was sired by an Exotic Shorthair, another breed that carries the longhair gene. Exotics and any shorthaired cats were legitimate outcrosses for the Scottish Fold until the latter was accepted for champion competition, at which point British and American shorthairs became the only sanctioned crosses. Exotics, however, remained a legitimate Fold outcross in ACFA for one or two years after the Fold's acceptance, and they remain an illegitimate Fold outcross in all associations to this day.

'In retrospect,' says one British cat fancier who was

Silver Tortie Tabby (patched Torbie) Van Scottish Fold Longhair

present at the Fold's creation, 'I'm not sure it was such good advice [telling the Rosses to work with shorthaired Folds only]. The longhairs I have seen have been just lovely.'

A Fold breeder in America told *Cats* magazine in 1984 that 'there is nothing prettier than a Scottish Fold with long hair. I wouldn't be surprised if they were eventually recognized. There are longhaired Manx, longhaired Siamese, and longhaired Abyssinians. I can't see that there aren't going to be longhaired Folds.'

As of May 1, 1987, there were. In the preceding fall the Scottish Fold Breed Section of The International Cat Association voted thirty-nine to one in favour of accepting the Scottish Fold Longhair for championship competition beginning with the 1987-88 show season.

No one is certain where or by whom the first Longhair Folds were shown in new breed classes in TICA, but the name most frequently mentioned is Hazel Swadberg in Renton, Washington. She exhibited a number of Longhairs in the Northwest Region in 1982. The following year a *Cats* magazine contributing editor learned about the longhaired Fold and with the help of two TICA judges was soon able to obtain recognition for these engaging cats.

SCOTTISH FOLD LONGHAIR

Not recognized by the GCCF

Standard, courtesy of the The International Cat Association. Differences in the Standards of other registries are indicated at the end of the text.

HEAD: 15	**EYES:** 15
EARS: 30	**BODY:** 10
TAIL: 20	**COLOUR:** 10

RECOGNIZED CATEGORY/DIVISIONS/ COLOURS: Traditional category, all divisions, all colours.

GENERAL: The Scottish Fold occurred as a spontaneous mutation in farm cats in Scotland. The breed has been established by crosses to British Shorthair and domestic cats in Scotland and England. In America, the outcrosses are the American and British shorthairs. All bona fide Scottish Fold Longhairs trace their pedigree to Susie, the first fold-eared cat, discovered by the founders of the breed, William and Mary Ross.

HEAD: Well rounded with a firm chin and jaw. Muzzle to have well-rounded whisker pads. Head should blend into a short neck. Prominent cheeks with a jowly appearance in males.

EYES: Wide open with a sweet expression. Large, well rounded, and separated by a broad nose.[2] Eye colour to conform to coat colour.[3]

NOSE: Nose to be short with a gentle curve. A brief stop is permitted, but a definite nose break is considered a fault. Profile is moderate in appearance.

EARS: Fold forward and downward. The smaller tightly folded ear preferred to a loose fold and a large ear. The ears should be set in a caplike fashion to expose a rounded cranium. Ear tips to be rounded.

BODY: Medium,[4] rounded and even from shoulder to pelvic girdle. The cat should stand firmly. The body should be well padded. There must be no hint of thickness or lack of mobility in the cat due to short, coarse legs. Toes to be neat and well rounded. Overall appearance is that of a well-rounded cat with medium bone; fault cats obviously lacking in type. Females may be slightly smaller.

TAIL: Tail should be medium to long but in proportion to the body. Tail should be flexible and tapering. Longer, tapering tail preferred.[5]

COAT: Semilong; standing away from the body; ruff and britches desirable. The texture of the coat is soft and full of life.

PENALIZE: Definite nose break.

DISQUALIFY: Tail that is foreshortened. Tail that is lacking in flexibility due to abnormally thick vertebrae.

Allowable Scottish Fold Longhair outcross breeds:[6] British Shorthair, American Shorthair, Scottish Folds.

[1] This breed is called the *Longhair Fold* in CFF and the *Highland Fold* in ACFA.
[2] CFF: 'The overall appearance should be of innocence or surprise.'
[3] CFF: 'Eye colour does not need to conform to coat colour. Allowance should be made for development of eye colour up to the age of eighteen months.'
[4] CFF: 'Medium to large in size.'
[5] CFF: '... ending in a modified, blunt tip [and] with a full plume.'
[6] In all associations where the breed is recognized.

Siamese

ORIGIN

From the earliest days of the cat fancy, the Siamese has been recognized—even by those who have no interest in cats—as a breed unlike any other. The first known reference to a cat with the Siamese pattern has been found in the *Cat-Book Poems*, a centuries-old manuscript preserved in the Thai National Library in Bangkok. This anonymous work contains verses that describe white-haired cats with black tails, feet, and ears—a recognizable portrait of today's seal point Siamese. The *Cat-Book Poems* was rescued from the ancient Siamese city of Ayudha, which was 417 years old when it was destroyed by Burmese invaders in 1767. We can assume, therefore, that the Siamese breed is well over two centuries old, and perhaps a good deal older.

Another reference to cats with the Siamese pattern occurred in 1793 in the writings of the naturalist Simon Pallas. These cats, which Pallas had observed in central Russia, had darker extremities than the cats from Siam—and light chestnut bodies where the 'Siamese' bodies were white. Pallas' cats may have descended from imported Siamese, or perhaps the recessive Siamese gene had mutated spontaneously in Russia, too. In either case, climate would have accounted for the differences in colour between Pallas' cats and the ones in the *Cat-Book Poems*. The formation of pigment in the Siamese is directly related to temperature. The colder the environment, the darker the markings and body colour.

Beyond these references to Siamese, all theories about the breed's derivation are just that, including the belief that Siamese originated in the Khorat province in northeastern Siam (now Thailand). Yet whatever its origin, the breed had arrived in England by 1871. Catalogues from the Crystal Palace shows for 1871 to 1887 list nineteen Siamese entries.

Not all the Royal Cats of Siam, as they were also called in those times, resembled the Siamese we know today. In 1889 Harrison Weir reported that 'Mr Young, of Harrogate, possesses a chocolate variety of this Royal Siamese cat.' According to Weir, Young had purchased his cat—which had a rich, dark-brown body and darker points—from an English gentleman who had obtained the cat from Singapore. While allowing that 'this peculiar colour is very beautiful and scarce,' Weir insisted that 'the light grey or fawn colour with black and well-marked muzzle, ears, and legs is the typical variety.' For its part, Young's chocolate Siamese appears to have resembled the current Burmese, whose ancestors are also thought to have originated in Siam.

There is no doubt—and little wonder—that Siamese attracted the attention of royalty and the élite, for no breed of cat could then compare with the unique colour and pattern of the Siamese. Even its voice and personality identified this as a breed apart. Siamese were treasured among wealthy and titled persons in Siam, who protected their cats by keeping them indoors and who were seldom willing to allow unaltered Siamese cats to leave the country. A Mrs Vivian of Dover, England, who imported Siamese in 1885 and 1886, wrote that her cats were believed to have come from the King's palace in Siam, 'where alone the breed are said to be kept pure.' The first imported cats known to have originated in the King's cattery were Pho and Mia, two seal points who were presented by the King to Owen Gould, the departing British consul general, in 1884. Gould, in turn, gave these cats to his sister, a Mrs Veley, who showed them at the Crystal Palace the following year.

DEVELOPMENT

Frances Simpson, a well-known English judge and author during the late nineteenth and early twentieth centuries, declared that Siamese were 'perhaps the most difficult cat to breed and rear' in England. Another writer predicted that because of their delicacy Siamese were 'never likely to be common.' They were especially susceptible to enteritis and respiratory problems. Nevertheless, the Siamese' intelligence, personality, and distinctive appearance were sufficient to ensure its popularity and proliferation.

For many years the seal point was the only variety of Siamese considered desirable. Blue points were not recognized until 1934, chocolate points gained recognition in 1952, and lilac (or frost) points in 1955. Since the genes that produce these colours were present in the native Siamese population long before the breed became fashionable, the delayed recognition of the non-seal varieties must be blamed on snobbery and stubbornness. When a blue point was exhibited at an English show in 1896, the judge disqualified the cat. Whether this was a true blue point or a self-blue Korat—yet another breed found in Siam—is not known; but there must have been some crossbreedings between Siamese and the self-coloured blue cats in Siam, for blue point kittens appeared in many litters born to the earliest Korats imported to this country.

By the turn of the century interest in Siamese had spread to the United States, and the breed began to appear at American shows. Volume I of the Beresford Cat Club book, published in 1900, contains the names of Lockhaven Siam and Sally Ward, two Siamese that were owned by Mrs Clinton Locke of Chicago, founder of the Beresford Cat Club, the first cat club in the United States, which later evolved into the American Cat

Blue Point Siamese

Association. Mrs Locke acquired cats from Lady Marcus Beresford, a legendary fancier in Great Britain, and one Siamese was imported by the United States Postmaster General.

The Siamese cat continued to develop in England and in the early 1920s the Siamese Cat Club began to publish the Siamese Cat Register. In the second edition of the register, which appeared in 1927, about 540 cats were listed. At the beginning of the register there is a brief listing of some of the original Siamese, including the legendary Pho and Mia. The list also includes Stumpy, a male imported by Mrs Hannan and owned by Mrs Veley which was described as having a bobbed tail.

The origins of the Siamese cat were obviously of great interest at that time and as a preface to the register, the editor included various discussions which had appeared in a magazine called *Cat Gossip* asking such questions as 'Is the Siamese the sacred cat of old Egypt? Is the Siamese identical with this cat?' However, the popular belief seemed to be that the Abyssinian cat originated from Egypt and was not in any way like the Siamese; a theory which would almost certainly be supported today.

The preface also includes an article about the origin of the Siamese cat by Lilian Veley. In her discussion of the origin of the kinked tail, it is obvious that this characteristic was believed to be unique to the Siamese cat. We now know that any breed may suffer from this defect. However, at that time it was not thought to be a defect, in fact it appears that a large number of Siamese cats had kinked tails and also the renowned squint, of which Mrs Veley said 'The squint is of quite recent development, is heritable and is going far towards spoiling the beautiful eyes which are a feature of the Siamese cat.'

Almost all the cats in this register have no colour description, although one, Adastra was obviously a Chocolate Point as it won the Chocolate Point class at the Siamese Cat Club Show in 1926. At least four cats are described as blue pointed, all but one coming from the same parents but of more than one litter. Two of these cats were born in 1924, Bluboi and Mystic, followed by two more of the same breeding as Mystic in 1925.

The advertisements in the back of this issue included one prefix known to the present day, the 'Prestwick' prefix of Mrs Duncan Hindley. The advertisements also include a photograph of 'Saintly' performing the well known Siamese trick of opening a door; he is seen balanced on the doorknob negotiating the latch, a sight familiar to many Siamese owners today.

The Blue Point Siamese was recognised officially in 1936 but had appeared at cat shows since the mid-1920s and in 1926 the Siamese Cat Club introduced a class for Blue Point Siamese. It is difficult to gauge from the very limited breeding information that is available whether the blue colour appeared as a natural mutation or resulted from outcrosses to solid colour blue cats. During the Second World War, the number of Siamese, as with all other cats, dwindled dramatically and the number of Blue Points became very small. Mrs Hargreaves of 'Laurentide' prefix decided to outcross to a Russian Blue cat to bring new blood into the Siamese Blue Point lines. These original outcrosses are now to be found six or seven generations back on many Blue Point pedigrees and can be recognised by their names, the F1 generation all including the name 'Ephone' to the F3 generation which featured the word 'Ephree'.

The Chocolate Point cats had obviously been appearing from the early days of the Siamese but the colour was not officially recognised until 1951. Much of the work towards recognition of the chocolate colour was done by Miss Val Prentis, who was for many years the Siamese registrar.

Finally, the Lilac Points were granted recognition in 1961, although again the colour must have appeared at an earlier stage and possibly was not recognised. The Blue Point stud Champion Fernreig Zyn was kept at stud by Mr and Mrs Lamb until he was nearly fourteen years of age and in his very last litter, he sired a female that was recognised as a Lilac Point; it seems unlikely that this was the first Lilac Point he sired after such a long career at stud.

Meanwhile, many breeders had been examining the possibility of introducing further colours into the Siamese breed. The first Red Point Siamese was bred by Dr Nora Archer in the early 1950s and the challenge was taken up by Miss Ray, under her 'Penwyn' prefix. Work on the breed continued for many years without hope for recognition. However, in the early 1960s the Tabby Point Siamese were introduced as a result of outcrosses to a Shorthair British Silver Tabby. Their pale coats and tabby markings appealed to many Siamese breeders, including several leading members of the Cat Fancy. This resulted in Championship status being granted to both the Tabby Points and the Red Points in 1966; this was followed by recognition of all colours of Tortie Points and Cream Points, so accepting all these colours as Siamese unlike the situation in many countries overseas where the Tabby and Red groups are not accepted within this description.

The type of the Siamese cat has changed gradually over the many years of its existence from a round headed cat only slightly slimmer than its British counterpart to a slim and elegant animal with a long whip tail and long head. The development of the Siamese head has given cause for concern in recent years as on occasions the head shape has become so narrow that a weak chin with an uneven bite began to appear. The ideal Siamese cat should have a long wedge but with plenty of width between the ears and a good firm chin. The introduction of the standard list of faults which penalized cats showing weak chins and many other faults has done a great deal to correct this situation.

The Siamese cat is no longer the most popular breed in the United Kingdom but it certainly has a very strong following and still accounts for nearly one third of all registrations.

SIAMESE

General Type Standard

The Siamese Cat should be a beautifully balanced animal with head, ears and neck carried on a long svelte body, supported on fine legs and feet with a tail in proportion. The head and profile should be wedge-shaped, neither round nor pointed. The mask complete, connected by tracings with the ears (except in kittens), the eyes a clear brilliant blue. Expression alert and intelligent.

BODY AND TAIL: Medium in size, body long and svelte, legs proportionately slim, hind legs slightly higher than front legs, feet small and oval, tail long and tapering and free from any kink. The body legs and feet should all be in proportion giving the whole a well balanced appearance.

HEAD AND EARS: Head long and well proportioned, carried upon an elegant neck, with width between the ears narrowing in perfectly straight lines to a fine muzzle, with straight profile, strong chin and level bite. Ears rather large and pricked, wide at base.

EYES: Oriental in shape and slanting towards the nose, but with width between.

POINTS: Mask, ears, feet and tail dense and clearly defined colour, matching in basic colour on all points, showing clear contrast between points and body colour. Mask complete and (except in kittens) connected by tracings with the ears.

COAT: Very short and fine in texture, glossy and close-lying. Colours as per individual colour standards, any shading to appear on back and sides. Bib, chest and belly to be pale.

SIAMESE COLOURS

(See page 170 for a full description of the colours listed below.)

Seal Point (24)
Blue Point (24a)
Chocolate Point (24b)
Lilac Point (24c)
Red Point (32a)
Cream Point (32c)
Seal Tortie Point (32bl)
Blue Tortie Point (32b2)
Chocolate Tortie Point (32b3)
Lilac Tortie Point (32b4)
and all the above-listed colours in tabby point pattern.

Siamese allowable outcross breeds: Siamese cats may be bred by mating to Siamese or to Oriental Shorthairs, but outcrosses to Orientals of silver, cinnamon or caramel background are not allowed. When Siamese result from matings to Orientals the cats appear on the supplementary register.

Singapura

ORIGIN

Cats undergo considerable change in appearance as each breed evolves over the years, but seldom does the official history of a breed change. The Singapura is an exception.

In 1971 Hal Meadow, a geophysicist who lived in New Orleans, was sent to Singapore on business. There he found four, brown-ticked cats in the Lo Yang district. He paid a crewman on a ship that was bound for the United States to transport these cats to his friend Tommy Brodie, a woman living in Houston, Texas. There were no import or export papers sent with the animals, nor was there any other record of their origin.

DEVELOPMENT

Meadow's friend Tommy Brodie had once bred Abyssinians and had also been a Cat Fanciers' Federation allbreed judge. Intrigued by the brown-ticked cats from Singapore, she allowed three of them to reproduce. The fourth had died in the meantime. She kept no records of these transactions because she did not intend to establish a new breed from these cats.

In short, but not necessarily chronological, order: Hal Meadow and Tommy Brodie were married; Hal and Tommy Meadow went to live for a while in

Singapura

Singapore after Hal Meadow had been transferred there on business; three of the original imports from Singapore produced children and grandchildren; and Hal and/or Tommy Meadow decided to establish a new breed from these cats. But the nature of Hal Meadow's work in Singapore in 1971 had been politically sensitive. Therefore, he insisted that Tommy not reveal the origins of the cats he had sent her.

When the Meadows went to Singapore in 1974, they took several cats with them. Three of these were grandchildren of the cats that Hal Meadow had found on the island in 1971. These grandchildren were called Tess, Tickle, and Pusse. When the Meadows left Singapore and returned to the United States in 1975, they announced that they had found Tess, Tickle, and Pusse on the streets in Singapore and that they intended to establish a new breed based on this unique, naturally occurring Singapore street cat.

Cat publications in the United States dutifully printed Tommy Meadow's articles about the origin of the breed she had founded. All the registries in North America duly recognized the Singapura for championship competition. The Meadows' revisionist history of the creation of their breed, which they maintain was warranted by the nature of Hal Meadow's work, would have remained the official story. However an American named Jerry Mayes went to Singapore in the mid-1980s to find additional street cats to bring back to the United States, and the history was rewritten.

When Mayes' enquiries about street cats in Singapore provoked suspicious glances, he began an investigation. He discovered that the import papers filed by the Meadows when they had entered Singapore as husband and wife contained the singular names of three 'brown Abyssinian' cats: the aforementioned Tess, Tickle, and Pusse.

Eventually Mayes brought this information to the attention of Sandra Davie, a reporter for the Singapore *Straits Times*. Davie phoned Tommy Meadow during the summer of 1990, and during their conversation, which Davie claims to have taped, Meadow admitted fabricating the story about finding cats on the streets of Singapore in 1974. She admitted the same thing to the American Cat Fanciers' Association board of directors in an executive session in February 1991. Davie's interest in the story was prompted by the fact that the Singapore tourist board was about to launch a gigantic promotion based on these tiny cats. The board would have been embarrassed if it turned out that the Singapura, newly designated mascot of its native land, had actually been bred in somebody's basement in the United States and then transported to Singapore, as some people in Singapore and the States were beginning to suggest.

When the Meadows appeared before the CFA board in February 1991, they were able to substantiate with passports and visas Hal Meadow's presence in Singapore twenty years earlier. They did not substantiate, at least according to the minutes from the executive session, the existence of the cats that Hal Meadow shipped from Singapore in 1971.

There are some people who continue to question the origin of the Singapura. Meanwhile, some cat fanciers maintain that the Singapura, which is called Singapore's national treasure by that country's tourist promotion board, should be called Houston's national treasure instead. Those sceptics want more proof than Tommy Meadow is currently offering—which is nothing more than her already discredited word—that her husband did send cats to her in 1971. Yet there are more disturbing questions about this breed. They concern its future, not its past. To date, the Singapura has been derived from only four cats: the three that Hal Meadow shipped to America in 1971, and another import from Singapore that arrived later. There are no allowable outcrosses for this breed, and the Singapura registry is already closed in the Cat Fanciers' Federation, which means that no additional imports from Singapore can be registered. The registries in other associations—with the exception of the Canadian Cat Association and The International Cat Association—are virtually closed, too, because they require anything from a three- to a five-generation pedigree on cats imported from Singapore. No one in Singapore has been breeding cats long enough to satisfy this requirement. Only CCA and TICA, which allow the registration of imported Singapuras, have a policy that will allow the needed expansion of this breed's gene pool. Meanwhile, the number of Singapura litters registered in CFA dropped from fifty five in 1989 to twenty eight in 1990.

A few Singapuras have been imported into the United Kingdom and have been registered but there are not enough cats or breeders for recognition of the breed to be considered.

SINGAPURA

Not recognized by the GCCF

Standard, courtesy of the Cat Fanciers' Association of America. Differences in the Standards of other registries are indicated at the end of the text.

HEAD: (25)	**BODY, LEGS, and TAIL:** (20)
Ears 10	Neck 3
Head shape 4	Proportion 10
Width at eye 4	Legs and feet 5
Muzzle shape 4	Tail 2
Profile 3	
EYES: (10)	**COAT:** 15
Size and placement 6	**COLOUR:** 15
Shape 3	
Colour 1	**MARKINGS:** 15

GENERAL: The appearance of an alert, healthy, small to medium-sized, muscular-bodied cat with noticeably large eyes and ears. Cat to have the illusion of refined, delicate colouring.

HEAD: Skull rounded with rounded width at the outer eye, narrowing to a definite whisker break and a medium-short, broad muzzle with a blunt nose. In profile, a rounded skull with a very slight stop well below eye level. Straight line nose to chin. Chin well developed.

EARS: Large, slightly pointed, wide open at the base, and possessing a deep cup. Medium set. Outer lines of the ear to extend upward at an angle slightly wide of parallel. Small ears a serious fault.

EYES: Large, almond shaped, held wide open but showing slant. Neither protruding nor recessed. Eyes set not less than an eye width apart. Colour hazel, green, or yellow with no other colour permitted. Brilliance preferred. Small eyes a serious fault.

BODY: Small to medium overall size cat. Moderately stocky and muscular. Body, legs, and floor to form a square. Midsection not tucked but firm.

NECK: Short and thick.

LEGS AND FEET: Legs heavy and muscled at the body tapering to small, short, oval feet.

TAIL: Length to be short of the shoulder when laid along the torso. Tending towards slender but not whippy. Blunt tip.

COAT: Fine, very short, lying very close to the body. Allowance for longer coat in kittens. Springy coat a fault.

MARKINGS: Each hair to have at least two bands of dark ticking separated by light bands. Light next to skin and a dark tip. Dark tail tip with colour extending back toward the body on the upper side. Cat to show some barring on inner front legs and back knees only. Allowance to be made for undeveloped ticking in kittens. Spine line not a fault.

PENALIZE: Dark coat colouring next to skin, definite grey tones, barring on outer front legs, necklaces, non-visible tail faults.

DISQUALIFY: White lockets, barring on tail, top of the head unticked, unbroken necklaces or leg bracelets. Very small eyes or ears. Visible tail faults.

SINGAPURA COLOUR

Colour to be dark-brown ticking on a warm, old-ivory ground colour. Muzzle, chin, chest, and stomach to be the colour of unbleached muslin. Nose leather pale to dark salmon. Eyeliner, nose outline, lips, whisker apertures, hair between the toes to be dark brown. Foot pads a rosy brown. Salmon tones to the ears and nose bridge not a fault. Warm, light shades preferred.

Singapura allowable outcross breeds:[1] none.

[1] In all associations where the breed is recognized.

Somali

ORIGIN

The origin of the Somali begins with the origin of its shorthaired littermates, the Abyssinians. For many of their early years the Abyssinians were, of necessity, hybrid cats. By 1900, fewer than twenty years after the Abyssinian had been listed as a separate breed in England, many authorities concluded that it was simply the result of chance matings among ordinary ticked tabbies, and the name Abyssinian was replaced for a time by 'Ticks' or 'British Ticks' or 'Bunny Cats.' This decision was supported by records that subsequently appeared in the 1900-1905 stud book of the National Cat Club in England. Each of the twelve Abyssinians listed there had at least one parent of unknown origin.

It is certainly possible that some of those unknowns were either longhaired cats or shorthaired cats which had inherited the recessive longhaired gene from one of their parents. And it is probable that breeders in England, struggling to develop the Abyssinian, resorted to outcrossing as the easiest way to cope with limited stock and the setbacks occasioned by two world wars. Indeed, the list of stud cats in the 1947-48 GCCF records contains just four Abyssinian males, two of them unproven. Breeders seeking mates for their females at that time obviously had to look elsewhere for eligible suitors.

DEVELOPMENT

Whatever the origin of the longhaired gene, there is no doubt that longhaired Abyssinian kittens were man-made. They were not the result of a spontaneous mutation as some Abyssinian breeders stubbornly insisted. Nor was England alone responsible for introducing this gene to the breed. American breeders also helped to enlarge the Abyssinian gene pool—and to enhance those qualities that needed strengthening—through outcrossing. Nevertheless, Abyssinian breeders behaved true to form as cat fanciers and refused to recognize their longhaired kittens as natural Abys. Such kittens were sold without papers as quickly and quietly as possible.

One day in 1969 a year-old longhaired Abyssinian named George—who had been given away at the age of five weeks—was brought by his fifth owner to a private shelter in Gillette, New Jersey. Evelyn Mague, the woman who operated the shelter, is an Abyssinian breeder. In fact, she later discovered that she owned the Abyssinian male that had sired the much-travelled George. Mague thought that George was 'the most beautiful cat' she had ever seen, but because he was unaccustomed to being around other cats, she arranged for him to be neutered and vaccinated. Then she placed him in a single-cat home.

Mague resented the way George had been treated. Although his parents had been pedigreed cats from some of the finest Abyssinian lines of that time, he was treated no better than a street cat because he had been born with long hair. Mague was determined to find and show another longhaired Aby, and to start a campaign to get these cats accepted. When Aby breeders would not hear of calling these cats longhaired Abyssinians, Mague chose the name Somali because Somalia forms the eastern and southeastern borders of Ethiopia, formerly called Abyssinia.

Finding another longhaired Aby was not difficult. In order for two shorthaired cats to produce a longhaired kitten, each of those shorthairs must possess a longhair gene. Since Mague had inherited George's mother when his breeder left the business of breeding cats—and since she already owned George's father—she was able to produce additional Somalis with little difficulty: one out of every four kittens on average. Breeding Somalis to Somalis, of course, will produce nothing but longhairs.

After running an ad in *Cats* magazine for a year, Mague heard from a breeder in Canada who had bought some longhaired Abys from a Canadian judge

Usual (Ruddy) Somali

and had been working with them for four or five years. Gradually Mague found other Aby breeders with longhairs, and in 1972 founded the Somali Cat Club of America (SCCA). Registration and championship status for the Somali soon followed. The now defunct National Cat Fanciers' Association was the first to recognize Somalis.

Genetically, the only difference between a Somali and an Abyssinian is one gene: that which determines coat length. There was little sense in creating a new breed for these cats. They should have been an Abyssinian variety. There is even less sense for insisting, as most associations do, that shorthaired kittens born from Somali-Abyssinian crosses must be registered as Somalis and cannot be shown.

The first Somali cat to be shown in England appeared at the Kentish Cat Society show in 1981. Dr Margaret Freyne imported a cat named Black Iron Vagabond, who became the father of the British Somali breed. Vagabond was an extremely friendly cat who seemed to enjoy being shown and won the hearts of everyone who saw him at cat shows. It was probably the outgoing personality that Vagabond possessed which made the Somali breed very popular from its inception. At the 1989 Supreme cat show, the Somali Neuter Sitah Kissmayu won the Best Provisional Breeds Neuter and the Best Kitten was Pyjamarama Dandy Lion. These awards were won in the final year of the Provisional status for the Somali cat; it received its Championship status in June 1990, when the Sorrel and the Usual Somali became eligible for full Challenge Certificates. Dr Margaret Freyne's 'Mycene' prefix has been well known throughout the Cat Fancy in the United Kingdom and appears on the pedigree of the majority of Somali cats.

The GCCF registers short haired kittens as Somali Variants and these cats may not be shown. The first two colours of the breed to reach championship status in 1991 are the usual, and the sorrel. All other colours have only preliminary recognition.

SOMALI

(General Type Standard)

The overall impression of the Somali is that of a well-proportioned, medium sized cat of foreign type, with coat of medium length, and firm, muscular development, lithe, showing an alert lively interest in all surroundings, with an even disposition and easy to handle. The cat is to give the appearance of activity, sound health and general vigour, with a good weight for size.

HEAD: A moderate wedge, the brow, cheek and profile lines all showing a gentle contour. A slight rise from the bridge of the nose to the forehead, which should be of good size with width between the ears, flowing into the arched neck without a break. A shallow indentation forming the muzzle is desirable, but a pinch is a fault. In profile the head shows a gentle rounding to the brow, a slight nose break is essential, leading to a firm chin. The muzzle shall not be sharply pointed and there shall be no evidence of snipiness or whisker pinch.

EARS: Ears set wide apart and pricked, broad at base, comparatively large, well cupped and tufted.

EYES: Almond shaped, set well apart, large, brilliant and expressive. Skull aperture neither round nor oriental. Eyes accentuated by dark lidskin, encircled by light coloured 'spectacles'. Above each eye a short dark vertical 'pencil' stroke with a dark 'pencil' line continuing from the upper lid towards the ear.

LEGS AND FEET: Legs in proportion to torso, feet oval and tufted between toes. Five toes in front and four at the back.

TAIL: The tail has a full brush, thick at the base and slightly tapering. Its length to balance with the torso.

COAT: The texture is very soft to the touch, extremely fine, dense and double coated with at least with 3 bands of ticking. The coat is medium length, except over the shoulders where a shorter length is permitted. The texture and length of coat may lead to a natural separation of the fur, mainly on the chest, for which the cat should not be penalized. Preference is to be given to a cat with ruff and breeches, giving a full coated appearance to the cat.

N.B: The Somali is extremely slow in showing mature

ticking, and allowances should be made for kittens. It should be noted that ticking is not so apparent in a medium length coat in comparison with ticking in a short coat.

SOMALI COLOURS

USUAL (63): Overall impression is of a rich golden brown ticked with black. Colour has radiant or glowing quality. Darker shading along the spine and top of tail desirable. Underside of body and inside of legs and chest to be of an even rich apricot tone harmonizing with the top coat, without ticking, barring, necklaces or belly marks. Tail ending black at the tip, with complete absence of rings on tail. Preference given to unmarked ruddy colour. Ears tipped with black or dark brown. NOSE LEATHER: Tile Red. FEET: Black or brown paw pads with black or brown between the toes and extending upwards on the back legs. Toe tufts on front and rear feet, back or dark brown. EYES: Amber, hazel or green—the more richness and depth of colour the better.

SORREL (63a): Warm glowing copper ticked with chocolate. The base hair to be deep apricot. Deeper shades preferred. Ears and tail tipped with chocolate. NOSE LEATHER: Pink. FEET: Pink pads with chocolate between the toes and extending upwards on back legs. Toe tufts on front and rear feet chocolate. EYES: Amber, hazel or green—the more richness and depth of colour the better.

SOMALI Preliminary

(The following descriptions should be read in conjuction with the existing SOP for Usual and Sorrel Somalis.)
Chocolate (63b, Preliminary)
Blue (63c, Preliminary)
Lilac (Dilute Chocolate 63d, Preliminary)
Fawn (Dilute Sorrel 63e, Preliminary)
Usual Silver (63s, Preliminary)
Sorrel Silver (63as, Preliminary)
Chocolate Silver (63bs, Preliminary)
Blue Silver (63cs, Preliminary)

Somali allowable outcross breeds: Abyssinian.

Tonkinese

ORIGIN

The one breed to originate in Canada, the Tonkinese, is a hybrid cat that was first accepted for championship competition by the Canadian Cat Association in 1965. This breed was developed in the early 1960s by a Canadian cat fancier named Margaret Conroy, who decided to cross a seal point Siamese and a sable Burmese to create a cat with some of the qualities she liked best in each of the breeds. She hoped for a cat that would be intermediate in type and have a temperament falling between that of a Siamese and a Burmese. Conroy believed that Siamese were becoming too stylized and extreme for popular taste. Although Conroy could not have foreseen this, the Burmese would eventually acquire a new and controversial look, thereby creating a demand in the market for a cat like the Tonkinese, with some of the characteristics of the old style Siamese.

Nearly a decade before Mrs Conroy 'officially' developed her new breed, Milan Greer, a pet shop owner in New York City, had worked towards the same goal. Greer used colourpoint Siamese and Burmese in his plan and claimed to have produced five generations of cats that he called Golden Siamese before dropping the project. When Margaret Conroy began working on her Siamese-Burmese crosses, she also used the name Golden Siamese for a few years. Records indicate that *Tonkinese* (first spelled with an *a* instead of an *i*) was suggested later by cat fanciers who wanted to avoid any suggestion that this hybrid was either a Siamese or Burmese.

DEVELOPMENT

With help from breeders who shared her belief in the virtue of moderation—'I don't like to fool with Mother Nature; it bothers me,' says one Tonkinese advocate—Conroy wrote a standard for an 'intermediate' breed and presented this standard to the Canadian Cat Association. The cat described in her blueprint was neither slinky, like the Siamese, nor stocky, like the Burmese. Instead, the Tonkinese was designed with medium torso, moderately slim legs, well-developed muscles, a head with a modified wedge, and medium ears set as much on the side as on the top of the head.

By the end of the sixties, Margaret Conroy was no longer breeding cats, but by then the Tonkinese had gained popularity in the United States, and in 1972 the now-defunct Independent Cat Federation became the

Lilac (Platinum) Tonkinese

first registry there to recognize Tonkinese for Championship competition. Eventually all the other registries in the United States followed suit.

In developing the Tonkinese, Margaret Conroy had virtually reinvented the wheel. In 1930 a female cat named Wong Mau, from whom all Burmese cats are descended, arrived in the United States. Wong Mau was a brown hybrid with darker points on her face, legs, feet and tail. Bred to a sealpoint Siamese, she produced both Siamese cats and other offspring that resembled her, with darker bodies than the Siamese and with less contrast between point colour and body colour. It was not until Wong Mau was bred to one of her sons, or when two of her offspring were bred together, that the uniform, sable-brown Burmese colour appeared. It is obvious, therefore, that Wong Mau—in addition to being the matriarch of the Burmese breed—was also the precursor of today's Tonkinese. In fact, she was a Tonkinese cat long before the breed was invented, and the 'light' phase kittens that Dr Joseph Thompson, Wong Mau's owner, referred to in his writings were possibly the earliest examples of this strain.

Just as Wong Mau did not breed true for colour neither does the Tonkinese today. Furthermore, not every color produced by Tonk-to-Tonk breedings is accepted for championship competition. All registries recognize the Tonk in natural mink, blue mink, platinum mink, champagne mink, and honey mink colors. A few other associations, most notably the American Cat Fanciers' Association and The International Cat Association, accept Tonkinese in solid mink and pointed colors as well.

The addition of *mink* to the universally accepted Tonkinese colors is somewhat confusing. Though many people believe that *mink* describes the feel of the Tonkinese coat, Jane Barletta, who pioneered the breed in the United States, reports that *mink* actually describes the original Tonkinese pattern: a medium brown that shaded to a lighter hue on a cat's underparts and to a dark-brown color at its extremities. To obtain balanced Tonkinese colors, breeders are challenged by the necessity of restricting the expression of the gene for point coloration to a medium tone while avoiding any solid-color appearance that would make the Tonkinese look like a spoiled Burmese.

Although Siamese and Burmese breeders initially derided at first about their cats' look-alike cousins with the similar name, 'that sort of hostility has been toned down considerably over the years,' says Tonkinese breeder and TICA judge Mark Fensterstock. 'Most Siamese and Burmese people accept the Tonk as another legitimate breed. In fact, there are a number of people who breed both Burmese and Tonkinese.'

For its part, the public has never shown anything but enthusiasm for the Tonkinese. 'When I go to a cat show,' says Fensterstock, 'and people see my cats—especially if I have some pointed Tonkinese with me—they'll say, "Oh, that's like the Siamese we had for fifteen years." There's a big demand for Tonkinese among people who had its old style component breeds for a long time and now can't find them anymore. These are people who like the more moderate, less extreme look.'

While the Tonkinese is an intermediate cat by design, there is one outstanding feature about the breed: its brilliant, aqua-colored eyes. This is one area where the Tonkinese prefers license to limitation. A distinctive 'blend' of the blue Siamese and gold Burmese eye colors, the Tonkinese' aqua eyes range from aquamarine to turquoise.

TONKINESE

Not recognized by the GCCF

Standard, courtesy of the
Cat Fanciers' Association of America.
Differences in the Standards of other registries are indicated at the end of the text.

HEAD: (25)
Profile 8
Muzzle 6
Ears 6
Eye shape and set 5

BODY: (30)
Torso 15
Legs and Feet 5
Tail 5
Muscle tone 5

COAT: 10

COLOUR: (35)
Body colour 15
Point colour 10
Eye colour 10

GENERAL: The Tonkinese cat was originally the result of a Siamese-to-Burmese breeding. The ideal Tonkinese is intermediate in type, being neither cobby or svelte. The Tonkinese should give the overall impression of an alert, active cat with good muscular development. The cat should be surprisingly heavy. While the breed is to be considered medium in size, balance and proportion are of greater importance.

HEAD: A modified wedge, somewhat longer than it is wide,[1] with high, gently planed cheekbones; the brow, cheek, and profile all showing clean, strong contours. In profile there is a slight convex curve of the forehead, from the top of the head to just above the eyes. A slight stop at eye level.[2] Good width between the eyes.

MUZZLE: Blunt; as long as it is wide. Slight whisker break, gently curved, following lines of wedge. In profile, the tip of the chin lines up with the tip of nose in the same vertical plane.

EARS: Alert, medium in size.[3] Oval tips, broad at the base. Ears set as much on the sides of the head as on the top. Hair on the ears very short and close lying. Leather may show through.

EYES: Open, almond shape.[4,5] Slanted along the cheekbones toward the outer edge of the ear.[6] Eyes are proportionate in size to the face.[7]

EYE COLOUR: Aqua. A definitive characteristic of the Tonkinese breed, best seen in natural light. Depth, clarity, and brilliance of colour preferred.

BODY: Torso medium in length, demonstrating well-developed muscular strength without coarseness. The Tonkinese conformation strikes a midpoint between the extremes of the long, svelte body types and the cobby, compact body types. Balance and proportion are more important than size alone. The abdomen should be taut, well muscled, and firm.[8]

LEGS AND FEET: Fairly slim, proportionate in length and bone to the body. Hind legs slightly longer than front. Paws more oval than round. Trim. Toes: five in front and four behind.

TAIL: Proportionate in length to body.[9] Tapering.[10]

COAT: Medium short[11] in length, close lying, fine, soft and silky, with a lustrous sheen.

BODY COLOUR: The mature specimen should be a rich, even, unmarked colour, shading almost imperceptibly to a slightly lighter hue on the underparts. Allowance to be made for lighter body colour in young cats. With the dilute colours in particular, development of full body colour may take up to sixteen months. Cats do darken with age, but there must be a distinct contrast between body colour and points.

POINT COLOUR: Mask, ears, feet, and tail densely marked, but merging gently into body colour. Except in kittens, mask and ears must be connected by tracings. Allowance made for slight barring in young cats.

PENALIZE: Palpable tail fault. Extreme ranginess or cobbiness. Definite nose break. Round or crossed eyes.

DISQUALIFY: Yellow eyes. White locket or button. Visible tail kink.

TONKINESE COLOURS[12]

BLUE MINK: Body soft, blue grey, shading to lighter hue on underparts. Fawn overtones permissible but not preferable. Points: slate blue, distinctly darker than body colour. Nose leather: blue grey (corresponding to intensity of the point colour). Paw pads: blue grey (may have a rosy undertone).

CHAMPAGNE MINK: Body buff cream. Points: medium brown. Nose leather: cinnamon brown (corresponding to the intensity of the point colour). Paw pads: cinnamon pink to cinnamon brown.

HONEY MINK:[13] Body golden cream, preferably with an apricot cast. Points: light to medium, ruddy brown. Nose leather: caramel pink. Paw pads: caramel pink.

NATURAL MINK: Body medium brown, shading to lighter hue on underparts. Ruddy highlights acceptable. Points, nose leather: dark brown (corresponding to intensity of the point colour). Paw pads: medium to dark brown (may have rosy undertone).

PLATINUM MINK: Body pale, silvery grey with warm overtones. Not white or cream. Points: frosty grey, distinctly darker than the body colour. Nose leather: lavender pink to lavender grey. Paw pads: lavender pink.

Tonkinese allowable outcross breeds:[14] none.

1 TICA: 'Head and ears give impression of equilateral triangle.'
2 CFF: 'A clearly defined nose stop.'
3 ACA, ACFA, TICA: 'Pricked forward.'
4 ACFA, CFF: 'Slightly rounded on the bottom.'
5 TICA: 'Peach pit. Half almond on top, slightly rounded on bottom.'
6 ACFA, TICA: 'Set at least an eye's width apart.'
7 ACA, ACFA: 'Medium in size, in proportion to the head.'
8 TICA: 'Back rises slightly from shoulder to rump.'
9 ACFA: 'Medium to medium long, in proportion to body.'
10 TICA: ' ... gently to a slightly blunted tip.'
11 CFF: 'Short.'
12 ACFA and TICA accept the following additional Tonkinese colours: natural, blue, champagne, and platinum solid; natural, blue, champagne, and platinum pointed.
13 ACFA does not recognize this colour.
14 In all associations where the breed is recognized.

Turkish Angora

ORIGIN

The Angora is certainly as recognizable as any other longhaired breed in the world; and even though its fortunes do not compare with the Persian's, the two cats share a parallel history. Nearly two and a half centuries ago Angora cats existed in the region surrounding the city of Angora, now called Ankara. At the same time another variety of longhaired cat was associated with the province of Chorazan in Persia. According to early observers, there was virtually no difference between Angora and Persian cats then. The French naturalist Count de Buffon, writing in the mid eighteenth century, observed that Persian cats, 'except in colour ... have a perfect resemblance to the cat of the Angora.' Persians were all grey. Angoras occurred in black, white, deep red, light fawn, mottled grey, and even smoke colours.

White Turkish Angora

DEVELOPMENT

After Persians and Angoras had made their way to England in the nineteenth century, a certain contrast became evident between them. The Angora's head was smaller, more narrow, and less round; its eyes were less round; its bone was less substantial; its tail was more fanlike and pointed at the tip; and its coat was not so heavy as the Persian's.

Still, Persians and Angoras were judged by the same standard. Gradually, Persian type won out; and by 1903 Frances Simpson, an English cat breeder and judge, declared, 'There are two distinctive breeds: the *Long-haired* or Persian Cats, and *Short-haired* or English and Foreign Cats.' But the Governing Council of the Cat Fancy, formed in England in 1910, decreed that Persians should continue to be called *longhairs*, a practice that survives in England today. The same practice also survived in the United States until the mid 1950s, when all pedigreed longhairs became *de facto* Persians, and Angoras became all but extinct.

Though effectively disenfranchised for a while, the Turkish Angora would soon be revived. In 1962 Mrs. Liesa F. Grant imported a pair of Angora cats from the Ankara Zoo. These and subsequent importations by other American breeders comprised the stock used to reconstruct the Angora as a separate breed in the United States.

From the 1940s the Ankara Zoo has maintained a breeding colony of Angora cats, and for a time so did the zoo in Istanbul. Since the zoos were the primary and most reliable sources of Turkish Angoras, the Cat Fanciers' Association—the first registry in North America to recognize the Turkish Angora, would not register any Turkish imports not born in the zoo. What's more, CFA was unwilling to register nonwhite

Angoras until 1978, some time after the other associations had recognized the breed in a variety of colours. It is no surprise that 76 percent of the 2,108 Turkish Angoras registered by CFA in the United States between January 1, 1958, and December 31, 1990, were white. The Turkish Angora is not recognized in the United Kingdom.

Because the Angora had not been subject to controlled breeding for approximately fifty years before the breed was revived in the United States, the breed remained true to its original type. There was almost no difference at all between the Angoras of the 1900s and the ones imported to the United States in the 1960s.

Now that breeders are making selective choices in their breeding programmes, changes are occurring in Turkish Angoras that are not in keeping with the true Angora type. Modern Angoras are much too high on their hind legs, and have ultralong bodies. They are too fine in bone and have suffered a loss of coat length. Hopefully, the interest in other Angora colours will return proper type to the breed.

TURKISH ANGORA

Not recognized by the GCCF

Standard, courtesy of the Cat Fanciers' Association of America. Differences in the Standards of other registries are indicated at the end of the text.

HEAD: 35	**COLOUR:** 20
BODY: 30	**COAT:** 15

GENERAL: Solid, firm, giving the impression of grace and flowing movement.
HEAD: Size, small to medium. Wedge-shaped.[1] Wide at top.[2] Definite taper toward chin.[3] Allowance to be made for jowls in stud cat.
EARS: Wide at base, long, pointed, and tufted. Set high on the head and erect.
EYES: Large,[4] almond shaped.[5] Slanting upwards slightly.
NOSE: Medium long, gentle slope. No break.
NECK: Slim and graceful, medium length.
CHIN: Gently rounded. Tip to form a perpendicular line with the nose.
JAW: Tapered.
BODY: Medium size in the female,[6] slightly larger in the male. Torso long, graceful, and lithe. Chest, lightly framed.[7] Rump slightly higher than front.[8] Bone, fine.[9]
LEGS: Long. Hind legs longer than front.
PAWS: Small and round, dainty. Tufts between toes.
TAIL: Long and tapering, wide at base, narrow at end, full. Carried lower than body but not trailing. When moving, relaxed tail is carried horizontally over the body, sometimes almost touching the head.
COAT: Body coat medium long,[10] long at ruff.[11] Full brush on tail. Silky with a wavy tendency. Wavier on stomach. Very fine and having a silklike sheen.[12]
BALANCE: Proportionate in all physical aspects with graceful, lithe appearance.
DISQUALIFY: Persian body type. Kinked or abnormal tail.

TURKISH ANGORA COLOURS

(See page 170 for a full description of the colours listed below.)

Particolour colours: bicolours (black and white, blue and white, red and white, or cream and white), blue cream, calico, dilute calico, tortoiseshell. **Smoke colours:** black smoke, blue smoke. **Solid colours:** black, blue, cream, red, white.[13] **Tabby colours:** blue (classic and mackerel), brown (classic and mackerel), cream (classic and mackerel), red (classic and mackerel), silver (classic and mackerel). **Other Turkish Angora colours:** any other colour or pattern with the exception of those showing hybridization resulting in the colours chocolate, lavender, the Himalayan pattern, or these combinations with white.

Turkish Angora allowable outcross breeds:[14] none.

1 ACFA: 'Modified wedge shape.'
2 ACFA, CFF, TICA: 'Top of skull is medium wide.'
3 ACFA, CFF, TICA: 'No whisker pinch.'
4 TICA: ' ... but in proportion to the head.'
5 ACA: ' ... to almost round.'
6 ACFA: 'Medium to small in females.'
7 CFF: 'Chest to be narrow and deep, never rounded.'
8 ACA, ACFA: 'Upper leg should lie at close angle to the body with the lower leg straight.'
9 TICA: 'Medium to fine.'
10 TICA: 'Semilong.'
11 ACFA: ' ... and undersides.'
12 ACFA: 'Seasonal variations in coat are acceptable.'
13 ACFA, CFF: 'Colour spot on whites is allowed up to two years.'
14 In all associations where the breed is recognized.

Turkish Van

ORIGIN

The Turkish Van is a mostly white, semi-longhaired cat with a wide body, heavy bones, and a distinctive colour pattern. The Van was named after the Lake Van district in western Turkey, but there is no evidence that the breed originated in this area, nor is it the only place in Turkey where Van cats have been found. 'There is no repository of Turkish Van cats in Turkey,' says one Van fancier, 'and no one has ever found anybody in Turkey who bred for these cats specifically. In fact, the Turkish Van is really an Armenian cat. It is revered by the Armenian people, who settled in the Lake Van district and who pronounce *Van* to rhyme with *Don*, not *Dan*.'

Furthermore, while Turkish Vans have existed near Lake Van for centuries, if you went to this isolated region looking for a Van cat, you would be shown an odd-eyed white most likely a longhair that resembles the cat we know as the Turkish Angora. The reason for this confusion is a proclamation made by Mustafa Kemal Ataturk, who founded the modern Republic of Turkey in 1923. Ataturk declared that his successor would be someone who had been bitten on the ankle by an odd-eyed, white cat. This prediction understandably increased the popularity of odd-eyed white cats throughout Turkey.

DEVELOPMENT

The evolution of the Turkish Van as a breed began in 1955 when Laura Lushington and Sonia Halliday, two British women vacationing in Turkey, brought a pair of Van kittens back to England. These kittens differed in conformation as well as colour from most of the Angora type cats around Lake Van. The Van kittens are substantially boned while the Angoras are delicate; Vans are heavily muscled while the Angoras are lean; and the Turkish Vans' heads are a bit shorter and wider than the Angoras'.

The Van's most distinguishing feature—its unusual pattern—is caused by a piebald spotting gene. This dominant gene accounts for the presence of white in bicoloured and tricoloured cats. When the gene governing a trait is dominant, a kitten will exhibit that trait, e.g., a bicoloured or tricoloured coat, as long as the kitten inherits a copy of that gene from one of its parents. The van pattern, spelled with a lowercase *v*, is also found in other breeds, including Persians, Cornish Rex, Scottish Folds, and American Shorthairs.

When the two cats brought back to England by Laura Lushington and Sonia Halliday produced a litter of kittens that resembled their parents, the ladies were convinced they were working with a separate breed of cat, a breed for which they began to seek recognition. They imported two more Vans in 1959, and by 1969 Turkish Vans were accepted for championship competition in Great Britain. The following year the first Vans officially arrived in the United States. Other Vans may have arrived unofficially before that, brought into the country by military personnel returning from tours of duty at the American air base in Turkey. There is reason to believe that these unofficial Vans were frequently imported as Turkish Angoras and that some were bred into Angora lines.

As of May 1, 1985, the Turkish Van was eligible for championship competition in The International Cat Association, the first—and so far the only—North American registry to accept this breed. The progress of the breed has been slow in the meantime. Part of the reason is the difficulty of finding Van cats in Turkey. Another factor is the temperament of the Turkish Van. Though much improved as the result of selective breeding in the United States, the Van still suffers from a reputation for being somewhat troublesome in the showring.

Red and White Turkish Van

TURKISH VAN

(General Type Standard)

HEAD: Short wedge, nose long, straight but with a barely perceptible dip in profile.
EYES: Large and oval.
EARS: Large, well feathered, fairly close together and set high on head.
BODY: Long and sturdy; the males are particularly muscular and strong. Legs medium in length. Feet neat, well rounded and tufted.
TAIL: Full brush, length to balance with the body.
COAT: Fur should be long, soft and silky to the roots. No woolly undercoat. It should be noted that the winter coat of the Van is longer and heavier than the summer coat.
CONDITION: Well groomed and immaculately prepared with no trace of greasiness, staining or tangles in the coat. Ears completely clean and free from all wax.
COLOR: White with no trace of yellow. The markings are a blazed head patch, and a rump patch extending to the tip of the tail. One or more random spots of color are permitted on the upper body, flanks, and outside of legs to the ankles. The markings may be broken by patches of white. Nose leather and paw pads are pink. Eyes may be yellow to amber, blue, or odd-eyed, all with pink rims.
NOTE: The foregoing description is the ideal. Occasional small auburn or cream 'thumbprints' irregularly placed on the cat are undesirable but should not necessarily disqualify any otherwise good specimen.

AUBURN TURKISH VAN (13D)

General Standard as above

COLOUR: Chalk white with no trace of yellow, auburn markings on the face but not below the level of the eyes or beyond the base of the rear of the ears. The auburn on the face should be separated by a vertical white blaze. White nose. Ears should be white with delicate shell pink inside. The brush is auburn and faintly ringed and the colour may extend a very short distance up the back. The rings are more distinctive in kittens. Nose leather and paw pads are pink. EYES: Light amber in colour with pink rims.

Auburn Turkish Van - Blue Eyed (13d b1)(Preliminary)
Auburn Turkish Van - Odd Eyed (13d od) (Preliminary)
Cream Turkish Van - 13df (Preliminary)
Cream Turkish Van - Blue Eyed (13df bl) (Preliminary)
Cream Turkish Van - Odd Eyed (13df od) (Prelimary)

Allowable Turkish Van outcrosses: none.

American Curl

In June 1981 a black, longhaired, stray kitten with unusual, swept-back ears turned up at the house of Joe and Grace Ruga in Lakewood, California. Six years later the descendants of this kitten, whom the Rugas had named Shulamith, were competing in championship classes in The International Cat Association.

The Curl's ears are the product of a spontaneous mutation with incomplete dominant expression. If a kitten inherits one gene for curled ears and another for straight ears, that kitten will still develop curled ears. In addition to its signature ears, the Curl can claim one other distinction: it is the only pedigreed cat that must be outcrossed only to non-pedigreed varieties. This has hampered the standardization of the breed. Setting type is difficult enough in a new breed that depends on established breeds for outcrosses. Trying to set type by crossing to cats obtained from shelters—or wherever else suitable, non-pedigreed cats might be found—makes the job ten times as difficult. The American Curl is not recognized by the GCCF.

Black and White American Curl

Bengal

The present-day Bengal was created in the late 1970s by Mrs Jean Mill of Covina, California, who wanted to reproduce the spotted pattern, colours, and facial qualities of the Asian Leopard Cat. Mill inherited eight females, the products of crosses between Asian Leopard Cats and domestic shorthairs, from a researcher at the University of California at Davis. She then added two male cats to this group: a feral, orange domestic with deep brown rosettes from a zoo in Delhi, India, and a brown—spotted—tabby domestic shorthair from a shelter in Los Angeles.

Ten years later there were two hundred Bengals in the United States, and the breed was being registered by The International Cat Association. Once TICA was satisfied that the Bengal exhibited a normal sterility profile and that it was no different on a cellular level from domestic cats, the breed became eligible to compete in championship classes as of May 1, 1991. Like the Ocicat, another man-made spotted variety, the Bengal does not always breed true for pattern. The Bengal is not recognized by the GCCF.

Leopard Spotted Bengal

Burmilla

When explaining the domestication of cats, zoologists often say that humans played a supporting role in that production. The cat, in its wisdom, found a vacant evolutionary niche and exploited it deftly.

In Great Britain in 1981, a chinchilla Persian male and a lilac Burmese female exploited a niche in their respective mating schedules to produce a mixed-breed litter of kittens. The youngsters—who developed comely green eyes and handsome black or brown tipping over a shimmering, silver base coat—were most attractive. As often happens, cat fanciers conceived of them as the foundation members of a new breed, which was duly christened the Burmilla.

Within three years of its inception the Burmilla was being championed by a breed club in England. In 1990 it advanced to preliminary status in its native land, where it is one of the most popular new breeds. Meanwhile, the Burmilla has also attracted the first stirring of interest abroad.

Black Tipped Burmilla

Javanese

Javanese are to Colourpoint Shorthairs what Balinese are to Siamese: the longhaired counterpart. The Javanese, accepted for championship competition beginning May 1, 1987, is one breed for which 'new' implies no mystique, no clouded or grey area, and surely no chance for fantasizing. Nor does the name have anything to do with the cat's place of origin.

It is obvious how and why this breed should have appeared. When breeders crossed American Shorthairs to Siamese in order to produce new Siamese colours, a number of those Americans had long hair in their backgrounds. Consequently, Javanese have long hair in theirs.

Four registries do not make any distinction between the Javanese and Balinese breeds. In these registries any Siamese with long hair is called a Balinese. Efforts to combine the Javanese and Balinese breeds have always been voted down in the Cat Fanciers' Association in America and the Canadian Cat Association, because some Balinese breeders like to think that their cats are as pure as the Siamese. They will not consider a merger of any kind, even though the coat texture, length, and feel of the Balinese and Javanese coats are identical. The Javanese is not recognized by the GCCF.

Tortie Point Javanese

Oriental Longhair

Ebony Oriental Longhair

The Oriental Longhair, accepted for championship competition by The International Cat Association since 1985, is the final stage in the evolution of the Siamese cat. As we have seen, when Siamese were first shown in England during the nineteenth century, seal point was the only colour acceptable. By the mid 1930s blue points were officially recognized. Twenty years later chocolate points and lilac points (sometimes called frost points) were added to the list.

While these 'new' Siamese colours were being developed, some breeders were working with additional colours and also with longhaired Siamese variants. Known formally as Balinese, the latter were recognized by the Cat Fanciers' Federation in 1961 and in all other registries by 1970. Meanwhile, enterprising breeders in England and the United States were crossing Siamese to several other shorthaired breeds to produce the Oriental Shorthair: a cat of Siamese conformation whose colour is not restricted to its extremities. Now accepted by all federations, the Oriental Shorthair was first recognized in 1976 by the Cat Fanciers' Association. Nine years later, TICA completed the Siamese evolutionary cycle by adding the Oriental Longhair to its list.

Despite some diehards' persistent lip service to natural mutations, the progression from Siamese to Oriental Longhair was no accident. For reasons discussed in other breed profiles, long hair and additional colours were added to the Siamese gene pool over the years by outcrosses to a number of other breeds. Finally, after the Oriental Shorthair had been developed, a few breeders created the Oriental Longhair in the late 1970s and early 1980s.

To accomplish this, they crossed a Balinese and an Oriental Shorthair. This mating produces all shorthaired kittens unless the Oriental is carrying a longhaired gene, in which case, half the kittens will have short hair. By crossing two nonpointed, shorthaired Balinese-Oriental Shorthair hybrids, it is possible to arrive at the Oriental Longhair. It is also possible to reach this destination by crossing a nonpointed, shorthaired Balinese-Oriental Shorthair hybrid to a Balinese. In either case, some of the kittens may be pointed and some may have short hair.

The Oriental Longhair was a challenge to produce, and it remains a challenge to work with. Breeding to an Oriental Shorthair to improve type will produce all shorthaired kittens—and a lost generation—unless the Oriental is carrying a longhaired gene. Breeding to a Balinese to maintain long hair will produce Oriental Longhairs carrying a pointed gene, which could come back to haunt successive breedings. And if the Oriental Longhair is already carrying a pointed gene, half the kittens from a cross to a Balinese will be Balinese.

'There are so many variables to manipulate in producing Oriental Longhairs,' one breeder observes, 'that you can't flirt with this breed just because you're working with one of its parent breeds. You're either an Oriental Longhair breeder, or you aren't going anywhere.' Which might explain why the Oriental Longhair, as of 1991, was recognized by only one association and has only received preliminary recognition in the United Kingdom. In recent years development on the breed has been in the doldrums but now a new breeders group is being set up to develop this attractive cat.

Snowshoe

The Snowshoe is a pointed cat with carefully drawn white markings on its face, chest, belly, and feet. This hybrid was developed in the late 1960s by Dorothy Hinds-Daugherty of Philadelphia. Though Mrs Hinds-Daugherty disappeared from the cat fancy after working with the Snowshoe for several years, we can infer that creating this breed required much patience and at least two matings between Siamese, bicoloured American Shorthairs, and their offspring.

After she had created and named her new breed, Mrs Hinds-Daugherty left its future to others. The first Snowshoe Standard was written by Vikki Olander of Norfolk, Virginia, who was influential in securing registration status for the Snowshoe in 1974 from both the American Cat Association and the Cat Fanciers' Federation. The breed has been recognized for championship competition by CFF since May 1, 1983. It is not recognized in the United Kingdom.

Seal Point Snowshoe

Sphynx

A cat resembling the modern-day Sphynx was exhibited in the early 1900s as the New Mexican Hairless cat. Although hairless cats had appeared previously as spontaneous mutations in South America and in North America and Europe afterwards, efforts to gain championship recognition for this breed were not made until hairless cats appeared in Ontario, Canada, in the 1960s.

The Sphynx reached provisional status in the American Cat Fanciers' Association by 1970, but progressed no further because the CFA board was concerned about the breed's genetic difficulties–viz., its failure to develop an adequate immune system because of decreased T-cell function. The Sphynx was accepted for championship competition in 1971, however, by the now defunct Crown Cat Fanciers' Federation.

At the moment The International Cat Association is the only registry in North America in which Sphynx compete in championship classes. According to the TICA standard, the Sphynx has short, fine down on its body, and short, tightly packed, soft hair on its muzzle, tail, and feet.

Sphynx advocates claim that the cats being shown now are not subject to the same immune system deficiencies that once troubled the breed. It is perhaps too soon to make such claims, and even if the breed's health problems are no longer life threatening, its maintenance problems are extremely troublesome. Since the Sphynx has no coat to absorb the natural oils a cat's body normally exudes, Sphynx must be bathed or towel washed frequently—otherwise, it is very easy to tell by the grease spot where a Sphynx spent the night.

In May 1991 the Executive Committee of the GCCF decided not to recognize the Spynx breed because it did not consider that they would prove viable in an average pet home.

Blue Cream Sphynx

Colour

Cats come in every colour imaginable. Those colours which officially permit pedigreed cats into the show ring have formal, sometimes confusing names. The colours of non-pedigreed cats have simple, descriptive names—like *grey tiger.* Everybody knows what that means. Few people know what *chocolate tortie tabby point* means.

Breed Standards include a full description of all colours recognized by an association. For breeds like the Korat that occur in one colour only, and for those like the Abyssinian that occur in few colours, we have printed complete colour descriptions along with the breed profiles. For breeds that come in many colours, like the Devon Rex, Persian, and Exotic Shorthair, we have simply listed those colours, without descriptions, at the end of the breed Standard. If you would like to know more about any colour that was not described fully in that section, consider the following.

There are roughly half a dozen basic cat colours. When one of those colours occupies the hairs on a cat from the tips to the roots, that cat is called solid or sometimes *self* coloured. The hair shafts on some cats, however, are tinted to varying degrees along their tips while the rest of the hair shaft down to the cat's body is white. These cats are called shadeds or smokes, depending on how much of the hair shaft is occupied by colour and how much is white. Still other cats have their colour arranged in one of five tabby patterns. Furthermore, all of the above—solids, shadeds, smokes, and tabbies—can also occur with white. And some colours—such as chestnut, with shades of red, which together equal a chocolate tortoiseshell—can occur with one another. Or with one another and with white. Finally, there are pointed cats, whose basic colour is confined to their faces, ears, legs, and tails.

Space prohibits a full description of each of the colours found in Oriental Shorthairs, Maine Coons, Cymrics, and other multicoloured breeds. Yet any of these colours in any one of those breeds will be easily understood by reference to the list of basic colours and patterns below.

For example, chocolate tortie tabby point is a Siamese colour. By finding chocolate in the 'Basic Colours' section, we learn that this is a rich, chestnut-brown colour. The word *tortie,* short for *tortoiseshell,* turns up in the 'Patterns' section, where we learn that tortoiseshells have unbrindled patches of light and dark red mixed in with their basic colour. The footnote for *lynx* in the 'Tabby' section lets us know that there are tabby markings in this pattern, and *pointed* is our clue that the basic colour on this cat is confined to its extremities—if *Siamese* hadn't already brought that to mind.

BASIC COLOURS

BLACK: dense, coal black from the roots to the tips of the fur. Free from any tinge of rust on the tips, or smoke on the undercoat.

BLUE: even, pale blue from the nose to the tip of the tail. Sound to the roots. Though a light shade is preferred, a sound darker shade is more acceptable than an unsound lighter one.

CARAMEL: cool toned bluish fawn.

CHOCOLATE: rich warm chestnut brown.

CINNAMON: warm cinnamon, brown sound throughout.

CREAM: one level shade of buff cream without markings. Sound to the roots. Lighter shades preferred.

EBONY: see black.

FAWN: warm rosy mushroom. Sound throughout. Pinker shades preferred.

LAVENDER: frosty grey with a pinkish tone. Sound throughout.

LILAC:[1] see lavender.

RED: rich, warm red; without shading, markings, or ticking. Lips and chin are the same colour as the coat.

WHITE: pure, glistening white.

SHADINGS

SHELL OR TIPPED:[2,3] undercoat is white. The coat on the back, flanks, head, and tail is sufficiently tipped with the cat's basic colour to give a characteristic, sparkling appearance. Face and legs may be very slightly shaded with tipping. Chin, ear tufts, stomach, and chest are white.

SHADED:[4] undercoat is white with a mantle of tipping in the cat's basic colour that shades down from the sides, face, and tail from a deep hue on the ridge to white on the chin, chest, stomach, and under the tail. Legs are the same tone as the face. The general effect is much darker than a shell shading.

SMOKE: white undercoat, deeply tipped with the cat's basic colour. Cat in repose appears to be that basic colour (e.g., red, black, blue, etc.). In motion the white undercoat is clearly apparent. Points and mask of the primary colour, with narrow band of white at the base of the hairs next to the skin which may be seen only when fur is parted.

CHINCHILLA GOLDEN: undercoat is apricot deepening to gold. Coat on the back, flanks, head, and tail is sufficiently tipped with black or seal brown to give a golden appearance. Legs may be slightly shaded with tipping. Chin, ear tufts, stomach, and chest, are cream. Rims of eyes, lips, and nose are outlined with black or seal brown.

CHINCHILLA SILVER: undercoat is pure white. Coat on the back, flanks, head, and tail is sufficiently tipped with black to give a characteristic, sparkling-silver appearance. Legs may be slightly shaded with tipping. Chin, ear tufts, stomach, and chest, are pure white. Rims of eyes, lips, and nose are outlined with black.

SHADED GOLDEN: undercoat is apricot deepening to gold with a mantle of black or seal brown tipping that shades down from the sides, face, and tail from dark on the ridge to cream on the chin, chest, stomach, and under the tail. Legs are the same tone as the face. The general effect is much darker than a chinchilla. Rims of eyes, lips, and nose are outlined with black or seal brown.

SHADED SILVER: undercoat is white with a mantle of black tipping that shades down from the sides, face, and tail from dark on the ridge to white on the chin, chest, stomach, and under the tail. Legs are the same tone as the face. The general effect is much darker than a chinchilla. Rims of eyes, lips, and nose are outlined with black.

PEWTER: white shaded with black giving the effect of a pewter mantle. Darker than a shaded silver.

PATTERNS

Tabby Patterns

CLASSIC TABBY: markings are dense, clearly defined, and broad. Legs are evenly barred with bracelets coming up to meet body markings. Tail is evenly ringed. There are several unbroken necklaces on the neck and upper chest, the more the better. Frown marks on the forehead form an intricate letter 'M.' Unbroken line runs back from the outer corner of the eye. Swirls on cheeks. Vertical lines over the back of the head extend to the shoulder markings, which are in the shape of a butterfly with both the upper and lower wings distinctly outlined and marked with dots inside the outline. Back markings consist of a vertical line down the spine from butterfly to tail with a vertical stripe parallelling it on each side. These three stripes are well separated by stripes of the ground colour. There is a large, solid blotch on each side, encircled by one or more unbroken rings. Side markings are the same on both sides. There is a double, vertical row of buttons on the chest and stomach. Hocks are the same colour as the markings.

MACKEREL TABBY: markings are dense, clearly defined, narrow pencillings that encircle the body. Legs are evenly barred with narrow bracelets coming up to meet body markings. Tail is barred. Necklaces on neck and chest are distinct, like so many chains. Head barred with an 'M' on the forehead. Unbroken lines run back from the eyes. Lines run down the head to meet the shoulders. Spine lines run together to form a narrow saddle. Hocks are the same colour as the markings.

TORTIE TABBY: this is a brown, silver, or blue tabby with patches of varying shades of red or cream in its coat.

SPOTTED TABBY: markings on the body are spotted. They may vary in size and shape, but preference is given to round, evenly distributed spots. Spots should not run together in a broken mackerel pattern. A dorsal stripe runing the length of the body to the tip of the tail is considered a serious fault. The markings on the face and forehead shall be typically tabby markings. The underside of the body has 'vest buttons.' The legs and tail are barred.

TICKED TABBY: body hairs are ticked, but free of stripes, or blotches, except for a darker, dorsal shading. Lighter underside may show tabby markings. Face, legs, and tail must show distinct tabby striping. Cat must have at least one distinct necklace.

Pointed Patterns

On pointed cats the basic colour is confined to the face, ears, legs, and tail. The body is usually pale cream, fawn, or white. The latter may have either a bluish, creamy, ivory, or glacial overtone. Body colour and point colour are wedded in the pointed cat. For example, a blue point must have a bluish white, not a cream or a fawn, body.

NON-TABBY POINTED COLOURS Blue, blue tortie,[5] chocolate, chocolate tortie, red, lilac, lilac tortie[5], seal, tortie.

TABBY POINTED COLOURS Blue, blue tortie,[6] chocolate, chocolate tortie, cream, lilac, lilac tortie, red, seal, seal tortie.

Other Patterns

BICOLOUR: a white cat with unbrindled patches of one of the following colours: black, blue, red, or cream. Also, a white cat with patches of blue cream, tortoiseshell, or one of the tabby, shaded, or smoke colours.

BLUE CREAM: blue mingled or patched with shades of cream. The patches are clearly defined and well broken on the body and extremities.

TORTIE AND WHITE: a white cat with unbrindled patches of black and red. White predominates on the underparts.

BLUE TORTIE AND WHITE: a white cat with unbrindled patches of blue and cream. White predominates on the underparts.

TORTOISESHELL: unbrindled patches of red and cream combined with some other colour such as black or chestnut. The patches are clearly defined and well broken on the body and extremities. A blaze of red or cream on the face is desirable.

VAN: a white cat whose colour is confined to its head, tail, and legs. One or two small, coloured patches are permitted on the body.

[1] The American Cat Fanciers' Association calls this colour frost.
[2] In the Devon Rex and Oriental Shorthair breeds this shading is called silver, which is not the same as the colour chinchilla silver that is found in the Exotic Shorthair and the Persian.
[3] When the basic colour is red, this colour is also known as shell cameo.
[4] When the basic colour is red, this colour is also known as shaded cameo or red shaded.
[5] These colours are called blue cream and lilac cream in some breeds.
[6] This colour is called blue tortie lynx in some associations.

Addendum

HOW NEW BREEDS AND COLOURS ARE ACCEPTED

A new breed or colour must meet certain requirements before it can qualify for championship competition. First, the breed must be accepted for registration. In order for this to happen, a certain number of breeders (anywhere from six to twelve, depending on the association) must certify that they are working with the new breed, and a proposed Standard—along with several photos of representatives—of the breed must be submitted to an association's executive office. An association may also request that breeders bring cats from the new breed to a board meeting. If the board of directors is satisfied that the proposed new breed is sufficiently distinct from existing breeds and that it is free from genetic or health complications, then the board will grant registration status.

At this point most associations will allow the new breed or colour to compete in the provisional class at shows. This gives judges a chance to become familiar with the breed, and it gives people involved with the breed a chance to do a little public relations work for their cats.

Finally, after a minimum number of persons (as many as twenty-five, depending on the association) is verifiably working with the breed, has registered anywhere from fifty to one hundred representatives of that breed, and the required number of cats has been shown in provisional classes, the breed is advanced, with board approval, to championship status. This process takes, on average, from four to seven years, depending on the association.

CORRESPONDENCE BETWEEN COAT COLOUR AND EYE COLOUR

In several associations eye colour must conform to coat colour in breeds where more than one eye colour occurs. When this rule is enforced, the following correspondences prevail:

American Shorthair/American Wirehair

Eye Colour	*Coat Colour*
blue	white
odd eyed	white
green/blue-green	chinchilla, shaded silver
green or hazel	silver tabby
brilliant gold	all other colours

British Shorthair

Eye Colour	*Coat Colour*
blue	white
odd eyed	white
green or hazel	silver tabby
gold or copper	all other colours

Cornish Rex

Eye Colour	*Coat Colour*
blue	white
odd eyed	white
green/blue-green	chinchilla, shaded silver
green or hazel	silver tabby
gold or copper	all other colours

Devon Rex

Eye Colour	*Coat Colour*
blue	white
odd eyed	white
green/blue-green	chinchilla
green or hazel	silver tabby
gold or copper	all other colours

Maine Coon Cat

Eye Colour	*Coat Colour*
blue	white
odd eyed	white
green, gold, copper	all other colours

Manx/Cymric

Eye Colour	*Coat Colour*
blue	white
odd eyed	white
green/blue-green	chinchilla, shaded silver
green or hazel	silver tabby
brilliant copper	all other colours

Persian/Exotic Shorthair

Eye Colour	*Coat Colour*
blue	white
odd eyed	white
green/blue-green	chinchilla, shaded silver, chinchilla golden, shaded golden
green or hazel	silver tabby
brilliant copper	all other colours

Scottish Fold/Scottish Fold Longhair

Eye Colour	*Coat Colour*
blue	white
odd eyed	white
green/blue-green	chinchilla, shaded silver
green or hazel	silver tabby
brilliant gold	all other colours

Turkish Angora

Eye Colour	*Coat Colour*
blue	white
odd eyed	white
amber	all other colours

Care and Housekeeping

BASIC SUPPLIES

According to Russian folklore, a person who brings home a cat should throw it immediately onto the bed. If the cat settles down promptly, that means it will stay with its new owner. Perhaps this works in Russia, but cats are more apt to become homelovers if their new owners have laid in some basic supplies and have conducted a scrupulous safety check of the premises. First the supplies.

Litter tray. At least one. Roughly nineteen by fifteen by four inches. Litter trays come in several styles: open, enclosed, or outfitted with a raised, detachable rim that helps to contain litter when the feet hit the sand. Whatever the style, a tray should be steadfast, durable, and washable.

Litter. 'Absorbent' and 'dust free' are the buzzwords here. Most brands are. Some also contain deodorant—whose efficiency is in the nose of the beholder.

Litter scoop. At least one. The sturdier the better. Some of the thinner kinds snap too easily. Don't be caught without a spare.

Litter tray liners. Convenient for quick packaging and disposal of the entire contents of the tray. Optional at home; most desirable during hotel stays.

Food and water dishes. Reusable plastic can retain odours even if it's washed carefully. Disposable plastic is a rude joke on the environment. Glass or metal dishes and bowls are the proper choice. Glass should be sturdy enough so that it won't break, crack, or chip if a cat knocks it over. Glass and metal should be solid enough so that they aren't likely to be tipped over. Vinyl place mats underneath food and water dishes will protect the surface where a cat eats.

Scratching post. Better than Scotch Guard for protecting furniture. Provides an acceptable fabric on which a cat can exercise its natural tendency to scratch. The post should be well anchored so that it won't tip over when a cat uses it, and tall enough so that cats can stretch themselves while scratching. The scratching surface should be made from a strong, stalwart material like sisal or hemp.

Grooming tools. A good currying should be part of every cat's routine—daily for some longhairs that are going to shows, less frequently for housebound shorthairs. Cats enjoy being groomed, especially if they're introduced to the routine when they're young. Cats also benefit internally from being groomed because the more dead hair that's removed from their coats, the less they'll swallow when they groom themselves, and the fewer hair balls they'll develop. Pet shops or vendors at cat shows carry a full arsenal of grooming aids: shampoos and rinses, nail clippers, brushes, combs, powders, ointments, sprays, hair dryers, grooming tables, cotton wool balls, and so forth. If the pet shop doesn't have cotton wool balls and buds, the chemist's will.

Toys. The pet shop, cat show vendor, and supermarket stock a generous selection of feline diversions. Cats especially like plastic balls with bells inside, but the ball should be sturdy enough so that the cat can't remove the bell and swallow it. A few of a cat's other favourite things include small stuffed toys, preferably in the shape of mice, and the occasional dose of catnip straight. Again, the cute, little eye on the toy mouse should not be loose, or it may wind up in the cat's stomach. A most popular toy is the Kitty Tease, which looks like a miniature fishing pole with a small bow tied to the end of the line. While the owner dangles the bow in the air, cats display their natural athletic ability by leaps and bounds.

Shop bought toys are not the only ones that cats enjoy. A crumpled piece of paper, an empty film canister, a cardboard box turned upside down with holes cut at either end, a plain brown paper bag, a pen sitting on a table . . . the possibilities are limited only by an owner's and a cat's imaginations. But shop bought or homemade, toys should not have dangling

Grooming equipment for every coat length

strings that cats might swallow or become entangled in, loose bits or pieces they can chew off and ingest, or sharp edges on which to get cut. Cellophane, plastic wrap, and aluminum foil should be avoided always.

Beds. Even when cats are given elaborate beds, they may want to sleep somewhere else—on a window sill or comfortable chair or their owners' pillows. Many people wait until a cat has chosen the spot where it wants to sleep before buying a bed and putting it there.

Cage. The person with one cat has little need for a cage. The thoughtful, multiple cat owner scarcely needs cages either. The only times a cat might need to be caged are: from the time it's born until the time it's mastered toilet training, when it needs to be isolated because it's sick, or when it has just been brought into a new cattery and its owner wants to be satisfied that it isn't infectious before letting it meet the other cats. Most breeders recommend a three-week isolation period in this case. If possible, sick cats or new cats in isolation should have the run of a small room—of which other cats cannot get within sniffing distance. Hands, dishes, and water bowls should be scrubbed and disinfected carefully after shut-ins have been petted or fed, and these cats should always be last in the feeding queue.

THE MENU

From a cat's perspective, food is *the* most important item on the shopping list. Before people bring a new cat home, they should find out what it has been eating, and, if its diet has been sound, should continue with that product. If they choose to deviate from an established regimen, they should introduce new food a little at a time in increasing amounts for a week to ten days until the switchover has been accomplished without fuss, or hunger strikes.

The supermarket or pet-supply shop provides an extensive menu that will suit any cat's palate and nutritional requirements. Companies that manufacture the many brands of cat food must satisfy an exacting set of conditions—and usually use ingredients that would be acceptable in the human food chain. Trading Standards legislation must be complied with—with respect to identifying ingredients and substantiating nutritional claims made on pet food labels. Most cat foods provide 100 percent complete nutrition for a particular stage or for all stages of a cat's life. Any food that delivers complete and balanced nutrition for all

Cats often find empty baskets inviting

stages of a cat's life is a safe choice. It will provide the vitamins, minerals, and other nutrients a cat normally requires.

With so many products available, there is no excuse for a cat becoming addicted to one kind of food to the exclusion of all others. Owners should vary the menu from time to time, switching around from beef, chicken, turkey, and fish in either fresh or tinned form. Cheese and eggs can also be used to enliven the menu and are enjoyed by many cats.

HOW MUCH TO FEED

Contrary to marketing clichés, cats eat to satisfy their energy needs first, not their finicky palates. Energy, while it is not a nutrient itself, is a vital property of the three classes of nutrients: proteins, fats, and carbohydrates.

Cats can neither create nor destroy energy. They can, however—through the series of chemical reactions known as metabolism—intercept, convert, and distribute the energy contained in food. The National Research Council estimates that the metabolizable energy[1] needs of cats range from 250 kilocalories per kilogram of body weight for ten-week-old kittens to 70 kcal/kg of body weight for sedentary adults fifty weeks of age or older. In plain English that's 113 Calories[2] of metabolizable energy per pound of body weight for kittens and 32 Calories per pound for couch potatoes. A more active adult requires 36 Calories of metabolizable energy per pound; pregnant females need 45. Despite some breeders' agitated endorsements of vitamin potions, nutritionists report that pregnant females need more Calories, not more vitamins.

Every cat should have its own feeding dish

People who add vitamins to canned food are not only wasting money, they also risk throwing the existing vitamin balance in the food out of kelter. This could prevent a cat from absorbing some of the essential vitamins that were already present in the food.

Among the three types of cat foods—dry, semimoist, and canned—there is more gross energy and, hence, more metabolizable energy by weight in dry food than in the others. Accordingly, a ten-pound, inactive, adult cat would satisfy its daily metabolizable energy requirements by consuming approximately 3.5 ounces of dry food, 3.8 ounces of semimoist food, or 11.9 ounces of canned.

Fresh water should be available to cats always. When most kittens reach twelve weeks, they have outgrown the need for milk. As they mature, they no longer manufacture the enzymes required to metabolize milk. Once this occurs, milk may upset most cats' stomachs.

Kittens should be fed three times a day until they are six months old, and twice a day until they are a year old. From then on, one meal a day is sufficient—especially if cats have dry food on which to nibble. If there is no one at home to serve lunch to a kitten, set

[1] Metabolizable energy is the difference between the gross energy that goes into a cat as food and the wasted energy that goes out of a cat in its faeces and urine.

[2] Kilocalorie, when shortened to Calorie, is uppercased. For example, the five-hundred-plus calories (sic) in a fast-food cheeseburger are actually kilocalories and should be spelled Calories. A small *c* calorie, a thousand of which make up a kilocalorie, is the amount of heat energy needed to raise the temperature of one gram of water one degree centigrade.

out a bowl of dry food next to the kitten's water bowl before leaving for work.

The amount of canned food given to kittens should equal the amount they will eat during the first thirty minutes after they have been fed. For a twelve-week-old kitten, that's two to three tablespoons of canned food at room temperature. Pick up and discard any food not eaten in thirty minutes. If it is more convenient to feed dry food exclusively, select a product with the lowest ash content to minimize the possibility that a kitten will develop urinary problems later in life. Again, be sure the dry food is nutritionally complete, and observe the feeding instructions on the packet, especially about the supply of drinking water.

Food dishes should be washed after every meal. Water bowls should be washed daily.

THE CAT-PROOF HOUSE

Before bringing a cat home new owners should look at their houses the way they would if they were adopting an inquisitive two-year-old baby with super athletic ability. Cats are natural hunters. They are also natural explorers, wanting to investigate new objects, new openings, and whatever catches their eye in their domain. Therefore, the doors to any rooms that are out of bounds should be closed. Any small, breakable, or valuable items in the rooms a cat will be visiting should be safely out of reach. The cat should not have access to unscreened, open windows, and all window screens should be secure. Owners should see that no electrical cords are frayed; and if a cat develops a taste for them, they should be unplugged when not in use or wrapped in heavy tape or covered with plastic tubing, which can be purchased at an car supply shop. Unused electrical outlets should be fitted with the plastic, plug-in covers used for children.

In the kitchen and bathroom, keep all chemicals, cleaners, and toilet articles in cabinets that can be locked or closed securely. Keep the lids on all waste bins fastened. It is also a good idea to keep the toilet seat lid down. In the dining room, owners might want to take the table cloth off the table until a cat learns that climbing certain mountains is unacceptable.

In all rooms make sure there aren't any poisonous plants within the cat's reach. Some of the more common house plants that are poisonous to cats are: poinsettia, philodendron, caladium, dieffenbachia, English ivy, hydrangea, Jerusalem cherry, mistletoe, and holly. A veterinary surgeon can supply a more complete list.

WELCOMING A NEW ARRIVAL

After a person has bought every item on the shopping list and a few impulse items as well, has filled the litter tray with a couple of inches of litter, and has placed the tray in a convenient place, it's time to bring the new cat home. Whenever possible, this should be done at the start of a weekend or holiday when there's more time to spend with the newcomer.

Orientation can be a trying experience for a cat, and especially for a kitten. Normally a kitten has been taken away from mother, playmates, and the only home the youngster has ever known. Some cats adjust easily. After they've been taken from their carriers and placed in their new litter trays, they look around as if to say, 'Nice place. What's for dinner?' But other cats—the majority, if the truth be known—are not so self-possessed. Don't be surprised if a cat acts timid at first, looks around, then dives under the sofa. Pull up a chair and a cup of coffee and carry on watching television or reading the newspaper as though it were a normal day. The calm will be reassuring, and the cat's curiosity will prevail. No cat has ever permanently refused to come out from under a sofa. Once a cat has mastered the immediate surroundings—even if they comprise the underside of a couch—a natural instinct to explore will beckon. There's plenty of time for getting acquainted then.

The transition to a new home will go more smoothly if the cat's former owner can provide one of its favourite toys, a sleeping blanket, or even a small amount of soiled litter to sprinkle in the cat's new tray. These items give off familiar, comforting smells.

If there are other animals at home, do not include them in the welcoming party. Close the door to the room the cat will be exploring initially, or confine the other animals to another section of the house. Cats need to develop a sense of trust toward a new owner and a sense of comfort in new surroundings. This happens more easily if there are no distractions or challenges from other pets wanting to get acquainted with the cat.

A cat being introduced to a multi-pet household should spend the first few days and nights in a room or rooms with a closed door. Most breeders recommend that other cats should not even be allowed to sniff under the door and possibly transmit germs until three weeks have passed. Then allow the newcomer a few more days to make the acquaintance of the other four-legged members of the house by exchanging greetings with them under the door. If they meet each other this way before they meet face to face, chances are the introductions will be less fraught with peril.

Young children can pose challenges to a cat's safety and sense of security. Explain to children that they should be careful to watch where they walk and play

The Household Cat: non pedigree cats are judged in household pet classes, where beauty, cleanliness, and personality are decisive

when the cat is around. Caution them not to pick the cat up if they are not old enough to handle the cat properly. Cats should always be supported forward and behind when they are being held or carried. Explain, too, that cats are often frightened by loud, unfamiliar sounds. Ask children to speak and play quietly until the cat gets used to them. Reinforce this advice by setting a good example for the children to follow.

The first place a cat's feet should touch in a new home is in the litter tray. Ninety-nine-point-nine percent of all cats have been thoroughly trained in the use of the tray by the time they are twelve weeks old, and even in unfamiliar surroundings a natural instinct for cleanliness will direct a cat to the tray—providing that he knows where it is. Always keep the tray in the same place, somewhere that is quiet and easy for the cat to find. For the first few days after its arrival, place the cat in the tray after meals and naps to reinforce natural instincts. And when the cat uses the tray, praise quietly.

If an accident occurs, clean the soiled spot with a disinfectant cleaner that contains neither ammonia nor phenol and sprinkle a bit of vinegar on it to remove odour. A cat's attention stray is about twenty seconds long, it will *not* serve any purpose to drag a cat to the spot for a scolding. If caught misbehaving, a stern *No!* is in order. When finished, the cat should be carried to the tray and shown where to conduct business. In the rare event that accidents are repeated, perhaps the litter tray is too far away for the cat's convenience. If your cat's territory covers more than one floor, there should be a litter tray upstairs and down.

Dirty trays are another cause of accidents. Cats are creatures of cleanliness and habit. All waste products, solid and moist, should be scooped out of the litter tray and disposed of each day. Replace discarded litter with a fresh supply as necessary. Once a week or sooner discard all litter in the tray, and wash the tray thoroughly with a mild, non ammonia-based cleanser.

Once a cat is comfortable with a particular kind of litter, stick with that brand. Switching litter products may upset the cat's reliance on the tray; and this, too, might result in accidents.

Accidents of another sort can be prevented by a little common sense. When closing any door in the house—the refrigerator door, cupboard doors, the washing machine or oven—check to see that the cat isn't on the wrong side of it. Keep sewing supplies out of reach. After ironing, put hot irons out of harm's way. When cleaning, rinse all cleansers and chemicals thoroughly from any surfaces the cat may walk on. What gets on the cat's paws usually winds up in its stomach. Keep the bathroom door closed when running hot water for a bath. In general, keep an eye out for any potential accident waiting for a cat to make it happen.

Usually cats will have had their vaccinations before going to their new homes. Thus, trips to the vet will be limited, under normal circumstances, to visits for yearly checkups and booster shots. There might be times, however, when a cat becomes ill and a trip to the vet is advisable. (See chart on pages 187-88)

Once a cat has adjusted to a new home, everyone—including the cat—will settle into a comfortable routine that constitutes one of the more civilized and pleasant aspects of life. A cat having the run of the house will probably want to sleep where the owner sleeps. When people are reading, a cat will want to help turn the pages—or to sit on them; and when people are watching television, a cat will occasionally try to tag the characters on the screen. A cat will, in short, help to lighten the task of getting through each day. It is our responsibility—and it should be our pleasure—to return the favour.

WIELDING THE FINE-TOOTHED COMB

Grooming is an essential part of owning a cat, and should begin when kittens are young. Although cats deserve their reputation for cleanliness and personal hygiene, breeders have produced some varieties—viz., Persians and other longhairs—with profuse coats that are thicker and longer than nature would have designed. And regardless of coat length, virtually all breeds shed. Regular grooming removes dead hair from a cat's coat, and eliminates the necessity of removing that hair from the furniture—or from the floor in the form of a hair ball—later on.

A good way to get kittens used to being handled and to make it more pleasant to handle them is to start by clipping their nails. Hold the kitten's leg in one hand. Gently grasp the kitten's foot between thumb and forefinger. Press the top of the foot with the thumb, spreading the toes until the nails are extended. With the nails thus accessible, clip each one carefully to avoid cutting into the quick—the visible, pink vein in the nail.

THREE IMPORTANT QUESTIONS

Q: Should I have my cat neutered?

A: Absolutely, unless the animal was purchased for breeding. When male cats reach maturity, they are inclined to spray their urine to attract females. This is an odour that no amount of vinegar will overcome. When female cats go into season, they will sometimes stop using their litter trays, and they will frequently keep the family awake at night with their calling. Most vets recommend neutering or spaying when a cat is between seven and ten months old.

Q: Should I let my cat go outdoors?

A: Only if you have a completely closed-in yard that your cat cannot escape from, other animals cannot enter, and fleas totally avoid or if you live in an isolated area and are prepared to cope with fleas etc. Otherwise your cat should remain indoors, where it's safe, dry, warm in the winter, cool in the summer, and is not likely to be hit by a car, victimized by a larger animal, or subject to the many accidents that befall outdoor cats.

Q: Should I get my cat declawed?

A: No, and most vets will refuse to perform this operation. One way to save your cat's claws and your furniture is by training the cat to use a scratching post. Training should have begun when the cat was four weeks old; but you didn't have the cat then, so if no interest is shown in the scratching post you bought, you'll need to do some remedial training. Rubbing the post with catnip may help but if not, wave a toy directly in front of the scratching post so that your cat's nails dig into the post as they grab for the toy. Two or three times after realizing how good it feels to sink its claws into the post, the cat will get the idea. Then wave the toy farther up the post so that the cat is encouraged to climb up to reach it. Play this game two or three times a day for a few days, and the cat will soon be climbing the post like King Kong going up the Empire State Building.

Giving the ears a light dusting with boric acid powder keeps them clean and protects them from ear mites. This remedy, which has been passed on by breeders since the 1940s, is still effective today.

Owners of shorthaired cats often think it is not so necessary to bathe their cats, but all cats do better with a good bath from time to time. With Persians and other longhairs, of course, it is important to comb and bathe more frequently.

Don't expect to get by with surface grooming just because you're going to bathe the cat afterward. Thoroughly brush and comb from the base of the coat outward until there is no dead hair coming off in the comb or brush. It is important in the Oriental breeds and the Burmese, where the hair is supposed to lie close and tight, to remove any loose hairs from the coat. Usually a rubber brush and hand stroking will do wonders.

Curlycoated cats need to be groomed also, but care must be taken not to strip their coats. Since the hairs are fine and not very thick, they could be pulled out with too fine a comb. A wire pin brush, the kind used on a delicate-coated show dog, is best here. Apply the brush carefully while blow-drying the cat after a bath. This will help to lift the hairs without removing them.

Never bathe a matted animal, as washing a matted cat will intensify the mats, creating more of a problem. When small tangles or mats develop in the coat, they can usually be broken up and removed with the fingers and the wide end of a metal comb. Never try to cut mats out with a pair of scissors. Most often it is the cat that gets cut. If a mat is too large to work out by hand, clip it off with a pair of electric clippers or ask for help from your vet.

Place the cat in a sink or bath that has a drain and a spray-hose attachment. Never leave a cat sitting in a tub of dirty water. Gently wet the cat all over from the head down, then apply shampoo. Tearless shampoo is always the safest kind to use. Lather the cat thoroughly—let the shampoo stand if the label says to—then rinse repeatedly until all shampoo has been removed from the coat. The quickest way to develop a dander or flakey condition on the coat is to leave dried soap (shampoo) particles behind—which never seem to brush out. Towel dry the cat to get as much water out of the coat as possible. This will cut down on drying time. Use a hair dryer, preferably one with a stand, and a metal comb to finish drying the cat.

New cat owners frequently ask how often they should bathe a cat. In fact, most novice exhibitors don't bathe their cats often enough. There is no harm done to the coat if a cat is bathed weekly. The coat actually improves with each bathing. All the loose, dead hair is gone, new growth is free to develop, and the cat remains in its show coat longer than it would have otherwise. Reluctance to bathe a cat often enough is a carryover from the days when breeders worried that too much bathing would remove hair from the coat.

Frequently handled kittens become more sociable

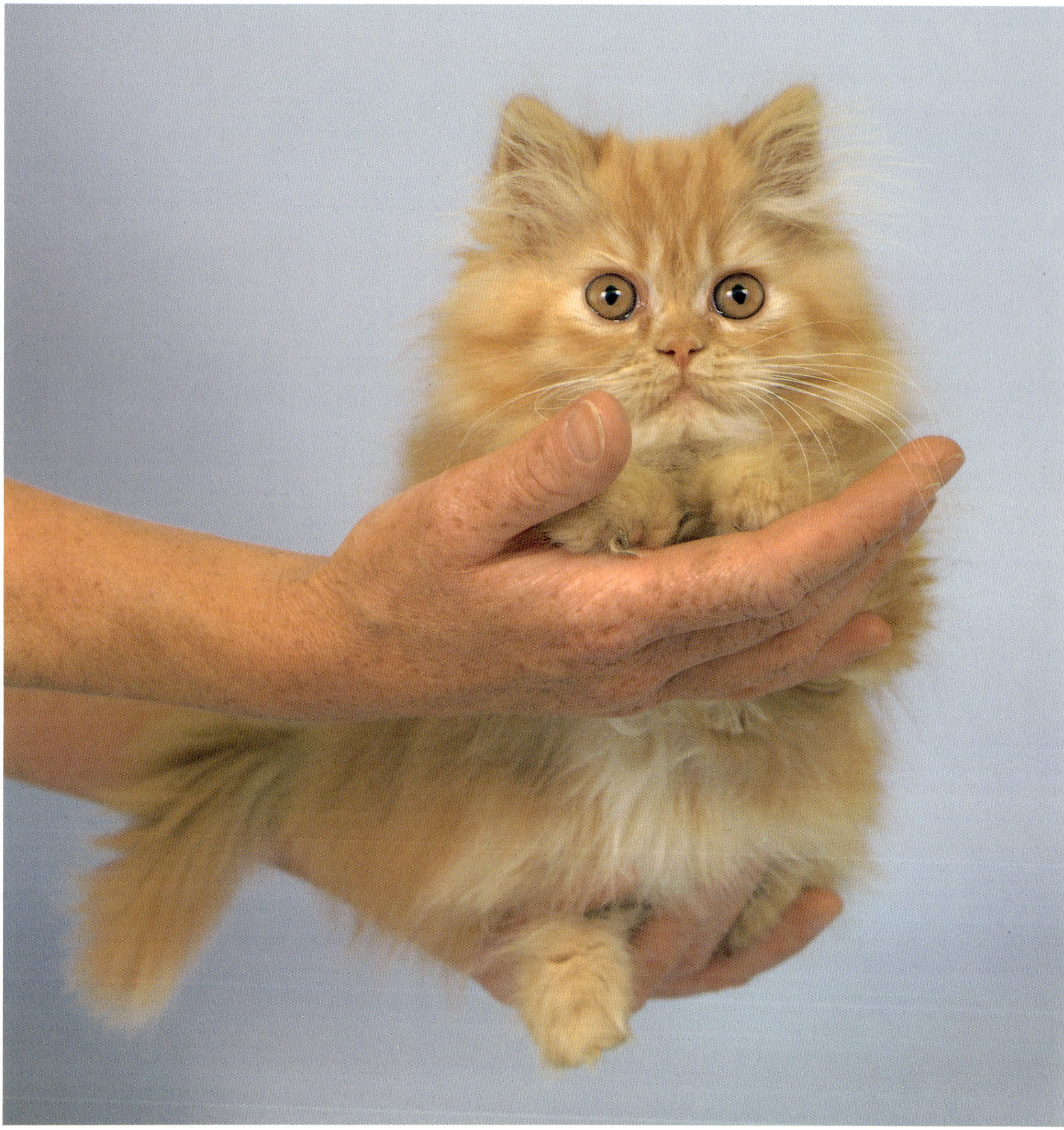

Cats should always be supported from the front and the back

Only dead hair is removed by bathing. By not bathing frequently enough, breeders were allowing the build up of dead coat. When they finally gave a bath, they produced a bag full of hair all at once, leaving the cat sparsely coated in many areas.

It is generally best to bathe a cat four or five days before a show. The concern about taking natural oils out of the coat by bathing is not well founded if the cat is confined indoors. Oils are intended to protect those animals who live outdoors from moisture and rain.

After bathing a cat, a little white talcum powder can be used to help keep the hairs separated. This must be brushed out–carefully until there is no powder left before a cat is presented for judging. The use of

GROOMING A PERSIAN

Clip a cat's claws before clipping the cat. Never attempt to clip a cat before testing the cat's reaction to the sound of the clipper. Hold the cat securely and hold the clipper away from the cat when you turn it on. If the cat remains calm, clip a small portion of the fur on its back, while holding the cat so that it's facing away from you. Always clip with the lie of the coat. Use a number 10 or number 15 blade for clipping. Start with a number 10 blade and switch to a number 15 if you find that there are some areas of the cat where the number 10 is not working as well as it should. Generally, a number 15 clipper is better if you are trying to remove a mat that is tight to the skin.

Clipping always proceeds more quickly if there are two people working. Since the cat is somewhat thin skinned, be sure to stretch the skin properly so that it is flat with the blade, or else you might nick the cat while you are clipping. Most breeders leave a tuft of hair at the end of the tail and on the lower legs.

coloured powders is not ethical since they constitute an attempt to deceive the judge. Using coloured hair dyes and powders or any artificial means to alter the cat to fit the standard is another dishonest practice. What one achieves by misrepresenting a cat is a total mystery. The cat can't reproduce the alterations, so how could a person have any real feeling of accomplishment with an artificial win?

After the show season is over, many Persian breeders prefer to clip their cats down into a lion cut. Electric clippers are the most efficient way to do this. Clip the entire neck, body and tail, leaving a pom-pom on the end of the tail. The cat is more comfortable this way, and there is no hair to mat or contribute to the formation of hair balls. What's more, the house is free from the tumbleweeds of hair that cats dig from their coats during the shedding season.

With any longhaired cat one must always be sure to keep the hair cut away and combed out on the hindquarters so that the cat can eliminate freely. Many cats have suffered severely from an impacted bowel because of matted-over hair, which shows a serious neglect on the part of the owner.

Once cats are cleaned and ready for the show, they should be kept in a cage on clean towels and bedding—at home and in their carriers as well. After spending all that time on preparation, one would not want to turn a cat loose and undo all that hard work.

COPING WITH EMERGENCIES

For all the modifications and improvements that breeders have made in the appearance of the cat, they have yet to produce a maintenance-free model. 'Til death do you part, there will be times—other than the yearly checkup—when you will have to take your cat to the vet or veterinary surgeon: when a cat begins sneezing or coughing and continues to for several hours; when a cat has an unusual discharge from the eyes or nose; when it scratches or licks a spot on its skin repeatedly and you notice hair loss and scaly, irritated-looking skin in that area; when it refuses to eat for more than two consecutive meals; when it has continuing attacks of vomiting or diarrhoea; when it becomes listless or feverish or cries when it is picked up; when it urinates frequently or urinates outside the litter tray.

Since feline urologic syndrome (more bluntly known as *blockage*) occurs most frequently in older, neutered males, any deviation in their routine around the litter tray should be cause for concern. When older males begin visiting the tray more frequently than usual—and when they seem to be staying in the tray longer than they normally do—they may be suffering from urinary tract blockage. Owners who notice this behaviour should check the tray to see if their males have produced a smaller-than-usual wet spot. If so, they should waste no time getting their cats to a vet, for urinary blockage is painful and sometimes fatal.

Some people are disinclined to visit the doctor even when they are in great pain. This stubborn, it'll-be-all-right-in-a-while attitude should not be imposed on a cat. Indeed, it is better to err in the direction of hypochondria than grim-lipped stoicism where a cat is concerned. Thus, a good practice to follow if any troubling sign becomes evident in a cat is this: when in doubt, call a vet.

CAT OWNERS AND VETERINARY CARE

The Pet Food Manufacturers Association profile for 1991 showed that 4.6 million of the 21.5 million British households owned a cat. This means that 21 percent of all British households share their lives with at least one cat. The most recent survey by the British Veterinary Association was conducted in 1986 and revealed that the vast majority of cats in England were seen by a veterinary surgeon at some time in their lives: 91 percent of cat owners had visited a veterinary surgeon with their current pet and 69 percent had had their cat vaccinated. Unfortunately, many cats are only vaccinated before being boarded and do not receive annual booster and check-up.

WHEN TO TAKE YOUR CAT TO THE VET

SYMPTOM	AT ONCE	NEXT DAY
Any deep wound or wound still bleeding after pressure has been applied	x	
Seems drowsy after ingesting a foreign substance	x	
Stops breathing after chewing on a poisonous plant	x	
Temperature raised beyond 105	x	
Temperature between 103 and 105, and other signs of illness present		x
Increased water intake coupled with excessive urination, diarrhoea, lethargy, or raised temperature		x
Decreased appetite coupled with coughing, vomiting, diarrhoea		x
Sudden weakness in hindquarters	x	
General lameness in any leg lasting more than three days		x
Red, ulcerated sore on the lips or other part of the body	x	
Abscess that is warm and painful to the touch	x	
Any general swelling that is warm and painful to the touch		x
Runny nose accompanied by raised temperature, pale gums, weakness	x	
Runny nose accompanied by lethargy, pus in the eye, or rapid breathing		x
Coughing accompanied by raised temperature, difficult breathing, depressed energy level		x
Foul breath accompanied by increased water intake, increased urination, excessive appetite, lethargy		x
Evidence of trauma accompanied by shortness of breath, raised temperature, pale gums, lethargy	x	

SYMPTOM	AT ONCE	NEXT DAY
Vomiting accompanied by lethargy, frequent attempts to urinate, raised temperature, bloody stools	x	
Diarrhoea accompanied by bloody faeces, raised temperature, vomiting	x	
Diarrhoea accompanied by dehydration		x
Constipation accompanied by straining and failure to defecate	x	
Abnormally thin stools accompanied by raised temperature		x

Reproduction

FIRST CONSIDERATIONS

Breeding a beautiful, well-mannered cat can provide joy, satisfaction, and the feeling of achievement that accompanies any creative endeavour, but there is a great responsibility attached to this enterprise. Too many unwanted kittens are produced by irresponsible, uncaring people who breed cats for the wrong reasons: to feed their own competitive egos, to make some quick cash, or to let their children observe the mystery of birth. Instead they should take their children to an animal shelter and let them observe the mystery of homeless animals and euthanasia. With as many as one hundred thousand purebred cats in the United States ending up in shelters each year, and with millions of healthy mixed-breed cats being destroyed annually for want of responsible owners, the decision to bring more kittens into the world is not one to be made lightly. For most people it is not one that should be made or even considered at all.

Persons inclined to breed cats should ask themselves what they plan to do with the kittens. If their answers include winning fame and fortune in the cat world, they should consider a hobby that does not involve living creatures. Competition in the show ring is such that few breeders become overnight sensations, and the laws of genetics are such that few, if any, litters are filled with nothing but show-quality kittens. Nor is it realistic to expect to make money selling kittens. *The time and expense required to raise animals almost always exceed the monetary return.*

We produce kittens not only for the joy they add to our lives, but for the kind of lives we can provide for them. If we cannot make them as happy as they make us, we shouldn't set about making them in the first place. The responsible breeder never produces a litter for which he or she does not already have good homes—or the resolute intention of providing one. Do not include among these good homes the promises from family members or friends who say they want a kitten. These promises rarely become reality, and the people who made them will offer a dazzling variety of reasons why they can't take a kitten when the time comes.

If you have not skipped to another section of the book by now, perhaps you are the rare individual who is responsible and serious enough to accept the stewardship of raising kittens. You don't need a degree in animal husbandry to do so, but you should understand that much is often lost in the translation of reproductive theory into live births. Breeders, therefore, need a working knowledge of the behavioural, gonadal, and endocrine relationships involved in reproduction as much as they need good stock and good fortune in their breeding programmes. They need to know what can go wrong in a planned mating, and to realize that what can go wrong most likely will. They also need to know what to do when nature's plans are at variance with theirs.

THE OESTRUS CYCLE

As the days begin to lengthen following the winter solstice, the cat's eye—in a way not yet understood—responds to the increase in light by sending a neurochemical message to the brain. The brain then signals the hypothalamus to discharge gonadotropin releasing hormone (GnRH). This substance, in turn, signals the pituitary gland to release two additional hormones.

One is called follicle stimulating hormone (FSH). It travels through the bloodstream to the ovaries, where it prompts the development of follicles and the maturation of eggs within them. Once the FSH level in the bloodstream is elevated enough to cause follicle development—generally two to four follicles per ovary per oestrus—ten to fifteen days pass before the follicles reach maturity.

The second hormone released by the pituitary gland is called luteinizing hormone (LH). A small amount of this hormone, which is also dispensed per instruction from the hypothalamus, is needed to ensure the final development and maturation of the ovarian follicles. As those follicles begin developing, the ovaries secrete oestradiol-17B, also known as oestrogen, the hormone primarily responsible for the behaviour of a cat in season.

OESTRUS BEHAVIOUR

Female cats, unlike dogs, display little if any swelling of the vulva and scant vaginal discharge when they go into season. Therefore, breeders have to rely on other clues to determine when females are ready to be bred. Those clues commence with the arrival of *pro-oestrus*, a one- or two-day interval during which female cats behave as if they have spring fever. They become listless and more vocal than usual, flirt with other cats of either sex, and tread intermittently with their hind feet. In pro-oestrus, cats often respond super-affectionately towards humans and the occasional table leg. If they were introduced to male cats at this time, females might allow those males to mount them, but penetration would generally be proscribed.

With the arrival of full-scale oestrus, the female is ready for serious courtship. Willing, eager, and frequently demanding, she will accept a mate without much preamble. She advertises her intentions by howling endlessly, or so it seems, and by going about most of the day in the lordosis posture: front end down, back end up, tail swept recklessly to the side. She remains in this agitated, sometimes comical, state for six to ten days, on average, going out of season if she is not bred or if she is bred and does not conceive.

The Queen's Cycle

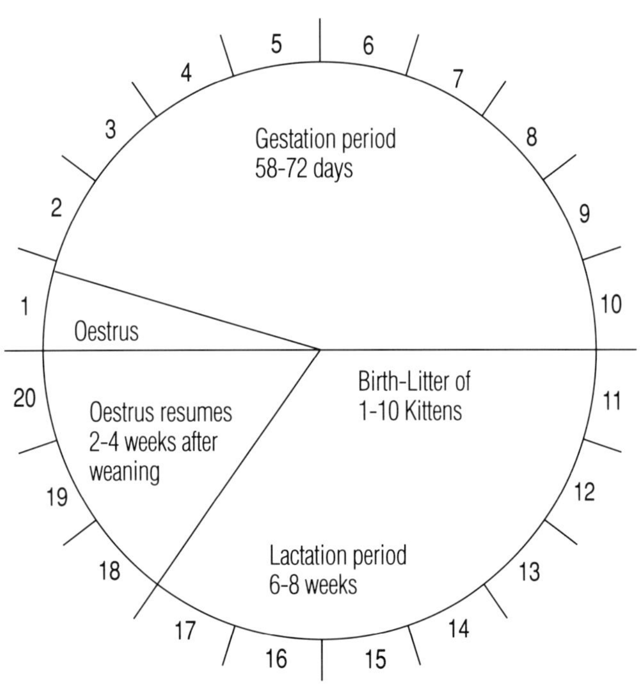

This cycle is repeated several times up to the end of March, when, for reasons not yet known, many females stop cycling for a spell. By June, unbred females resume cycling and continue doing so until autumn if they do not become pregnant. Towards mid-September most unbred queens are out of season. They remain in this fallow state, which is called anoestrus, until nature inaugurates the reproductive cycle once more the following January. However some foreign breeds remain in season for up to nine months each year.

OVULATION

Unlike all other mammals except the mink, ferret, and rabbit, the cat is an induced or reflex ovulator: females do not ovulate without copulatory stimulation. When the male achieves sufficient penetration, a signal is dispatched from nerve endings in the cervix to the brain via the nervous system. This signal is received by the hypothalamus, which then releases GnRH, causing the subsequent release of LH from the pituitary. When LH arrives in sufficient strength at the ovaries, it causes the follicles to rupture, releasing their eggs. This generally occurs between twenty-five to thirty-six hours after the mating-induced release of LH from the pituitary gland, but it can occur as many as fifty hours later. Once they have been released, eggs make their way into the fallopian tubes towards the waiting sperm.

SELECTING A MALE

After a female begins cycling, i.e., going into and out of season regularly, she ought to be spayed or else bred in due course. If she is allowed to continue cycling without intervention, she might develop cysts on her ovaries, and from those she might develop cancer.

The only females that should be considered for breeding are healthy, well-adjusted, show-quality females that have been in season at least once, are beyond ten months of age, and have done well enough at shows to convince their owners—and the judges who have given them awards—that they have a contribution to make to their breeds.

There are several ways to locate the cat of your cat's dreams: visiting shows to see the cats being produced by today's studs; pouring over the yearbooks published by cat associations; or scanning the advertisements in various cat magazines and newsletters.

No matter what the source, two genetic principles guide the selection of a stud. He should be from a family or line of cats that has crossed well with the female's line in the past, and he should be accomplished in producing those qualities the female lacks. There's little chance of improving eye colour in a female's kittens if the male she's bred to produces mediocre eye colour as a rule.

Genetics being the gamble that it is, there is no way to guarantee top-quality kittens in any breeding venture. The best a breeder can do is minimize the chances of failure. Towards this end, the chosen stud should be at best a grandfather because it's easier to gauge a male's reproductive quality by looking at his children and their children as well. Too many people rush out to breed to the latest winner. This cat may develop into a top producer one day, but for now it's more reasonable to assume that his father already has.

While breeders have little jurisdiction over a cat's genes, the practical aspects of reproduction are more easily controlled. An owner should not send a female out for breeding to any cattery that does not request a current health certificate for that cat (including a negative test result for Feline Leukaemia Virus, taken within the previous 72 hours) and additional proof that all her vaccinations are up to date. Nor should an owner send a female to a cattery that is unwilling to provide those same assurances regarding its stud.

The stud-service contract is another document that

Somali mother with her kittens

should accompany all breeding transactions. This needn't be a lengthy manuscript filled with meaningless words, but it should spell out the fee involved, the responsibilities of the stud owner while the queen is in his or her care, the length of time the stud owner is willing to keep the queen, what happens if the queen is not bred during that time, what happens if the queen is bred but loses her kittens prematurely after she returns to her owner, what happens if the queen has only one live kitten, and any other contingency that either party feels strongly enough about to put in writing. Such a contract, freely signed by both parties, is a legally binding document. Oral agreements are also considered legally binding, but, as the saying goes, they're not worth the paper they're written on. Beware of agreements that give the stud owner the 'pick of the litter'—these are often difficult to fulfil to the satisfaction of both parties.

GESTATION

The cat begins life as a one-cell being approximately 1/250th of an inch in diameter. Three days later that cell divides in two. Those cells divide seven more times in the next two days, at which point the cat has become a blastocyst. Eleven or twelve days after fertilization, the blastocyst attaches itself to the uterine wall. Though it is only four millimetres long, the blastocyst now contains the oxidative enzymes necessary to assimilate a variety of nutrients supplied through the tissues in the uterine wall.

Kittens greeting their first mouse. From Harrison Weir's Our Cats and All About Them (1889).

Days thirteen to seventeen are a time of maximum sensitivity in kitten embryos, when 90 percent of all congenital malformations that are going to happen start to happen. Most of these malformations are caused by genetic, spontaneous, or teratogenic mishaps. There isn't much breeders can do about genetic or spontaneous misfortune once they've bred their cats, but teratogens—extrinsic influences that disrupt normal embryonic development—do fall under a breeder's control. Griseofulvin (an antifungal medication used to treat ringworm), modified-live panleucopenia vaccines, excess Vitamin A, and some steroids are among the substances that are always potentially harmful to the developing embryo. They are especially threatening from days thirteen to seventeen of gestation.

Though statistics are few regarding cats, we know that as many as two thirds of all fertilized human ova fail to survive the first two weeks of life. There is no reason to suspect that the odds are more generous to feline ova. Nevertheless, when the embryo enters the period of greatest vulnerability to outside influences, nature instructs it to begin setting aside the cells that will be used to form gametes when and if the embryo grows up to be an adult cat. These cells, which seem to participate only in the formation of gametes, appear in the embryo about the fourteenth day of gestation and are sequestered outside the embryo in a region attached to the gut. They soon migrate to that place in the embryo where gonads will develop, entering the gonads about the twentieth day of gestation. The pregnant female carries not only her children but also the seeds of her grandchildren.

About three weeks after conception, a female's nipples will begin to swell and to turn rose blush in colour—a process which the British call *pinking up*. Soon afterwards the female begins pinking up all over, radiating contentment and good health. As her nipples are beginning to glow, a mother's children are scarcely more than half an inch long. Yet they contain the earliest recognizable form of the liver, respiratory system, limbs, sense organs, skull, urogenital structures, and tail. By this time the period of maximum vulnerability for the entire embryo has passed. Also passing are the critical periods for the brain and spinal cord, days twelve to twenty-one, and the heart, days fourteen to twenty-three. By day thirty-six the critical periods for the skull and vertebrae, sense organs, limbs, palate, and reproductive organs have passed, too.

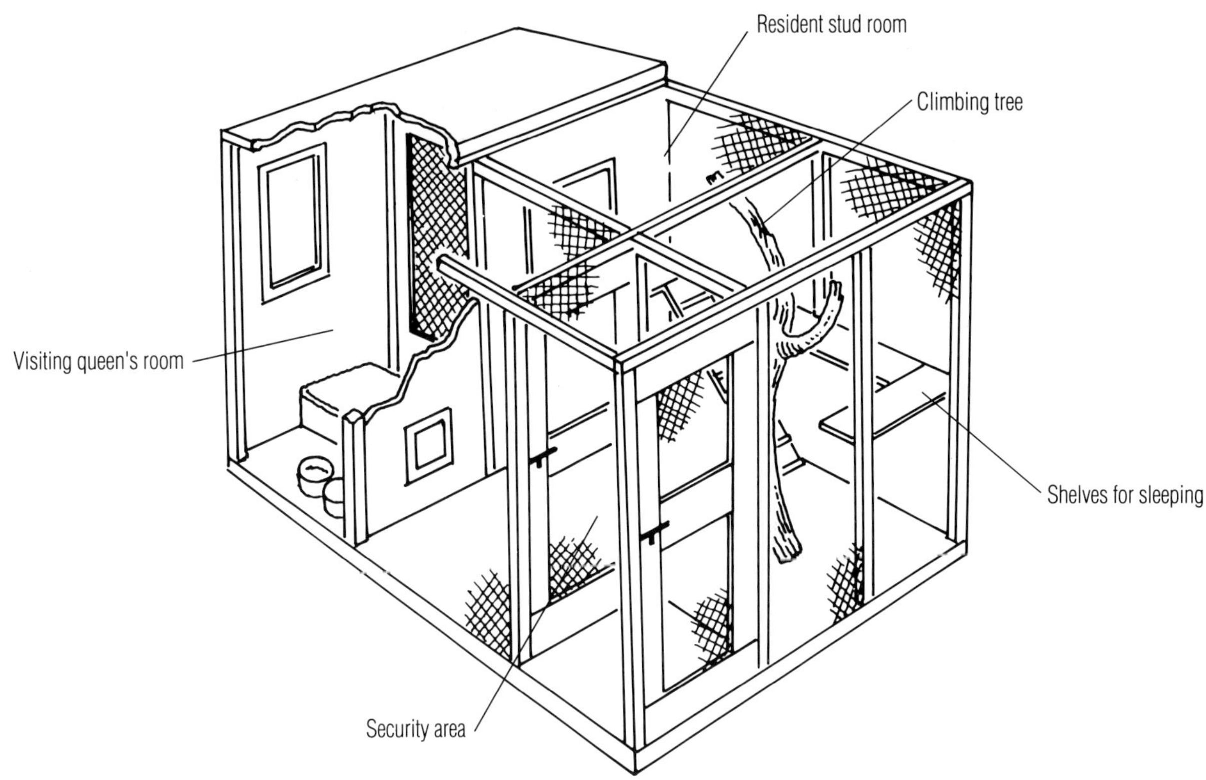

A spacious, multicompartment stud house

During this miraculous development the breeder is little more than a spectator, impatiently marking the days on the calendar. Somewhere between sixty-three and sixty-nine days following conception, on average, the first kitten will make its way into the birth canal. Until this great event, there is little that breeders need to do outside their normal routine of feeding and caring for their animals. A pregnant cat does not need extra vitamins, though she may well demand extra food, and will always appreciate a little extra loving at this time.

GHOSTS IN THE MACHINES

With luck and the cooperation of a competent stud owner, a novice breeder will become a grandparent without tribulation. Unhappily, problems can affect the first-time queen; and predictably, those breeders who produce subsequent litters will eventually have to cope with several difficulties.

To begin, some queens keep their seasons to themselves. When their hormones come calling, these females act as if they are much too refined for outward response. Or any response at all. Other females, especially first-time breeders, suddenly go out of season when they are sent to a male's residence to be bred. Still other queens, after breeding with one male by whom they produce nothing but pet-quality kittens, decide to bond with this mate for life. There are also females who mate willingly, but fail to become pregnant.

If females can not conceive of a way to frustrate the breeders' attempts at producing kittens, males are happy to oblige. A stud previously known to breed anything that moved—and a few things that did not—suddenly becomes discrete. Of course, the females he rejects are the ones he produced the best kittens with the previous year. Or a stud might continue to breed, but his conception rate will approach single digits.

THE SILENT HEAT

Ordinarily the signs that a female is in season are difficult to miss. But for some females a heat cycle is like the perfect crime, they leave no clues.

There is one straightforward solution to this problem: allow the female to live with her intended until their union has been consummated. This is more easily done by those experienced breeders who keep their own males. There are other, more scientific, ways of coping with silent seasons if extended cohabitation is not convenient. These include interpreting vaginal smears to identify changes in vaginal cytology that occur during the oestrus cycle; radio immunoassays to measure changes in hormone concentrations in the blood; and the direct viewing of the reproductive tract with a laparoscope. This latter technique has been used to monitor ovarian activity only with cats in laboratory-controlled reproductive studies. Vaginal smears and radio immunoassay may warrant consideration by the skilled breeder trying to cope with a valuable, top-winning female who gives no sign when she is in season.

THE STUD CAT

If breeding cats is a hobby, with a small *h*, and if you are fortunate enough to live close to someone with a superior stud that your female(s) get along with, you might breed a good cat or two each year and have fun showing them without having to own a male at all. But for several reasons, most of them having to do with convenience and with safeguarding their catteries from infection, many breeders choose to keep their own stud. The cautions exercised in choosing a mate for a female (see page 191) should be exercised to the *nth* degree in purchasing a male kitten, in buying or leasing a proven stud, or in keeping a kitten that you have bred for use in a breeding programme. In addition, a new breeder should not select a male that is too closely bred, that is, one with the same cats appearing over and over in his pedigree.

Male cats produce an especially high proportion of abnormal sperm cells, 25 percent on average, compared to males in other species. If a bull had more than 10 percent abnormality in his sperm, for example, he might not be considered a suitable prospect for stud. The more highly inbred a strain of cats, the more

A carpet helps breeding cats to maintain their footing and their concentration

The male often 'pedals' with his hind legs immediately prior to mating

abnormal sperm the members of that strain will produce. Sperm samples collected by electroejaculation from one inbred strain of lions revealed an abnormality rate approaching 75 percent.

With few exceptions, stud males cannot be permitted to have free run of the house. When they reach sexual maturity—generally between eight and sixteen months of age, depending on the breed—they begin to spray their urine to mark territory and to attract females. While female cats find something powerfully enchanting about male spray, humans simply find it overpowering. Thus the need to keep males confined. And to clean, deodorize, and disinfect their quarters daily.

The reason for confining a male is obvious, but there is no reason confinement should be abrupt. It is thoughtless to allow a young male to sleep in bed at night then to carry him into the basement one day and stick him into a pen. Far better to allow young kittens between weaning age and six or eight months of age to run free in the house during the day and to confine them at night in the quarters that will someday be their full-time home.

It is vital to provide a suitable pen for a stud male. At very least he deserves a large, walk-in enclosure equipped with a cat tree and shelves to climb, plenty of room to play and jump, adequate natural light, and a window from which to view the world. Remember that a male is destined to be confined for the duration of his breeding career, and perhaps his entire life. Think about this—and about how you would like to spend the rest of your life in a comparable space—when deciding how much room to give your male. Having been denied his freedom in order to serve his breeder's interests, a male cat should not be denied any comfort that can be made available to him. In fact, whenever possible a breeder should provide a stud male with an outside run.

BREEDING MANAGEMENT

In a cattery in which the stud male is not kept in solitary confinement, he will know the other cats in the house, and there should be little fuss involved when it is time for him to romance one of his ladies in waiting. When a new cat is introduced to the household or when a strange female is brought in for stud service, breeders must be far more vigilant chaperons.

Before placing a strange or a painfully shy female with a male, be sure to introduce them gradually. Coy, retiring, or aggressive females may need to be conditioned to accept a male's presence before they will accept his advances. They may also need to be protected from males who would rather fight than frolic. And this being the age of liberation, we should also mention that some males who suffer performance anxiety may need time to get used to the idea of having a new female in their living quarters.

These difficulties can most easily be surmounted if the cats are introduced to one another before the female is in season. There is no law against placing inexperienced breeders together. We have all heard stories about the nine-month-old male who impregnates the six-month-old female with whom he was running about the house. But many breeders prefer to have an inexperienced cat learn biology from an experienced one. Most often the male will be the teacher and the female the pupil in this situation.

School could begin with the female being caged for a few days in the male's quarters while the male is permitted to make her acquaintance through the bars of her cage. If the male's quarters are not large enough to accommodate a cage, the female could be placed in a large pen next to a male's, or be allowed to run loose in the room where his pen is. However the introduction is accomplished, the idea is to fit the female into the male's routine, not to make his majesty feel dethroned.

This conditioning should start a week or so before the female is expected to come into season. When you feel the time is right—and after you've clipped everyone's claws—allow the two cats to interact without restraint for fifteen to twenty minutes. Retire to a neutral corner during this time, but have a blanket and a broom handy just in case.

For many cats this is a very stressful time. Much understanding from the stud and the stud owner are necessary to bring about a successful mating. Some stud males and queens will tolerate a helping hand from humans. Others do not want any restraint or guidance, and some do not want people around at all. Contrary to normal procedure in the dog fancy, many cat matings are never witnessed, only heard.

HOW OFTEN IS ENOUGH?

If a female in season is compatible with her suitor, they should be left to their own devices whenever possible for three days. Queens respond to mating stimuli in a random fashion, and researchers have yet to determine whether one mating is sufficient to effect ovulation in all cats. It appears to be for some females, but it most likely is not for the majority of queens. What's more, cats who ovulate in response to a single mating this season may not do so the next.

Researchers further suspect that the vigour of

Tabby mother with her kittens showing the variable coat colours of the domestic cat

copulatory motion and the number of copulations per oestrus influence the strength of the message sent from the cervix to the hypothalamus, telling it to release the hormone necessary to bring about ovulation. Cats who do not ovulate after one mating were, perhaps, not sufficiently stimulated, and hence the hypothalamus was never told that it was time to release additional hormone. Or perhaps the hypothalamus did release the necessary LH, but its level in the bloodstream did not remain elevated long enough to ensure ovulation.

In a study conducted in the late seventies, four groups of twelve females were allowed to mate once on either the first, second, third, or fourth day of oestrus. Their conception rates were: 8.3 percent for the day-1 group; 16.6 percent for the day-2 group; 25 percent for the day-3 group; and 33.3 percent for the day-4 group. When three additional groups of females were allowed to mate three times a day on either the first, second, or third day of oestrus, the conception rate was 83.6 percent in each group. Therefore, the suggestion is that males and females be allowed to breed ad lib, if possible, for at least three days.

If a male is being used frequently in a cattery, and sexual exhaustion is a concern, a mating regimen in which cats were allowed to breed three times a day at three-or four-hour intervals during the first three days of oestrus has produced conception rates between 90 and 100 percent in several studies. This timetable ensures that functioning sperm, which only remains functional for two or three days, will be present in the reproductive tract in sufficient quantity when the female ovulates.

When two cats attempting to mate are not getting anywhere but tired—and the only result will be exhaustion on everyone's part—it is wise to separate them and wait until they are well rested before allowing them to try again. Some studs for some peculiar reason will attack a particular queen. In this case it is unlikely they will ever be compatible, and another stud should be chosen. Very often young, unproven males will attack a female or be too aggressive with their mates. It is important to supervise these early matings and to remember that it is never wise to use your hands or your feet to prise a male cat loose during a conflict. More than one stud owner has experienced a male's severe retaliation, and has ended up being bitten by her own cat. Such behaviour is most frequent from the foreign shorthair breeds, which are more hyper and excitable during breeding. Keeping a wide broom in reserve for emergencies is not a bad idea.

OESTRUS-INDUCING HORMONES

Breeders dissatisfied with nature's progress are often tempted to intervene in her affairs. Technologies are available for influencing the reproductive activities of female cats, and some breeders have experimented with various hormones designed to bring a reluctant queen into season. There are no formally approved pharmacological therapies for stimulating oestrus in female cats. Nevertheless, synthetic hormones have been used in the laboratory—and occasionally outside—to stimulate follicle growth and maturation and to bring about oestrus behaviour. Two synthetic gonadotropic hormones that appear safe and effective *if* they are used judiciously in consultation with a veterinarian are pregnant mare serum gonadotropin (PMSG), a potent compound obtained from the serum of pregnant mares, and follicle stimulating hormone pituitary (FSH-P), which is obtained from the pituitary glands of certain domestic animals.

These remedies are not for the beginner or for most experienced breeders, either. Reluctance is nature's way of telling us that some females should not be bred. The side effects of synthetic hormones are the drug manufacturers' way of telling us to be careful if we decide to use them. Treatment with FSH-P should not extend beyond five days because prolonged use might result in the formation of cystic follicles and interfere with ovulation. If the five-day treatment fails to produce a heat, the process should not be repeated, if at all, for another five or six weeks. A major problem with PMSG is that potency estimates of different preparations can vary significantly from one commercial lot to the next. There is, in addition, no available data concerning the safety of repeated PMSG use with the same queen.

Females can also be made to ovulate by exogenous stimulation. Two compounds effective in this regard are human chorionic gonadotropin (HCG) and gonadotropin releasing hormone (GnRH). The former is purified from the urine of pregnant women. The latter is a synthetic hypothalamic hormone. Neither substance will improve conception rates in queens receiving adequate mating stimuli, but they can be used in the cattery to ensure maximum ovulation in queens that didn't conceive in the past after being bred or with queens who produced only one or two kittens last year even though they had been observed breeding enthusiastically for several days. In these circumstances a person might want to take a female to the vet's for an injection of hCG as a safety measure after that female has been bred normally. The trick is to make sure you know when she is first bred so you can administer hCG right away. This is important because the female will still take at least twenty-four hours to ovulate, and you don't want sperm to go stale in the meantime. Normally you shouldn't need a second injection of hCG, but if you want to be safe, another shot could be administered twenty-four hours after the first one. Of course, you should allow a cat to continue mating after hCG has been administered.

CONCLUSIONS

In times past the activities of cat breeders were little noticed by the outside world except when the local club put on its annual show and a club member's cat got its picture in the newspaper. But times have changed, and with the increased concern over the surplus-animal population, some animal-welfare groups and municipalities are beginning to ask whether a person has the right to keep and produce as many cats as he or she pleases. They are also beginning to suggest that limits be placed on the number of animals per household, and that licenses and periodic inspections be required of people who wish to keep more than three or five or some minimal number of pets.

So far the cat fancy's reaction to these suggestions has been to increase the level of welfare advice to try and discourage indiscriminate breeding. One suspects that a stronger, more positive reaction ought to be forthcoming. For one thing, the cat fancy is still largely composed of individuals who breed cats on a limited and sensible basis. In 1990, most of the people who registered litters with the GCCF—registered just one or two litters. This level of activity should not be objectionable to any municipality. On the other hand, municipalities have the right—and cat federations have the obligation—to ask why anybody needs to produce more than twenty litters per year. If registries take the lead in policing their own members, as some registries are considering, the cat fancy will be spared the imposition of regulation from without.

DELIVERING KITTENS

The kittening box is a roll-up-your sleeves, get-your-hands-messy workplace where the faint of heart or the mildly curious need not apply.

Anyone with patience enough can learn to groom a cat. Lots of fanciers can recite pedigrees the way a minister quotes the Bible. Many people can buy a decent cat. But the person who makes the cat fancy go around is the one who is willing to get up every hour and a half during the night to check on a queen that's due to deliver; who is willing to miss a party or a relative's wedding to stay at home with an overdue mother; and who is determined enough to work for three quarters of an hour to get a weak kitten's heart going. It is sometimes the breeder's lot to cradle new life in a towel at three a.m. while a vet pulls kittens out of an anaesthetized female with a freshly made incision in her abdomen—and to get up every two hours around the clock to feed and clean kittens until they're old enough to take meals and use a litter tray on their own if their mother is unable or unwilling to nurse them.

During 1990 many thousands of people owned or leased females that produced litters of pedigreed kittens. No doubt most of these births were routine, as much as anything so miraculous can be routine, but it's the unexpected for which cat breeders have to prepare.

About the fifty-fifth day after a queen is first mated, she ought to be confined to a single room—preferably her owner's bedroom. Two or three days later, after she has settled in there, she ought to be confined to a cage in that room and be given generous periods of supervised free time. Left to her own instincts, a queen will sometimes want to have kittens in all the wrong places. If a queen needs assistance during delivery, a breeder shouldn't waste time coaxing her out from under a bed to provide it.

According to several textbooks, the standard gestation period ranges from sixty-three (or sixty-four) to sixty-nine days. Many experienced breeders begin taking their queens' temperatures on the sixty-first day after the first mating. If the temperature is where it should be for a day or two—around 101.5 degrees—then suddenly drops to 98 or 99 degrees, kittens will most likely arrive within twelve hours. Should the temperature be raised two or three degrees, call the vet at once.

The queen's delivery cage should be outfitted with one half of a large carrier or a cardboard box with three sides intact and the other side cut down, so that only a two- to three-inch strip is left at the bottom to prevent kittens from crawling out. Either of these makes a good nest in which the queen can raise her kittens. Both should be sprayed with a safe disinfectant and wiped dry before being placed in the cage.

Some breeders use cloth towels to line the kittening box, others use newspaper or paper towels. When they put this box into the cage, some breeders switch from litter to newspaper strips or paper towels in the litter tray in case a queen decides to start having her kittens there while the breeder is out of the room.

Queens beginning to get serious about delivering kittens signal their intent with a discharge caused by the passing of a placental plug. This discharge is followed before long by rapid breathing, trayting, deep purring, kneading with the paws, or frequent attention to the genital region. Breeders with longhaired cats should have clipped this area in advance. All breeders should have clipped their queens' nails about the time they were confined to their delivery cages.

Involuntary contractions soon follow the passing of the plug. When the queen begins to supplement these by bearing down in an effort to deliver, the breeder should note the time carefully. If the first kitten has not been born within an hour, call the vet and have a clean, towel-lined carrier ready.

When all goes normally, a dark, greyish-coloured bubble will emerge from the vagina. Once that bubble of new life appears, the clock should be reset to thirty minutes. If the queen cannot pass the kitten on her own by that time, take her promptly to the vet.

Sometimes a breeder can help pull the kitten free. Sometimes a breeder can damage the kitten in trying to do so. Never pull between contractions. Always pull with the contraction, and always pull gently.

Some breeders recommend giving the queen a shot of oxytocin at this point. This should be done only if a breeder has discussed the possibility with a vet in advance. Oxytocin should never be administered before a kitten is visible in the vaginal opening. A queen can die of a ruptured uterus is she's hit with a shot of oxytocin before her cervix is fully dilated, and it's no easy matter for a nonprofessional to tell when dilation has occurred. 'I never administer oxytocin before the first kitten is born,' says one breeder. 'If I have any problems before then, I'm off to the vet's.'

Once a kitten is 'on the ground,' as breeders say, the queen should begin licking it vigorously to clean it and to remove the placental membrane—or sack—surrounding the kitten. If the mother doesn't remove the sack from the kitten's face at once, do it for her so the kitten can begin breathing. The membrane should break and peel away if you rub the top of the kitten's skull gently with a small piece of clean cloth. If the membrane breaks, clean it away from the kitten's face. If it doesn't, take a pinch of membrane at the base of the skull between thumb and forefinger and pull it away carefully.

Hold the kitten face down in one prewashed and sterile hand while rubbing its back with a small, clean cloth. If the kitten is wriggling about and making a racket, give it back to its mother.

If the kitten is breathing with difficulty or not breathing at all, fasten a haemostat on the umbilical cord about six inches from the kitten. Grasp the cord on the side of the haemostat closer to the mother and pull gently. If the mother doesn't expel the placenta at once, don't waste time fussing with it. Cut the cord on the mother's side of the haemostat, remove the haemostat, dip the severed end of the cord into a bottle of white iodine, and try to revive the kitten. Aspirate any fluid in the kitten's mouth. Then hold the kitten in the palm of one hand, face towards you.

Make sure that the kitten's head is secure and

immobile between your thumb and forefinger. Place your other palm over the kitten's underside, with your forefinger over the kitten's heart.

Holding the kitten securely in both hands, swing your hands down abruptly a distance of two or three feet, massaging the rib cage over the kitten's heart with your forefinger as you do. Repeat this two or three times. Aspirate the kitten again, swing it downward abruptly between your hands two or three times more, aspirate, swing, aspirate—as often as you need to until the kitten begins breathing—or until it is sadly obvious that the kitten is not going to begin breathing at all. Do not think about throwing in the towel until at least half an hour has passed.

When the swing method does not revive a kitten after five or ten minutes, some breeders dip the kitten up to its neck into a bowl of very cool water and then into a bowl of very warm water in hope that the shock will kick start its breathing mechanism. Breeders who have discussed the possibility with a vet before hand sometimes put a drop of Dopram-V under the kitten's tongue to stimulate breathing at this point.

If a weak kitten does begin breathing on its own, give it back to its mother, but watch it carefully. If the kitten starts breathing slowly again or if it begins to feel cool to the touch, aspirate it again if necessary, massage it, and place it on a heating pad in a small box to keep it warm. Give it back to its mother in half an hour, but continue to monitor it carefully.

Meanwhile, the queen will normally be busy with other deliveries. Some queens chew the umbilical cords and eat every afterbirth compulsively. If not, cut the cords for them after five minutes or so, sterilize the severed end of the cord that is still attached to the kitten, and dispose of the afterbirth.

Be sure that all placentas are present and accounted for. A retained placenta can cause serious infection, may have to be removed surgically, and could mean that the breeder instead of the queen must raise the litter.

When the last kitten has been delivered, the queen will give an almost palpable sigh of relief and settle in to nursing her brood. At this point some breeders recommend giving the queen a shot of oxytocin to expel any placental material that might have been retained during the delivery. Ask the vet in advance about the advisability of doing this.

Monitor the kittens and their mother for another hour or so to make sure all kittens are nursing normally. If any are not, consult a vet or a good text on supplementary feeding and proceed accordingly.

THE DELIVERY SUPPLY LIST

1. The veterinary surgeon's emergency number
2. A generous quantity of soft cloths
3. An equally generous supply of towels
4. Small haemostat (presterilized in boiling water)
5. Scissors (presterilized in boiling water)
6. White iodine
7. Aspirator
8. Heating pad
9. Small box
10. Oxytocin
11. Dopram-V
12. Several syringes
13. An eye dropper
14. A clean, towel-lined carrier
15. A good text on supplementary feeding
16. Coffee

Showing

FINDING A SHOW AND OBTAINING AN ENTRY FORM

Prospective exhibitors who have never been to a cat show should visit one without their cats to see what showing is like. *Cats* or *Cat World* magazines, which are available at many newsstands, contain lists of shows throughout the United Kingdom or a show list covering the show year from 1 June to the 31 May can be bought from the GCCF office.

Owners who decide that they and their cats are ready for competition should write or phone the show manager to request a show schedule and an entry form for the show they've selected. Among other things, the schedule discloses the entry fee, show hall location, list of judges, and closing date for entries. The schedule also reminds owners that all their cats' innoculations should be current and prints information about show rules. It should be read very carefully. Shows often reach their quota before the advertised closing date, so it's best to enter at least two or three weeks prior to this deadline.

FILLING OUT AN ENTRY FORM

On the entry form, the exhibitor provides the name of the cat and that of its owner(s), and breed(s), its breed, colour, registration number, date of birth, parents, sex, the classes the cat will compete in. The details should always be copied from your registration or transfer certificate to avoid mistakes which could lead to disqualification after the show. If questions arise when an exhibitor is completing an entry form, show managers are happy to answer them at a reasonable hour. Once the blank is completed, the exhibitor mails it and the entry fee to the show manager. If confirmation isn't received within two weeks, the exhibitor should phone the show manager and ask politely if the entry has been received.

ENTRY CONFIRMATION

When the postman delivers the exhibitor's entry confirmation, it may contain a copy of the cat's listing in the show catalogue, and other information the show committee deems pertinent. The exhibitor should check the confirmation to make sure that all names are spelled correctly, that the cat's registration number is accurate, and that the cat or kitten is entered in the correct class. Many shows send out vetting in cards, tallies and admission tickets prior to the show.

PRESHOW GROOMING AND PREPARATION

'A cat kept in clean surroundings, well fed and cared for, needs very little preparation for the show pen.' This counsel, written in 1909, remains true today. Yet cats usually need bathing before a show. Some breeders prefer to bathe a cat several days in advance of a show to give the natural oils in the animal's coat—which may be removed by bathing—a chance to reappear. Others bathe their cats the day before a show. There is merit in both methods, and the way to find out which is best for a cat is by giving it a full-dress-rehearsal bath several weeks before the show and observing the cat for the next couple of days. If its coat looks great the day after its bath—and continues to look great for the next several days—the cat could be bathed between Tuesday and Friday of show week. If the coat looks dry or lifeless for a day or so after a bath but then regains its lustre, the cat should be bathed no later than Wednesday. If the cat looks fine the day after a bath but not so fine two days later, bathe as near to showtime as possible, preferably on Friday. Whenever a cat is bathed for a show, the owner should clip its claws on all four feet. Show rules and the judges' safety require this.

PROVISIONS FOR A SHOW

No matter how carefully a cat or kitten is bathed, it will need touch-up grooming—at least for its owner's peace of mind—at the show. Therefore, exhibitors should pack an assortment of combs, a brush, if it's part of the grooming routine, Q-tips, cotton balls, paper towels, facial tissues, grooming powder, if applicable,

A typical cat carrier

but not for use in the show hall, and any other accoutrements used in grooming sessions at home.

All entries are assigned a numbered pen where they remain when they are not being judged. Exhibitors are expected to bring a white blanket or white 'Vet-bed' type fabric for the cat to sit on. Cage size may vary from show to show, but most single pens are twenty-four inches long, wide, and tall.

Some shows offer double pens. For an extra fee the thoughtful exhibitor can order a double pen when sending in the entry form. This allows the cat more room to stretch out. The approximate dimensions of a double cage are twenty-four inches deep and tall and forty-eight inches wide. The exhibitor is also required to provide an open white plastic litter tray with litter, and a white drinking bowl. Cats are required to wear a cardboard tally round their necks on a narrow white tape or ribbon. The tally gives the pen number and can

The National Cat Club Show in Britain. At British shows the judges go from pen to pen accompanied by their steward to assess cats

In North American shows, cats are brought to the judging ring, where they are evaluated while exhibitors and spectators look on

be used to identify the cat if it escapes. A current vaccination certificate for Feline enteritis (Feline Panleucopaenia) is also required.

The number of incidental items packed for a show is a matter of personal comfort. Some exhibitors arrive with enough provisions for a month in the Kalahari Desert. Others bring only themselves, their cats, blankets and litter trays, a few grooming aids, a pen to mark the catalogue, and a good book. A few of the possible additions to that list include pipe cleaners or wire ties for fastening any loose corners of the pen, a towel on which to groom the cats, a can opener, adhesive tape, a first-aid kit, and the cat's favourite toy and food. Decorated pens are allowed at the Supreme show and prizes are offered for the best pens.

AT THE SHOW

Cats should be transported to shows in a comfortable, safe carrier, which are available at wholesale pet supply dealers, pet shops, and shows. The cat's journey will be more pleasant—especially if it is long or the cat is young—if the owner tapes a small litter tray to the floor inside the carrier. The rest of the carrier floor should be covered with a towel or blanket. In cold weather many exhibitors cover the outside of their carriers with fitted, quilted bonnets that resemble toaster covers. These covers, which shield the traveller from the cold, are available at shows or from companies that advertise in cat magazines. They can also be sewn at home, if the exhibitor is so inclined.

New exhibitors should arrive early for vetting in and at some shows obtain their cats' pen number and tallies, set up the pen, and get their cats and themselves settled in their new environment. The first order of business is arranging the pen with the blanket, a hot water bottle or heat reflecting pad under the blanket on a cold day, drinking water, a litter tray and the cat's favourite toy. Check the pen to ensure that it's fastened securely, the exhibitor should place the cat or kitten into the cage and take an admiring step back. Some exhibitors feed their cats as soon as the cats have finished exploring their cages. Other exhibitors, who fed their cats before bringing them to the show hall, wait until later in the day to provide food. Water should be available throughout the day.

The exhibitor should first check the catalogue to make sure that all the classes entered are correct. Judge changes are normally listed at the hall entrance and the list should be checked to make sure that a counter signature is not required if your cat is fortunate enough to win a challenge certificate. They should also check the catalogue to be sure their cat's name and all its biographical data are correct. If there are any mistakes, the master clerk should be told about them immediately.

JUDGING

In the United Kingdom cats are usually judged in their show pens by judges, accompanied by stewards, who visit each pen. The steward lifts the cat out of the pen onto a judging table, enabling the judge to examine the cat and decide on its merits. Both the judge and the steward disinfect their hands and the table after looking at each cat.

When each class has been judged, the judge enters the results on a results slip which is passed to the result table. One section of the slip is then placed on the awards board for the exhibitors to see how the judge has placed the class.

There is only one show in the United Kingdom which has ring judging. This is the Supreme Cat Show. Cats entered at this show must qualify by winning certificates or first prizes at Championship shows during the show season. Unlike normal cat shows there is only one class to be entered at the Supreme, as this is a knockout competition: each cat which wins its Open class is then considered for Best of Breed. The Best of Breed winners are taken back to the show ring and judged by a panel of three judges, so producing a Best of Variety winner in each of six sections: Longhair, British Shorthair, Foreign, Burmese, Oriental Shorthair and Siamese. There is also a section for the best of the Provisional breeds and non-pedigree cats.

Besides rosettes, medals are sometimes awarded to owners of winning cats

Individual shows are classified as either all-breed or specialist breed shows. In an all-breed show, all cats with Championship status may compete, but in a specialist breed show, only cats of the relevant breed may take part. Many shows have sections for Household Pets. These are non-pedigree cats that are also unregistered and have at least one unregistered parent.

The plate (left) was awarded for a top regional win. The bowl (right) was presented to the owner of the best cat in the show

CAT SHOWS IN GREAT BRITAIN

Most cat shows in Britain are held under the aegis, and according to the rules, of the GCCF.

There are three types of cat show—Exemption, Sanction and Championship. Exemption shows are held to help newly formed clubs acquire experience in running shows. They may then apply for a Sanction show licence. At Exemption and Sanction shows there are breed classes. Prizes are awarded for cats, kittens and neuters in first, second and third prizes. The GCCF may grant a licence for the staging of a Championship show to the organizers of Exemption and Sanction shows only when they have proved their competence at running such events.

A defining feature of all GCCF Championship shows is that entire cats over the age of nine months compete in open breed classes with cats of the same variety. The winner may be awarded a GCCF Challenge Certificate. At all Championship shows, adult cats may compete in their Open Class for a Challenge Certificate. Classes are divided into male and female. One certificate is awarded in each of these classes, and a cat placed first in the class does not automatically receive the certificate. This is awarded only if the judge considers the exhibit of sufficiently high quality to merit the award.

Three Certificates under three different judges, at three different shows are needed before the exhibit achieves the title 'Champion'. When this status has been won, the cat may be entered in subsequent shows in the Grand Champion Classes. Again, three Certificates at three different shows under three different judges are needed to gain the title Grand Champion. The same rules apply to Neuter Cats.

At the Supreme Show a 'Supreme' Certificate is awarded to the best entire cat and also to the best Neuter. From henceforth this prefix is used as part of any title the cat may win or has already won.

There are three principal cat shows held in Great Britain each year. The Supreme Show is held annually in May. The first Supreme was held in 1976 with the intention of starting a feline equivalent of the world famous Cruft's Dog Show. For this one show it is necessary for the exhibits to have qualified for entry by winning Certificates or first prizes at other GCCF shows.

The National Cat Club Show is probably the largest Championship Show in the world, with over two thousand entries. It is held annually in London at Olympia.

The Kensington Kitten and Neuter Cat Club show is held in London on the last Saturday in July. This club has a long history with many distinguished Presidents, including Constant Lambert and for the last fifteen years, Eric Wickham-Ruffle. This show regularly attracts visitors from all over Europe and Scandinavia.

It is not possible for United Kingdom shows to attract exhibitors from other countries because of the strict Rabies restrictions and regulations. All cats entering Britain must first spend six months in a quarantine cattery.

An international set of championship medals

Judging

The men and women who officiate at cat shows have demonstrated skill at breeding cats and a talent for exhibiting them. Prospective judges must have at least five to seven years consecutive breeding experience, depending on their association's requirements, before applying for admission to the judging programme. They must serve on show committees in several capacities and acquire their initial show-ring experience by clerking for judges at shows. Once accepted into the judging programme by their association's board of directors, judging trainees must pass examinations on breed standards and show ring procedures and apprentice successfully with certified instructors at a specified number of shows.

During a show, judges spend between one and two minutes evaluating each cat. They are often obliged to make more than two hundred of these ninety-second assessments per show, record their decisions in the judges' book, keep their impressions of the best cats straight in their minds—with the aid of a note pad—and pick the ten best cats in the show according to those ninety-second impressions.

By the time they carry a cat half a dozen steps from its cage in the show ring to the judging table, judges have already determined much about that animal. They know whether its coat feels dirty and tacky, or silky and clean. They know whether a cat is down on weight or too stout. They know whether it has the feel of an animal in peak show condition.

This author always has a quick look at a cat before taking it out of the cage. From then the judging process—a routine that does not vary from one cat to the next—is designed to confirm whether the first impression will be the final one. While standing the cat on the judging table, the author quickly runs one hand along the cat's spine from the shoulders to the base of the tail and from there to the end of the tail, feeling for kinks in the tail as he does. The tail length on most breeds that have tails should be equal to the length of the back. This quick, hands-on assessment reveals whether it does. Some judges bend the tail around to measure it against body length, but they lose some length in the tail in doing so.

Once judges put their hands on a cat, they should not move them more than necessary, for when they do, a cat is able to collect himself if he's in a mood to be difficult. Over the years the author developed a style of holding one of a cat's hind legs—the one farthest from the author's body—between the middle finger and forefinger of his left hand, palm facing inward, and one of the cat's front legs between the same fingers of the right hand. This enables the author to hold a cat at arms length to judge the top line and the belly line of its torso, to see whether its legs are in proportion to its body, and to roll the cat over in his hands while the cat is still in the air to check its underbelly and paw pads. Since cats do not always stand still to show off their finer qualities, the judge must put the cat into a position that allows the easiest examination.

As judges are handling a cat, they're constantly making evaluations, comparing that cat to its standard, a document that describes the ideal specimen in the breed (see Breeds section, page 37). Although each breed standard contains a scale of points that assigns a numerical value to eye colour, coat, head type, etc., those points are more of a guide to breeders trying to create a top-quality cat than they are to judges trying to evaluate one. No judge stands in the ring calculating how many points to award for each part of the cat. Anyone who did would end up being terminally confused.

This author believes it is easier to look for faults rather than virtues in judging a cat: not only the faults that are cause for disqualification according to the standard, but general flaws in the type or conformation of the cat. One assumes that the cat being presented to a judge meets the breed standard. It is the judge's job to discover where an individual cat's characteristics

IDEAL SPATIAL RELATIONSHIPS IN PERSIAN AND SIAMESE HEAD TYPE

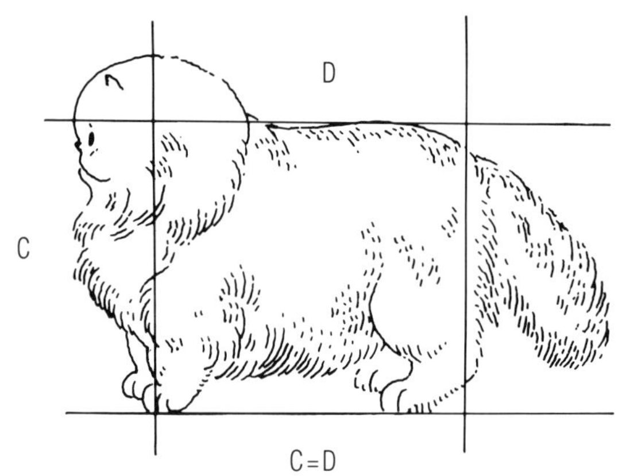

These dimensions above and at right apply to the American ideal of the Persian, Himalayan, and Exotic Shorthair. The dimensions below apply to the American ideal of the Siamese and other Oriental breeds.

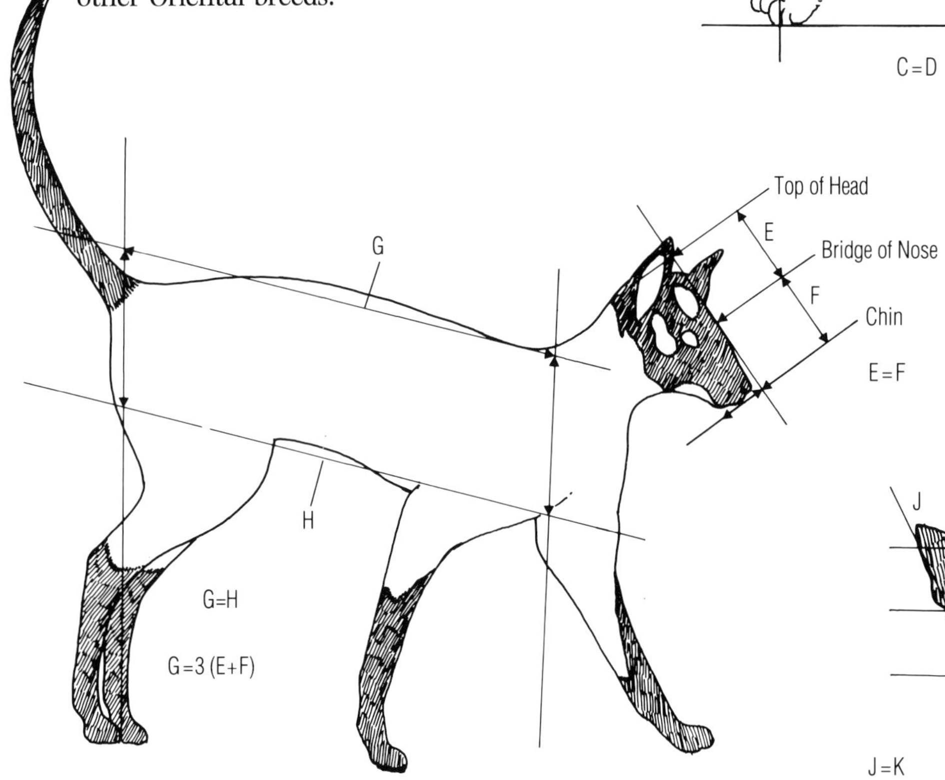

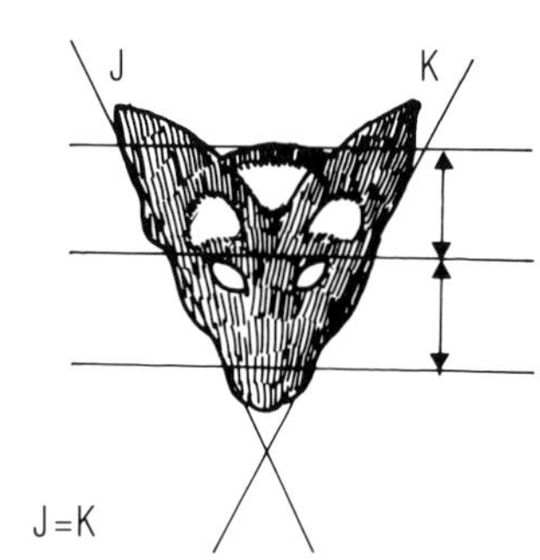

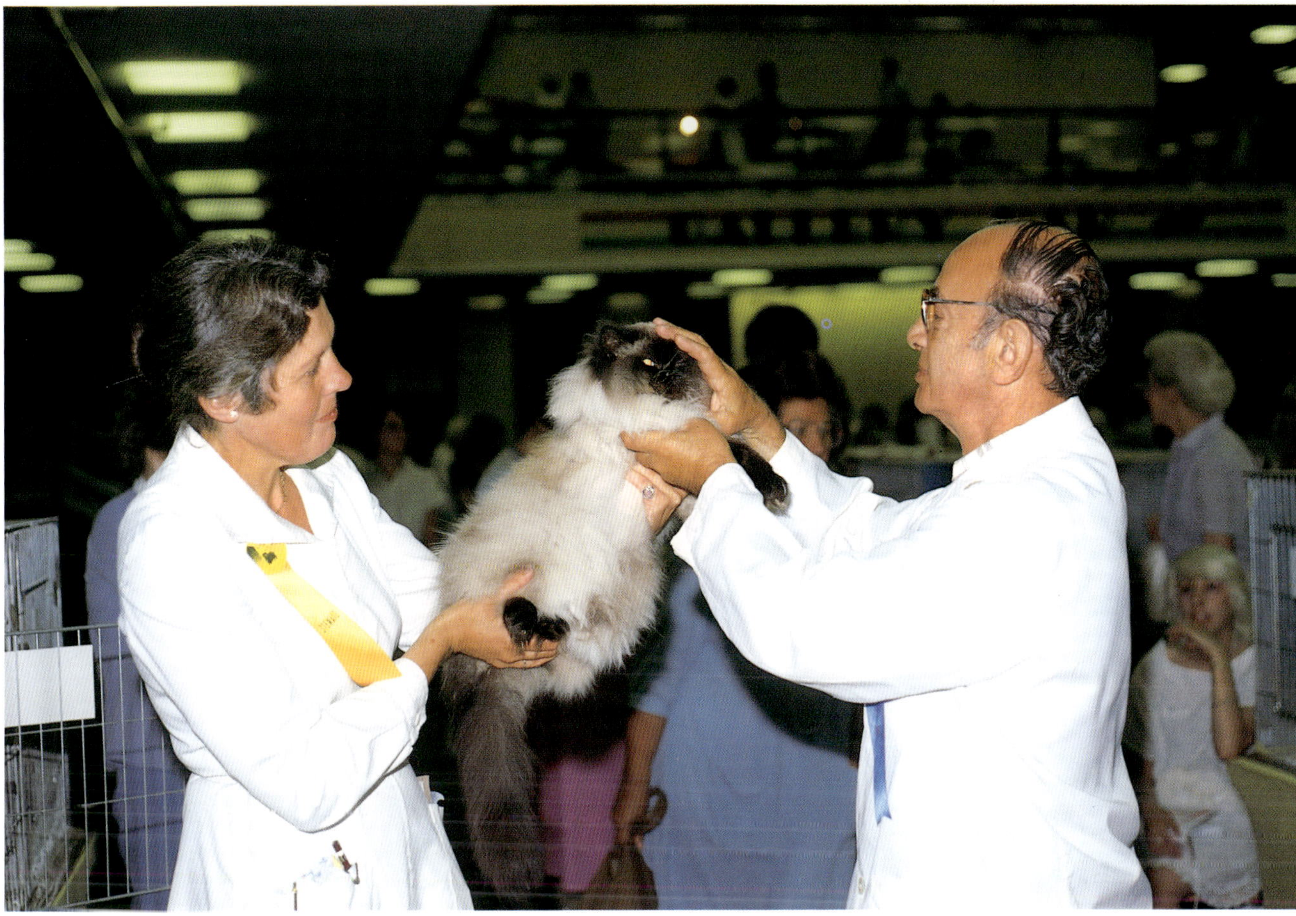

At a British show, a steward holds an entry while the judge assesses it

may not meet that standard precisely. Then, if one cat has two faults and another cat has three, the two-fault cat is the winner.

With so many cats of exceptional quality being shown today, it doesn't take much to separate them this way. For example, many Persians have tiny, narrow noses with their nostrils pointing straight out; but according to the standard, the nose is supposed to be broad and flat. The full coat on some Persians might cover a multitude of flaws, including large ears, long legs, and less-than-massive bone structure. Or perhaps a cat's eyes are too deeply set, or the eye aperture slants too much toward the ear. If judges look closely enough, they'll find these shortcomings and evaluate the cats accordingly.

Sometimes grooming is the tie breaker. A cat that is well presented has the best chance of advancing, and if all other things are equal, grooming can make the difference between a blue ribbon and a red one. This isn't to say that everyone who shows a cat has to be an artist with a comb and brush. Occasionally older fanciers can't groom the way they could before, or newer exhibitors have not learned all the skills they need.

Grooming is temporary, type is not. It's unfair to penalize one cat that's obviously superior to its competition simply because it isn't as well groomed.

Because cat judging is an art, not a science, there is room for subjectivity in judges' decisions, especially when they select the top ten cats in show. Unlike picking best of breed, an intramural competition, choosing cats for finals involves comparing apples and oranges, Siamese and American Shorthairs, Persians and Turkish Angoras. It's one thing to decide which of five Tonkinese fits the standard most closely, but it's quite another to decide if the best Tonkinese comes closer to meeting its standard than the best Exotic Shorthair does.

The author presenting a Persian cat in finals

This decision is further complicated because some breeds are older, more established, and more highly refined than others. In fact, within some breeds there are certain colours that are generally superior to others. Therefore, judges have to weigh the relative merit of achievements when they compare one breed to the next. The silver Persian is a case in point.

Judges who compare a silver Persian to its breed standard might see that the silver is short in the face, has a wide, flat nose, and round eyes—all of which the standard mandates. Nevertheless, the silver might not be as extreme or as massive as a blue Persian. In deciding which of those cats to place in the final—or which should be placed above the other for best longhaired champion, perhaps—judges must consider how difficult it is to produce a silver with a decent break to the nose.

If a judge believes that it was more difficult to achieve the quality of the silver than it was to achieve the quality of the blue—even though the blue is more extreme and massive than the silver—that judge could justify putting the silver over the blue. Another judge might not see it the same way, but that's what exhibitors are paying for—each judge's opinion. Unless judges encourage people working with cats in the more difficult or newer breeds, these breeds are never going to develop.

In addition to type, conformation, and presentation, there is one other critical attribute of a show cat: temperament. When this author started judging cats in 1953, they were much more difficult to handle than they are today. Indeed, their quality was frequently exceeded by their ferocity. It was not uncommon to see an owner put on heavy, leather gauntlets before placing a cat into the judging cage. Fortunately, cats were judged only twice during a show in those days, compared to the six to twelve to sixteen judgings (in some three-day shows) that exhibitors subject them to today.

Many judges believe that temperament and its chief component, charisma, are what separate the great cats from the good ones. Great cats just stand out. They are different enough to be unique, and yet still fit the standard; and there is always that little extra something about them, that air of self-possession. Great cats have presence. They display themselves properly. They show off well enough to accentuate their best qualities.

Like type and conformation, temperament is inherited—from the people around a cat as well as its ancestors. Invariably people who are highly strung and nervous have nervous cats. When a cat acts like a spoiled child and is jumpy and jittery, it is often because the personality of its owner is much the same. Unfortunately, when some people acquire cats that don't have a temperament problem, it doesn't take long for those cats to develop one.

Given the constraints under which they have to work, judges must become adept at thinking on their feet. They also have to have the courage to make their own decisions in the ring. Sometimes there are judges—though they don't constitute a great number—who are influenced by the reputation of the person showing the cat. These judges aren't necessarily dishonest, but if they don't know a breed well enough themselves, they assume that because a cat's owner is prominent, it must be a good cat.

Judges need to have a good, solid background—to have spent time showing cats and handling them—because the more judges know, the less influenced they are likely to be by the person showing the cat, or by other judges' opinions of that cat. When a judge knows cats, it is not in his or her heart to make an undeserving cat a winner.

In many regards judges are like appraisers. They put a value and a demand on a cat. Frequently, exhibitors who are uncertain of a kitten's value may enter that kitten in a show, hoping that the judges' decisions will determine whether the exhibitor should keep the kitten or sell it. Judges are also arbiters of taste. People breed to the winning cats, not to the losers, and the judge's opinion is a certification of value. That is why judges are responsible for ensuring that sound, healthy cats with the greatest likelihood of carrying on their breeds become the winners.

Besides their knowledge of breeds and standards,

THE CAT FANCIERS' ASSOCIATION, INC.
World's Largest Registry of Pedigreed Cats
1309 Allaire Avenue • Ocean NJ 07712 • 201-531-2390
BREED/DIVISION AWARDS • 1990-1991 Show Season
Page 1 of 2

Show: Empire ET
Date: Feb 10-91
Judge: Richard Gebhardt
Master Clerk: [illegible]

LONGHAIR	BEST	2ND	BEST CH
BIRMAN	78	71	71
EXOTIC SH	81	—	—
MAINE COON	85	89	85
SOLID PERSIAN	95	99	102
SHADED PERSIAN	114	113	113
SMOKE PERSIAN	115	—	—
TABBY PERSIAN	116	—	116
PARTI-COLOR PERSIAN	126	124	126
BI-COLOR PERSIAN	129	128	128
HIMALAYAN PERSIAN	132	134	132
TURKISH ANGORA	—	—	—

SHORTHAIR	BEST	2ND	BEST CH
ABYSSINIAN	140	146	139
AMERICAN SH	150	148	150
AMERICAN WH	—	—	—
BALINESE	155	—	—
BOMBAY	—	—	—
BRITISH SH	157	—	—
SABLE BURMESE	—	—	—
DILUTE BURMESE	—	—	—
CHARTREUX	—	—	—
COLORPOINT SH	162	160	162
CORNISH REX	166	163	163
CYMRIC	—	—	—
DEVON REX	167	—	—
EGYPTIAN MAU	—	—	—
HAVANA BROWN	168	—	—
JAPANESE BOBTAIL	—	—	—
JAVANESE	[illegible]	169	169
KORAT	—	—	—
MANX	—	—	—
OCICAT	174	172	172
ORIENTAL SH	177	178	177
RUSSIAN BLUE	180	—	
SCOTTISH FOLD	183	181	181
SIAMESE	186	185	—
SINGAPURA	—	—	—
SOMALI	190	189	187
TONKINESE	191	192	[illegible]

DISTRIBUTION: WHITE-Central Office; CANARY-Club; PINK-Judge
310©-4/90

A page from a judge's book, showing the numbers of the best and second best cats and the best champions in various breeds and divisions

judges must bring to their task an air of professional comportment. Their dress and behaviour should not call attention to themselves, for the cat is the star on the show bench. During a show, a judge must not fraternize with exhibitors in an attempt to be one of the gang. Nor should a judge speak to any exhibitors while classes are being judged. If this were allowed to happen, other exhibitors would have a right to feel resentful if their cats were not to do well, even if the judge's decisions were made impartially. Judges cannot expect every exhibitor to agree with their decisions, but their conduct should be such that every exhibitor respects them—and leaves the show feeling that the awards are earned by the cats, not their owners.

Judges also have a responsibility both to the letter and the spiret of the breed standards on which they base their evaluations. A judge is hired to apply, not interpret, while seldom enterely absent from a judge's considerations, ought never to be the deciding factor when it is time to give awards.

(Below) In Great Britain, Grand Challenge Certificates are awarded at Championship shows to cats of exceptional merit. Only cats who are already Champions/Premiers are eligible to enter these classes. Grand Challenge Certificates awarded by three different judges at three different shows are needed for the cat to win the coveted title of Grand Champion/Premier.

The award of the Grand Challenge Certificate is not automatic. If the judge decides that an exhibit is the best of all the cats entered, but not of sufficient merit to justify the award of a Certificate, it will only be given a first placing, and the Grand Challenge Certificate will be withheld. It is expected that the winner of one of these Certificates should be an almost perfect specimen of the breed.

The Governing Council of the Cat Fancy
SUPREME SHOW

GRAND CHALLENGE CERTIFICATE

Pen No. .... Name ....

Date .... Signature of Judge ....

Glossary

ACA: American Cat Association.

ACFA: American Cat Fanciers Association.

Agouti: the colour between the stripes on a ticked or tabby cat; for example, the warm toned, coppery brown, ground colour of the Brown Tabby.

Allele: one of two or more genes—each governing a different physical characteristic—that can occupy a particular locus (position) on a chromosome; for example, the genes determining coat length–either long or short—are alleles.

Anoestrus: a period during which a female cat is not in season.

Any other colour (AOC): formerly used by GCCF to mean any potential colour used in show schedules to cover classes from which certain colours have been excluded.

Any other variety (AOV): a term formerly used by GCCF to describe any cat that is the offspring of two registered parents but is not eligible for championship competition; also used in show schedules to denote a class which includes all remaining varieties in a section.

Awn hair: the coarser of the two types of secondary hairs; normally longer than down hair, but shorter than guard hair.

Back crossing: a form of inbreeding (see below) in which a cat is mated to its parent of the opposite sex.

Best of breed: the cat which, in the judge's opinion, comes closest to meeting the breed standard of all the cats in a given breed. Normally divided into Adult, Kitten and Neuter catagories.

Blaze: 1) in blue creams and tortoiseshells, a vertical division of two colours extending down the center of a cat's forehead and nose.

Bloodline (or line): the ancestors of a given cat; often used imprecisely to refer to any cat produced by a particular cattery.

Break: a distinct, unmistakable indentation affecting the bridge of the nose, occurring just below—or at a moderate distance below a point in between—the eyes. The break is often more noticeable when viewed in profile.

Breed: cats with similar physical characteristics.

Brindling: the random mixture of hairs of different colours in a cat's coat; usually not a term of approbation.

Brush: 1) to groom a cat with a similarly named instrument; 2) the tail on a longhaired cat.

CAB: The Cat Association of Great Britain.

Carnivore: an animal whose diet consists primarily, if not exclusively, of meat.

Carry: 1) to possess a recessive gene (see below) or genes governing a physical characteristic that is not apparent to the eye; a shorthaired cat, for example, may be carrying a longhair gene; 2) to harbour the virus or bacteria that could transmit a disease while exhibiting no symptoms of that disease; 3) to be pregnant with kittens.

Cat fancy: the loose confederation of cat-registering bodies, breeders, and exhibitors dedicated to the care, welfare, promotion, and exhibition of pedigreed and other cats.

Catalogue: a publication listing the entries for a cat show, together with the age, date of birth, title held (if any), parents' names, breeder's name, and owner's name for each entry. May also contain advertising, a list of exhibitors' addresses, and assorted information.

Cattery: a place where cats are bred and/or boarded.

Cattery name: the registered name of a place where cats are bred; may be used as a prefix by the breeder of a cat.

CCA: Canadian Cat Association.

Cell: the basic structural and functional unit of the body.

CFA: Cat Fanciers' Association.

CFF: Cat Fanciers' Federation.

Champion: a title that a cat earns, by beating cats of the same breed number in three open classes at three different shows under three different judges. A similar title is awarded to registered cats which then become known as *Premier*.

Chromosomes: minute, rod-shaped elements in the nucleus of a cell that control the inheritance of characteristics in the cell and in the entire cat.

Coarse: not smooth, refined, or harmonious in the arrangement of parts.

Cobby: close coupled; that is, short in the body, broad in the beam, and low on the legs.

Colour breeding: mating cats of the same colour and breed for at least three generations, or five, according to purists.

Condition: the state of a cat's well being; includes weight, muscle tone, cleanliness, radiant good health, and grooming.

Conformation: the configuration of a cat's torso, legs, and tail.

Congenital: existing at birth but not acquired by heredity.

Cross: 1) a mating between cats; 2) to mate or breed one cat with another which may not be related or may be of a different breed.

Dam: the female parent.

Depth of flank: the extent and substance of the flank—that area of the cat's side between the last rib and the hip. Most often used in reference to Manx and Cymric.

Dilute: a paler version of a basic colour. For example, blue is the dilute of black, cream the dilute of red.

Doctoring: 1) a British term synonymous with neutering; 2) in the United States a term used to describe the illegal alteration of a cat's colour or conformation.

Domestic: a non-pedigreed cat, usually a shorthair, indigenous to a particular country.

Dominant: prevailing over another. For example, the gene for folded ears is dominant over the gene for straight ears. Therefore, if a cat has one gene for folded ears and one gene for straight ears, the cat's ears will fold.

Double coat: a coat in which the awn hairs are as long as the guard hairs. Generally the awn hairs are intermediate in length between the longer guard hairs (see below) and the shorter down hairs (see immediately below).

Down hair: the shorter of the two types of secondary hairs, and the shortest hair in a cat.

Ear furnishings: hairs growing inside the ears.

Euthanasia: the act of humanely ending a cat's life.

Extreme: pronounced; possessing a desirable characteristic to an exaggerated extent.

Feral: when used correctly, a term that describes a formerly domesticated cat—or the descendants of formerly domesticated cats—now living in a wild state. Often used imprecisely to denote any cat that doesn't seem to belong to anyone.

Follicle: 1) the indentation in the skin from which hair grows; 2) the sac on the female's ovary in which an egg develops.

Foreign: a moderately tubular body conformation. The Abyssinian has a foreign body.

GCCF: the Governing Council of the Cat Fancy (United Kingdom).

Gene pool: the sum total of all the genes that exist in the cats of a given breed.

Genes: units of heredity that control the growth, development, function, and physical characteristics of the cat.

Genetics: the study of heredity.

Genotype: the genes an individual inherits from its parents; not to be confused with the individual's physical appearance (see phenotype).

Gestation: the period between conception and birth; normally lasts from sixty-three to sixty-nine days in cats.

Grand champion (Grand Premier): a title earned by a cat (after it has become a champion) by winning three Grand champion/Premier classes at three different shows under three different judges.

Ground colour: the colour occurring on the part of the hair shaft closest to the body.

Guard hairs: the outer—and longest—hairs in a cat's coat; sometimes called the primary hairs.

Heat: a period of sexual receptivity in a female cat.

Heterozygous: possessing a pair of dissimilar alleles (see above) for a particular trait.

Homozygous: possessing an identical pair of alleles (see above) for a particular trait.

Hormone: a chemical messenger sent into the bloodstream by a gland in order to affect development or function in another part of the body.

Hybrid: 1) a cat produced from a mating between cats of different breeds; 2) a breed derived by combining two or more breeds.

Hybrid vigour: an increase in health and vitality sought by mating one cat to another of a different bloodline or breed.

Inbreeding: a union between two cats that does not result in the introduction of any new genetic material to the offspring of those cats. Mother-son; father-daughter; and brother-sister matings constitute inbreeding. A knowledge of the traits—both good and bad—of the cats involved constitutes the wise use of inbreeding.

Intermediate certificates: awarded to cats with provisional recognition.

Kitten: for exhibition purposes, a cat between the ages of three and nine months.

Line breeding: a mating between related cats that have a common ancestor appearing at least once in the first three generations on both the sire's and the dam's side of the pedigree.

Litter: kittens born at the same time from the same mother.

Litter registration: enrolling a litter of kittens with a cat association.

Merit certificates: awarded to cats with preliminary recognition, assessed to have reached the necessary standard.

Mutation: a genetic mishap—usually caused by environmental conditions or a glitch in the replication process—that alters the normal inheritance of a characteristic.

Neuter: 1) a castrated male; 2) to remove testicles from a male cat.

New breed or colour: a competitive category for cats or kittens not yet accepted for championship competition.

Oriental: the most slim of the tubular body styles.

Outcross: 1) a breeding between two cats that do not have any ancestors in common for at least three generations; 2) a breed that can be used in the production of another breed of kittens. The Abyssinian, for example, is an allowable outcross for the Somali.

Papers: registration documents issued for a cat.

Pedigree: a document containing the known names, titles, colours, and registration numbers of the first three to five generations of a cat's predecessors.

Pen: in the show hall, the enclosure in which a cat remains when it is not being judged.

Phenotype: a cat's physical appearance; always influenced by heredity and sometimes by environment (that is, vitamins, diet, and grooming), too.

Pigment: colouration (or colouring matter) in a cat.

Pointed: a pattern in which a pale body colour contrasts with darker colour(s) confined to a cat's face, ears, legs, and tail.

Points: 1) the face, ears, legs, and tail of a pointed cat; 2) units earned in competition that count toward the attainment of a title or year-end award.

Prefix: A unique word purchased from a registering body to prefix the names of all cats bred by the owner.

Preliminary recognition: the first stage of official recognition by the GCCF. The cats are exhibited on assessment.

Premier: a title awarded to neutered cats *(see Champion)*

Pricked: the upright or forward inclination of a cat's ears.

Provisional: a class for cats or kittens not yet accepted for championship competition, but eligible for competition at cat shows.

Purebred: a cat whose ancestors are all of the same variety or allowable varieties; not a synonym for pedigreed.

Quarantine: a period during which a cat is isolated from other cats in order to prevent the spread of disease.

Queen: a female cat of breeding age.

Quick: the vein in a cat's claw.

Rangy: long in the body.

Recessive: 1) a characteristic that does not become apparent unless a cat possesses two genes governing that trait; 2) a gene governing a recessive trait.

Register: to enrol a cat, kitten, or litter with a registering body.

Registry: an association that records the lineage of cats, issues registration numbers, licenses shows, etc.

Ring: an area in which cats are judged at the Supreme Show.

Roman nose: a nose characterized by low-slung nostrils and an arch.

Rosettes: gaily coloured arrangements of ribbon that consist of a round centrepiece to which several long strips of ribbon have been affixed.

Rufous Polygens: a genetic factor that enhances the richness of a colour. The rufous influence can be seen in the usual Abyssinian, which would be a black agouti tabby otherwise.

Selective breeding: the purposeful mating of two cats in order to achieve a desired end or to eliminate an undesired one.

Self: solid; as in, 'The father is a self-red cat.'

Set type: to breed successive generations of cats containing a certain characteristic in the hope of producing cats that will not only possess that characteristic but will also pass it on to their offspring.

Sire: the male parent of a cat, the father.

Solid: all of one colour (see *self*).

Spay: 1) a female cat that has been sterilized surgically; 2) to render a female cat sterile by surgical means.

Spotting: 1) white areas in a cat's coat; 2) the discharge of fluid by a pregnant cat.

Spotting gene: the gene governing the distribution of white areas throughout a cat's coat.

Standard: document describing the breed ideal.

Stop: an indentation in the bridge of the nose occurring at a moderate distance below a point in between—the eyes (see *break*).

Stud: a siring male cat.

Stud book: a volume containing the names, sexes, and colours of cats, and birth dates and similar information (when known) about the cats' parents; records wins at championship cat shows.

Stud service: what a male cat provides when he breeds a female.

Supreme: a title awarded to the winning Adult, Kitten and Neuter at the Supreme Cat Show.

Titles: merit ranks earned by a cat in competition.

TICA: The International Cat Association.

Type: the arrangement of the overall parts of the cat in accordance with breed specifications.

UK: a title awarded to the winner of two UK Grand champion classes at the Supreme Cat Show.

Undercoat: the woolly down hairs on a cat; also used to denote the down and the longer awn hairs together.

Variant: a cat—with two registered parents—that is not eligible for championship competition because it varies from the breed standard in eye colour, coat length or colour, etc.

Appendices

CAT REGISTRIES

A cat registry performs many functions for its members. In addition to registering cats and recording their lineage, federations charter clubs, sanction shows, license judges, enforce by-laws and show rules, award titles to cats that have earned them in competition, approve breed standards, recognize new breeds and colours, publish breed standards and show rules, present national and regional awards annually to the highest-scoring cats and kittens in the association, and publish newsletters, magazines, and an annual yearbook.

There are two cat registry bodies in the United Kingdom. Each one is an independent association, with its own registration and show rules, its own judges, licensing requirements, breed standards, publications, and year-end award winners.

The Cat Association of Great Britain
Mill House
Letcombe Regis
Oxfordshire
OX12 9JD
(Founded 1983)

The Governing Council of the Cat Fancy
4-6 Penel Orlieu
Bridgwater
Somerset
TA6 3PG
(Founded 1910)

GCCF
NUMBER OF CAT SHOWS

	1990-91	1989-90	1988-89	1987-88
	91	98	100	97
Cats entered during season	35,650	38,274	34,355	Not available
Average number of cats per show	392	391	344	Not available

STANDARD LIST OF FAULTS FOR ALL BREEDS RECOGNIZED BY THE GCCF

Size and Condition: Withhold certificates or first prizes in kitten classes on any exhibit which, in the opinion of the judge, is not in excellent physical condition or is undersized for its age and breed.

The following list of defects applies to ALL BREEDS: Withhold certificates or first prizes in kittens for any of the following defects. It is considered that these defects are undesirable in breeding stock and may be detrimental to the individual cats:

Folded Ears: Where the top of the ear is folded forwards instead of being pricked.

Depression in Frontal Bone Area (skull depression): An indentation of the front of the skull above the eyebrows.

Entropion: Where the upper, lower or both eyelids turn inwards, allowing the lashes or hair to rub the surface of the eye.

Permanent Squint*

Reduced Nostril Aperture: Narrowing of the nostrils vertically, horizontally or both, which may cause breathing difficulties. It is often associated with flattened nasal bones and small nose leather.

Exaggerated Depression of the Nasal Bridge (stop): The nasal cavity is severely reduced, which may cause breathing difficulties. This is often accompanied by blocked tear ducts. The nose should not be excessively short.

Noticeably Undershot or Overshot Jaw

Narrow or Twisted Lower Jaw

Abnormal Angulation of Canine Teeth: When the mouth is closed the canine teeth should be nearly vertical, the lower canines fitting closely between the upper ones so that the anterior surface of the left upper canine and the posterior surface of the left lower canine almost touch, and similarly with the right upper and lower canines. The incisor teeth should form a straight line between the canines in both upper and lower jaws. The ideal bite is where the upper and lower incisors meet in alignment.

Deformity of Rib Cage
Fixed Deviation of the Sternum or Xiphisternum: The chest should be rounded or oval symmetrically from spine to breast bone when seen in cross-section. There should be no depressions or protrusions on spine or ribs. The sternum (breast bone) should follow a gentle convex curve with no deviation, depression or protrusion, and with no hook where the sternum ends.
Fixed Deviation (kink) of the Tail at any point*: Small bony excrescences need not debar the cat from being placed, but should be taken into consideration.
Luxating Patella in Adults: Where the kneecap can slip from the front of the joint towards the side.
Abnormal Number of Toes: Anything other than four toes on each foot and one dew-claw on each foreleg
Hernia: Consult the Duty Vet.
Monorchid or Cryptorchid Adult Males: Both testicles must be descended and positioned in the scrotum in entire adult males.

The defects are fully described, with illustrations, in the GCCF publication: '*Guide to the Defects Listed in the GCCF Standard of Points.*'

* Squints and kinks have been included in the list because they are faults in all breeds, although they are unlikely to affect the health of the cat or its progeny.

CAT WELFARE AND VETERINARY ORGANISATIONS

Animal Health Trust
PO Box 5
Newmarket
Suffolk
CB8 7DW

Blue Cross Animal Welfare Society
Information Officer
Field Centre
Shilton Road
Burford
Oxon
OX8 4PF

British Small Animal Veterinary Association
St George's Terrace
Cheltenham
Gloucestershire
GL50 3PT

Cat Action Trust
Mrs V Darkazally
PO Box 1639
London
N8 4RY

Cats Protection League
17 Kings Road
Horsham
West Sussex
RH13 5PP
Tel: 0403 65566

Feline Advisory Bureau
235 Upper Richmond Road
Putney
London
SW15 6SN
Tel: 081 789 9553

Joint Advisory Committee on Pets in Society (Jacopis)
1 Dean's Yard
Westminster
SW1P 3NR

Ministry of Agriculture Fisheries and Food (Animal Exports and Imports)
Mr CR Meredith
Animal Health Division
Government Buildings
Hook Rise South
Tolworth
Surbiton
Surrey
KT6 7NF

People's Dispensary for Sick Animals
Education Officer
PDSA Unit 6b
Ketley Business Park
Telford
Shropshire
TF1 4JD

Pet Health Council
4 Bedford Square
London
WC1B 3RA

Royal Society for the Prevention of Cruelty to Animals
Education Department
Causeway
Horsham
West Sussex
RH12 1HG

Wood Green Animal Shelters
(Critters Club)
Highway Cottage
Chishill Road
Heydon
Nr Royston

CAT MAGAZINES

Cats (Weekly)
5 James Leigh Street
Manchester
M1 6EX
Tel: 061 2360577

Cat World (Monthly)
Scan House
Southwick Street
Brighton
BN4 4TE
Tel: 0273 595944

Bibliography

Beadle, Muriel. *THE CAT: A Complete Authoritative Compendium of Information About Domestic Cats.* New York, S & S Trade, 1977.

Carlson, Delbert G., D.V.M., and Giffin, James M., M.D. *Cat Owner's Veterinary Handbook.* New York, Howell Book House, 1983.

Carr, William H.A. *The New Basic Book of Cats.* New York, Charles Scribner's Sons, 1978.

Eustace, May and Towe, Elizabeth. *Fifty Years of Pedigree Cats.* London, Pelham Books Ltd, 1967.

Fireman, Judy. *The Cat Catalog.* New York, Workman Publications, 1976.

Fogarty, Marna Sharron. *The Cat Yellow Pages: The Cat Owner's Guide to Goods and Services.* New York, Charles Scribner's Sons, 1984.

Gebhardt, Richard H. (editor); Pond, Grace; and Raleigh, Ivor; *A Standard Guide to Cat Breeds.* New York, McGraw, 1979.

Greer, Milan. *The Fabulous Felines* (or Dogs are passe). New York, Dial Press, 1961.

Hawcroft, Tim. *The Howell Book of Cat Care.* New York, Howell Book House, 1991.

Jennings, John. *Domestic and Fancy Cats.* London, L. Upcott Gill, 1893.

Jude, A.C. *Cat Genetics.* Neptune, New Jersey, T.F.H. Publications, 1977.

Kelsey-Wood, Dennis. *Atlas of Cats of the World.* Neptune, New Jersey, T.F.H. Publications, 1989.

McGonagle, John and Vella, Carolyn. *In the Spotlight, a Guide to Showing Pedigreed and Household Pet Cats.* New York, Howell Book House, 1990.

Muller, Ulrike. New Cat Handbook: *Everything About the Care, Nutrition, Diseases, and Breeding of Cats.* New York, Barron, 1984.

Pond, Grace. *The Complete Cat Encyclopedia.* London, W.H. Heinemann, 1979.

Pond, Grace. *The Complete Cat Guide.* New York, Doubleday, 1977.

Richards, Dorothy S. *A Handbook of Pedigree Cat Breeding.* London, David and Charles, 1980.

Robinson, Roy. *Genetics for Cat Breeders.* London, Pergamon Press, 1977.

Sayer, Angela. *A Guide to Breeding and Showing.* New York, Arco Publishing, 1983.

Siegal, Mordecai, ed. *The Cornell Book of Cats.* New York, Villard Books, 1990.

Simpson, Frances. *The Book of the Cat.* London, Sir Isaac Pitman and Sons, 1903.

Soderberg, P.M. *Pedigree Cats, Their Varieties, Breeding, and Exhibition.* London, Cassell & Company Ltd., 1958.

Stephens, Gloria. *Legacy of the Cat.* San Francisco, Chronicle Books, 1990.

Taylor, David. *The Ultimate Cat Book.* New York, Simon and Schuster, 1989.

Weir, Harrison. *Our Cats, and All About Them.* New York, Houghton, Mifflin and Company, 1889.

Wilson, Meredith. *Cat Breeding and Showing.* New York, A.S. Barnes & Company, 1972.

Wilson, Meredith. *Showing Your Cat.* New York, A.S. Barnes & Company, 1974.

Wilson, Meredith. *Encyclopedia of American Cat Breeds.* Neptune, New Jersey, T.F.H. Publications, 1978.

Winslow, Helen M. *Concerning Cats.* Boston, Lothrop Publishing, 1900.

Wright, Michael and Walters, Sally, ed. *The Book of the Cat.* New York, Summit Books, 1980.

Cat Breeder and Owner List

The Publishers thank the following breeders and owners
for allowing their cats to be photographed for this book:

Silver Classic Tabby American Shorthair
Grand Premier Angiras Thomax of Grandcru
Bred by Barbara Courtney
Owned by Eric and Helena Thom

Ruddy Abyssinian
Grand Champion Shechinah Daniel
Bred by Chris Strom and Kathryn Whitten
Owned by Bob and Chris Strom

Brown Classic Tabby American Shorthair
Grand Champion Carocats Kubla Khan
Bred and owned by Carol and Michael Rothfeld

Silver Classic Tabby American Shorthair
Grand Champion Tylona's Gloriana of Grandcru
Bred by Barbara Goulding
Owned by Eric and Helena Thom

Calico American Wirehair
Champion Silva Wyte Filigree
Bred and owned by Richard Gebhardt and John Bannon

Red and White American Wirehair
Champion Silva Wyte Billy the Kit
Bred and owned by Richard Gebhardt and John Bannon

Blue Point Balinese
Grand Champion Mikaso's Moon Struck
Bred and owned by Kathryn and Michael J. Sokolis

Blue Point Birman
Grand Champion Oxdowne Love Bug
Bred and owned by Betty Cowles

Bombay
Grand Champion Road to Fame's Blackberry Brandy
Bred by Herb and Suzanne Zwecker
Owned by Robert Unangst

Blue-and-White Van British Shorthair
Champion Excalibur Edward Langtry
Bred by Pamela Barrett
Owned by Susan Ross

Blue British Shorthair
Ankara Appolonia Kelling
Bred and owned by Heidi and Dick Mullin

Sable Burmese
Champion Road to Fame's Extremely Bold
Bred by Herb and Suzanne Zwecker
Owned by Robert Unangst

Blue Chartreux
Champion Steppenbleu Echo
Bred by Stephanie Pendleton
Owned by Frederick Andrews

Seal Lynx Point Colorpoint Shorthair
Grand Premier Lebianco Nicholas of Quarry Hill
Bred by Josephine Quinzi
Owned by Anne Vanasse

Blue-and-White Cornish Rex
Grand Champion Blu Sprs Prince Tamino
Bred and owned by Ellen Weiss

White Devon Rex
Champion Briarmar Clair de Lune of Anuket
Bred and owned by Adele Gay and Omar Gonzalez

Silver Egyptian Mau
Premier Coonfederacy's Ptah of Chesterpeake
Bred by Dorie Eckhart
Owned by Thomas and Linda Getz

Brown Classic Tabby Exotic Shorthair
Grand Champion Jovan The Legend
Bred and owned by Cheryl and Bob Lorditch

Havana Brown
Champion Hav-a-Hill Prince Charles
Bred and owned by Phyllis Hill

Red-and-White Japanese Bobtail
Nekomo Nagusami of Kemage
Bred by Allen Scruggs and Douglas Myers
Owned by Mathis/Scruggs/Myers

Korat
Grand Champion and Double Grand Champion Petlar Li'l Bo Peepers of Si Sawat
Bred by P. Greuel and L. Jones
Owned by Daphne Negus

Brown Classic Tabby Maine Coon
Champion Bakerstmews Michael Milken
Bred and owned by Carolynn Holmes-Sgro

White Manx
Grand Champion Mendocino Bearelegance of Mayflower
Bred by P. and R. Webster-Powell/R. Denton
Owned by Muriel Slodden

Brown Mackerel Tabby-and-White Norwegian Forest Cat
Supreme Grand Champion Maineline's Tord
Bred and owned by Steve and Louise Clair

Cinnamon Ocicat
Grand Champion Luvadot's Megabyte
Bred by Robert Parker
Owned by Robert and Grace Parker

White Oriental Shorthair
Grand Champion Leggs Amapola of Mayflower
Bred by Lynn Von Egidy/Mallary/Gonzalez
Owned by Muriel Slodden

Calico Persian
Grand Champion Anz Maggie the Cat
Bred by Anne Waddington
Owned by Waddington/Hannon/Watkins

Copper-eyed White Persian kitten
Kitty Charms Icy Sensation
Bred and owned by Darlene and June Feger

Red Classic Tabby Persian
Champion Charo's Flash Fire
Bred by Charmayne Phillips
Owned by Gerald and Charmayne Phillips

Chinchilla Silver Persian
Grand Champion Diadem Pollyanna
Bred and owned by Janice Reichle

Black Smoke Persian kitten
Jolair's Break Every Rule of Roann
Bred by James Newly and Ann Gonzales
Owned by A. Gonzales and R. Gingerelli

Tortoiseshell Persian kitten
Skyhy Moonlight Sonata of Baramere
Bred by Glen and Pat McNeil
Owned by Barbara and Merle Phipps

Cream-and-White Persian
Grand Champion Anz Mr. Dickens of Bekah
Bred by Anne Waddington
Owned by Rebecca Beckley

Flame Point Persian
Grand Champion Sulltans Shocking Pink
Bred by Nancy Sullivan and Lauren Jacobs
Owned by Nancy Sullivan

Blue Mitted Ragdoll
Champion Flashback
Bred by Susan Stephens
Owned by Susan Marshall and Eric Freeman

Russian Blue
Grand Champion Tylona's Sparkle Plenty
Bred By Laurel and Barbara Goulding
Owned by L. and B. Goulding and T. Schreck

Silver Classic Tabby Scottish Fold
Champion Aberdeen Angus
Bred and owned by Terry Havel

Silver-patched Torbie Van Scottish Fold Longhair
Quadruple Grand Champion Wynsome Vanity Fair
Bred by Phil and Mary Ann Maggitti
Owned by Connie Webb

Seal Point Siamese
Grand Champion Shabou Shannon
Bred by S. McKeehen-Bounds and G. Bounds
Owned by S. McKeehen-Bounds and Marion Butler

Singapura
Grand Champion Changi's Sahaja of angiras
Bred by Tommy and Hal Meadows
Owned by Bill and Barbara Courtney

Ruddy Somali
Grand Premier Roadraces' Stutz Bearcat of Grandcru
Bred by Carolyne Marriner
Owned by Eric and Helena Thom

Platinum Mink Tonkinese
Grand Champion Connacht's Shenanigan
Bred and owned by Frank Yaccino and Larry Rhinard

White Turkish Angora
Champion Cayman's Enchanting Princess
Bred and owned by Andrie Del Piano

Red-and-White Turkish Van
Champion Portacaeli Cabrera
Bred by A. Daly
Owned by Michael and Kitty Ann

Black-and-White American Curl
Supreme Grand Champion Carbon Copy of Fun Furz
Bred by Gerri Hamilton
Owned by Caroline Scott

Leopard-spotted Bengal
Champion Widwood Mustoflees of Belltown
Bred and owned by Roger and Karen Austin

Tortie-point Javanese
Champion Hunnapurr Sheezajehn
Bred and owned by Cathie Spina

Oriental Longhair
Talisyn's Chocolate Moose
Bred and owned by Steven Baylus

Seal-point Snowshoe
Cactus
Bred and owned by Jean Thompson

Blue-Cream Sphynx
Supreme Grand Champion Far from Pierrette
Bred and owned by Sandy Adler

Brown Spotted Tabby and White
St. Hubert's McKinley Domestic Shorthair
Owned by Marcy Zingler

Note: The titles presented here have been earned in several of the major show-giving federations.

The cats illustrated on pages 39, 64, 68, 87, 119, 122, 125, 164 were bred in Great Britain and are all of Grand Champion or equivalent status.

Photo and Illustration Credits

David Anstey 28, 29, 193
Jane Burton 146
By courtesy of the Trustees of the British Museum 15
By courtesy of the Natural History Museum 14, 16
By kind permission of British Museum Press 196
Chanan Photography 38, 49, 102, 143, 166, 203
Richard Gebhardt 208
Marc Henrie ASC (London) 6, 7, 8, 39, 64, 87, 118, 119, 121, 122, 125, 164, 183, 184, 191, 194, 195, 202, 209
Larry Johnson 42 153
Tetsu Yamazaki 94

INDEX